FAMOUS SPURGEON QUOTES

"Calvinism did not spring from Calvin. We believe that it sprang from the great Founder of all truth". (Sermons, Vol. 7, p. 298)

"We declare on scriptural authority that the human will is so desperately set on mischief, so depraved, so inclined to everything that is evil, and so disinclined to everything that is good, that without the powerful, supernatural, irresistible influence of the Holy Spirit, no human will ever be constrained toward Christ". (Sermons, Vol. 4, p.139)

"I believe that Christ came into the world not to put men into a salvable state, but into a saved state. Not to put them where they could save themselves, but to do the work in them and for them, from first to last. If I did not believe that there was might going forth with the word of Jesus which makes men willing, and which turns them from the error of their ways by the mighty, overwhelming, constraining force of divine influence, I should cease to glory in the cross of Christ". (Sermons, Vol. 3, p. 34)

"A man is not saved against his will, but he is made willing by the operation of the Holy Ghost. A mighty grace which he does not wish to resist enters into the man, disarms him, makes a new creature of him, and he is saved". (Sermons, Vol. 10, p. 309)

"I question whether we have preached the whole counsel of God, unless predestination with all its solemnity and sureness be continually declared". (Sermons, Vol. 6, p. 26)

"I do not come into this pulpit hoping that perhaps somebody will of his own free will return to Christ. My hope lies in another quarter. I hope that my Master will lay hold of some of them and say, 'You are mine, and you shall be mine. I claim you for myself.' My hope arises from the freeness of grace, and not from the freedom of the will".

The Plain Gospel of JESUS FOR PLAIN PEOPLE

& OTHER SERMONS ABOUT *The Gospel*

GREAT CHRISTIAN BOOKS
LINDENHURST, NEW YORK

PUBLISHER'S NOTE REGARDING ITS
RIGHTS WITH RESPECT TO THIS EDITION

Although *these sermons* were originally preached and committed to paper over several years in the latter part of the 1800's and therefore are now within the public domain, along with countless reprints, this special edition—its wording and graphics is the copyrighted property of Great Christian Books due to significant judicious editing to create a version suitable to modern readers as well as value added aspects. Therefore, no appropriation of the text or images from this edition is permissible under international copyright ordinances.

The Plain Gospel of JESUS FOR PLAIN PEOPLE

& OTHER SERMONS ABOUT *The Gospel* BY

C. H. SPURGEON

Great Christian Books
is an imprint of Rotolo Media
160 37th Street Lindenhurst, New York 11757,

ISBN 978-1-61010-048-9

©2024 Rotolo Media / Great Christian Books
All rights reserved under International and Pan-American Copyright Conventions. No part of this book maybe reproduced in any form, or by any means, electronic or mechanical, including photocopying, and informational storage and retrieval systems without the expressed written permission from the publisher, except in the case of brief quotations embodied in articles or reviews or promotional/advertising/catalog materials. For additional information or permissions, address all inquiries to the publisher.

Spurgeon, Charles Haddon, 1834–1892,
The Plain Gospel of Jesus for Plain People / by C. H. Spurgeon
p. cm.
A "A Great Christian Book" book
GREAT CHRISTIAN BOOKS an imprint of Rotolo Media
ISBN 978-1-61010-048-9,
Recommended Dewey Decimal Classifications: 230, 230.42
Suggested Subject Headings:
1. Religion—Christianity literature—Christianity & Christian theology
2. Christianity—Calvinist theology

I. Title

Book and cover design are by Michael Rotolo, www.michaelrotolo.com. This book is typeset in the Minion typeface by Adobe Inc. and is quality-manufactured on acid-free paper stock. To discuss the publication of your Christian manuscript or out-of-print book, please contact us.

Manufactured in the United States of America

CONTENTS

Introduction	9
1. The Plain Gospel for Plain People	11
2. The Heart of The Gospel	25
3. For Whom is The Gospel Meant?	39
4. The True Gospel—No Hidden Gospel	53
5. The Essence of The Gospel	67
6. The Parable of the Sower	81
7. The Glorious Gospel of the Blessed God	91
8. The Old, Old Story	107
9. The Two Effects of The Gospel	119
10. The Gospel's Healing Power	131
11. Preach The Gospel	147
12. Gospel Missions	161
13. The Doctrines of A Gracious Gospel	188
About the Author	229

INTRODUCTION

Charles Haddon Spurgeon, often referred to as the "Prince of Preachers," was one of the most influential Christian leaders of the 19th century. His powerful sermons, prolific writings, and unwavering commitment to the Gospel of Jesus Christ continue to inspire and guide believers around the world. This collection of Spurgeon's sermons focuses specifically on his articulation of the Christian Gospel, offering readers a profound exploration of the core tenets of faith as understood by this remarkable preacher.

Spurgeon's approach to the Gospel was characterized by its clarity, directness, and accessibility. He firmly believed that the message of salvation through Jesus Christ should be comprehensible to all, regardless of their educational background or social status. This conviction is evident throughout his sermons and writings, where complex theological concepts are explained with remarkable simplicity and power.

In this compilation, we begin with Spurgeon's sermon "The Plain Gospel for Plain People," delivered on June 12, 1887. This masterful exposition of Deuteronomy 30:11-14 sets the tone for the entire collection, emphasizing the accessibility and nearness of God's salvation. Spurgeon argues passionately that the way of salvation is not hidden in heavenly mysteries or wrapped in deep, unrevealed secrecy, but is brought close to people, easy to understand and grasp.

Throughout the selected works, several key themes emerge that were central to Spurgeon's understanding and preaching of the Gospel:

1. The depravity of human nature and the absolute necessity of God's grace for salvation.

2. The doctrine of predestination and God's sovereign choice in salvation, balanced with human responsibility.

3. The importance of preaching the whole counsel of God, including difficult or unpopular doctrines.

4. The simplicity and accessibility of the Gospel message, designed by God to be understood by all.

5. The transformative power of the Holy Spirit in bringing sinners to Christ.

Spurgeon's eloquence and passion are evident in every page, as he exhorts his listeners and readers to embrace the saving grace of Christ. His words carry a sense of urgency and deep conviction, reflecting his fervent desire to see souls saved and lives transformed by the power of the Gospel.

This collection not only provides insight into Spurgeon's theology but also serves as a practical guide for modern readers seeking to understand and articulate the essentials of the Christian Gospel. Whether you are a seasoned theologian, a new believer, or someone curious about Christianity, Spurgeon's clear and powerful exposition of the Gospel offers profound insights and challenges.

As you delve into these pages, prepare to be challenged, inspired, and moved by Spurgeon's unwavering commitment to the Gospel of Jesus Christ. His words, though spoken over a century ago, remain remarkably relevant and impactful in our contemporary world. May this collection serve as a beacon of truth, guiding readers to a deeper understanding of God's love and the transformative power of the Gospel.

In a world often characterized by complexity and confusion, Spurgeon's straightforward presentation of the Gospel stands as a testament to the enduring power of *simple truth*. As you engage with these timeless messages, may you find not only intellectual stimulation but also spiritual nourishment and a renewed passion for the "Old, Old Story" of Jesus and His love.

1

THE PLAIN GOSPEL FOR PLAIN PEOPLE

Preached on June 12, 1887
Scripture: Deuteronomy 30:11-14
From: Metropolitan Tabernacle Pulpit Volume 33

> "For this commandment which I command thee this day, it is not hidden from thee, neither is it far off. It is not in heaven, that thou shouldest say, Who shall go up for us to heaven, and bring it unto us, that we may hear it, and do it? Neither is it beyond the sea, that thou shouldest say, Who shall go over the sea for us, and bring it unto us, that we may hear it, and do it? But the word is very nigh unto thee, in thy mouth, and in thy heart, that thou mayest do it."
> —Deuteronomy xxx. 11-14.

OUR Lord Jesus Christ, in John's gospel, in the forty-sixth verse of the fifth chapter, says, "Moses wrote of me." Hence we may safely interpret much that Moses said, not only of the law, but also of the gospel; indeed, the law itself was given primarily to drive men to the gospel; it was meant to show them the impossibility of salvation by their own works, and so to shut them up to a salvation which is available even for sinners. The types of sacrifice and purification pointed to the method of pardon for the guilty by faith, and acceptance for sinners by a righteousness not their own. This is certainly one of the passages in which Moses wrote of the Savior yet to come.

We are not, however, left to conjecture this; for the apostle Paul, under the guidance of the Holy Spirit, has quoted this passage in the tenth chapter of his Epistle to the Romans. He has given us a sort of paraphrase of it; not quoting it with verbal exactness, but giving its sense, and then inserting his own interpretation of that sense; which interpretation, seeing that he spoke under the direct influence of the Spirit of God, may be accepted as decisive. The Spirit of God best knew what he meant by the words which he spake by Moses. Even if Moses himself may not altogether have meant the same, the Spirit's own meaning must stand. I believe, however, that Moses did intend that which Paul attributes to him, and that he saw in the whole revelation of God under the ancient dispensation the spirit, the essential spirit, of the gospel, which was more fully declared to us by our Lord Jesus Christ. In this instance he was not speaking of the law as given upon Sinai, if we view it as a covenant of works. I showed you this by reading the first verse of the twenty-ninth chapter, which is the preface to the passage now before us. There we read, "These are the words of the covenant, which the Lord commanded Moses to make with the children of Israel in the land of Moab, beside the covenant which he made with them in Horeb. We must understand Moses to be speaking now of God's way of salvation as it is set forth in the types, and sacrifices, and ordinances of the Mosaic dispensation—which Paul calls, "the righteousness of faith." Paul interprets him as speaking of the gospel itself, and using these remarkable words concerning salvation by grace.

What is meant by these words is this—that the way of salvation is plain and clear; it is not concealed among the mysteries of heaven: "It is not in heaven, that thou shouldest say, Who shall go up for us to heaven, and bring it unto us, that we may hear it, and do it?" Neither is it wrapped up among the profundities of deep, unrevealed secrecy: "Neither is it beyond the sea, that thou shouldest say, Who shall go over the sea for us, and bring it unto us, that we may hear it, and do it?" But the way of salvation is brought home to us, given to us in a handy form, and laid within grasp of our understanding; it is spoken to us in human language, and brought within the compass of human emotions. We can speak it with our mouths, and enjoy it with our hearts. It is a household treasure, not a foreign rarity. It is not so remote from us that only they can know it who travel far to make discoveries, neither is it so sublimely difficult that only they can grasp it who have soared to heaven and ransacked the secrets of the book sealed with seven seals. It is brought to our doors like the manna, and flows at our feet like the water from the rock. It is, as Moses says, "very nigh to us; yes," very nigh to each one who hears the gospel; for Moses puts it in the singular: "It is very nigh unto thee, in thy mouth, and in thy heart, that thou mayest do it."

I. And so I begin my discourse this morning with this first head: THE WAY OF SALVATION is PLAIN AND SIMPLE. You have neither to look skyward nor seaward to find it out: here it is before you; near as your tongue, inseparable from you as your heart. You have neither to rise to the sublime, nor sink to the profound; it lies before you an open secret. As saith Moses in the last verse of the previous chapter: "The secret things belong unto the Lord our God: but those things which are revealed belong unto us and to our children forever."

I think we might have expected this if we consider the nature of God, who has made this wonderful revelation. When God speaks to a man with a view to his salvation, it is but natural that in his wisdom he should so speak as to be understood. It is not wisdom which leads teachers to become obscure: if they teach at all, they should adapt themselves to the disciple's capacity. No doubt some men have obtained a reputation for wisdom because they have not been understood; but this was fictitious, and unworthy of true men. If they had possessed the highest wisdom, they would have aimed at making matters clear when their object was to instruct. As a general rule, when a speaker is not clear to his hearers it is because the thought is not clear to himself. This can never be supposed of him who knows all things, and sees all things as they are. The only wise God abounds to us in all wisdom and prudence in his manner of imparting to us the knowledge of his will: teaching, he does teach; and explaining, he does dearly explain. There may be, and there is, a sinful dulness in the minds of sinful men; but there is no such obscurity in the revelation itself as to excuse men for this blindness. God, who is infinitely wise, would not give to us a revelation upon the vital point of salvation, and then leave it so much in the dark that it was impossible for common minds to comprehend it if they desired to do so. God adapts means to ends, and does not allow men to miss of heaven from lack of plainness on his part.

We expect a plain and simple revelation, because God has made a revelation perfectly adapted for its end, upon which no improvement can be made. You must have noticed that when an invention first conies before the public eye, it is almost always complicated; and the reason for this lies in the fact that it is as yet in its infancy. As the invention is improved it is simplified. Almost every alteration in a piece of machinery which goes towards its perfecting, goes also towards making it more simple; and at the last, when the invention is complete, it is singularly simple. That which comes from the mind of God, being perfect, goes directly towards its desired end. I admit that certain parts of the divine revelation are hard to be understood, but these are intended for our education, that we may exercise our minds and thoughts, and may by the guidance of the Holy Spirit grow thereby. But in the matter of salvation, where the life or death of a soul is concerned, it is needful that the vision should be plain, and our wise and gracious Lord has condescended to that necessity. In all that concerns repentance and faith, and the vital matters of pardon and justification, there is no obscurity, but all is plain as a pikestaff. He that runs may read, and he that reads may run.

You might have expected this from God, because of his gracious condescension. When he deigns to speak with a trembling seeker, it is not after the manner of the incomprehensible doctor, but after the manner of a father with his child, desirous that his child should at once know his father's mind. He makes the way so plain that the wayfaring man, though a fool, shall not err therein. He breaks down his great thoughts to our narrow capacities: he has compassion on the ignorant, and he becomes the teacher of babes. Truly the knowledge which the Lord our God imparts to us is in itself sublime, but his manner of teaching is gentle; for he comes with precept upon precept, and line upon line, here a little and there a little. He does not come down to us half-way, but he stoops to men of low estate, and while he hides these things from the wise and prudent, he reveals them unto babes: "Even so Father: for so it seemed good in thy sight."

Remember, my brethren, that our great Lord always takes care that there shall be no provision made for the pride of men. The pride of intellect he hates as much as any other pride. No flesh shall glory in his presence. He taketh the proud in their own craftiness, while he lifts up the humble and the meek; therefore, we may expect that he will speak in terms that shall be open to shepherds and fishermen, whom others call unlearned and ignorant men; lest the wise men of this world should exalt themselves over the humbler sort. It is no design of the Lord God Almighty that a class of self-constituted superior persons should monopolize the blessings of the gospel through the truths of revelation being wrapt up in learned terms which the vulgar cannot understand. The various systems of idolatry endeavored to surround their false teaching with a mystic secrecy; but the word of our God is a revealer of things hidden from the foundation of the earth. We may be sure that when God dealeth with men he will do nothing which shall cause human wisdom to boast itself. None shall glory that, after all, their culture was the one thing needful to make the gospel of God effectual. Philosophy shall not pitch its tent in Immanuel's land and cry, "I am, and there is none beside me." It is after the manner of God, who boweth down to the humble and the contrite, that he should make his salvation the joy of the lowly. "Out of the mouths of babes and sucklings hast thou ordained strength because of thine enemies." Those who know the living God do not wonder as they read such words as these: "For it is written, I will destroy the wisdom of the wise, and will bring to nothing the understanding of the prudent. Where is the wise? where is the scribe? where is the disputer of this world? hath not God made foolish the wisdom of this world? For after that in the wisdom of God the world by wisdom knew not God, it pleased God by the foolishness of preaching to save them that believe."

We might also expect simplicity when we remember the design of the plan of salvation. God aims distinctly by the gospel at the salvation of men. He bids us preach the gospel to every creature. It had need be a simple gospel if it is to be preached to every creature. I thank God with all my heart that the sage is here put on a level with the child; for the gospel must be received by him as a little child receives it. If the grace of God be given to the least educated person in yonder village, he is as well able to receive the gospel as the most profound scholar in the university. Would any of you wish to have it otherwise? Could you be so inhuman? Must the gospel also be enclosed for an aristocracy? Must the cultured few be gratified at the expense of the ruin of the masses? God forbid. But it must be so unless the saving doctrine of the gospel can be perceived by the untutored many. Every generous heart delights to think that "the poor have the gospel preached unto them." Brethren, to save the many the truth must be very simple and easy to be understood; for the many are busy with needful labor. From morning to night their hands are going to earn the bread that perisheth, their thoughts must largely be taken up with their daily toil. I grant you that many are too much engrossed with the poor cares of common life; but still, to a large extent, they will by needful occupations be shut out from close study and steady thought, and they must have a salvation which can be grasped at once, and held without the strain of perpetual debate. If men cannot be saved without weeks and months of careful study, they will certainly be lost. As good have no salvation as one which is beyond ordinary comprehension. Our working men need a gospel which can be heard and thought upon while they earn their daily bread. It should be clear as the sun, and simple as the A B C, that they may see it, and then hold it in their memories. Give me a gospel which can be written in a line of a boy's copy book, or worked on a girl's sampler; a gospel which the humblest cottager may learn, and love, and live upon.

The mass of our fellow-men are not only very busy, but from their poverty and other surroundings they never will attain to any high degree of education. We are thankful for all that is done by School Boards and other agencies; but these operate for the present world rather than for eternal and spiritual things. Men may learn all that books can teach them, and not be a jot nearer the knowledge of heavenly truth. Heavenly knowledge is of another sort, and is open to those who gain no certificates and pass no standards. Those who know their Bibles true, and find therein the appointed Savior, have not reached that point by the learning of the schools: we may say of each one of them, "Blessed art thou; for flesh and blood hath not revealed it unto thee, but my Father which is in heaven." The word of life is meant for men as sinners, and not for men as philosophers; and hence the message is made plain and clear.

Moreover, we might expect the gospel to be very plain, because of the many feeble minds which else would be unable to receive it. Remember the children. How glad we are that our boys and girls can know and receive the Savior who said, "Suffer little children to come unto me, and forbid them not"! If in order to their salvation our children must all be learned divines, if they must understand the discussions of our monthly and fortnightly reviews before they can know the Lord, they are indeed in an evil case. Then might we close our Sunday-schools, being convinced that the children must perish, or at least must wait until they reach a riper age. Would you have it so? O sirs! I am sure you would not; rather would you help to gather in the lambs.

Remember, also, that many return to feebleness of mind in their old age. How many who displayed considerable strength of intellect in middle life find their faculties failing them as their years multiply! We want a gospel which an old man can grasp when sight and hearing are failing him, when the memory is weakened, and the judgment is enfeebled: we want a gospel which can be laid hold upon in second childhood, otherwise our venerable sires will miss the staff on which they have leaned so long, and other aged persons who have reached the eleventh hour without faith in Jesus must be abandoned in despair. Would you have it so? There is not one amongst us that would so desire it.

Remember, once more, the many feeble intellects which are to be found on all hands—not imbecile, but still not intellectual; not without thought and reason, but yet with an exceedingly narrow range of understanding. Shall these be shut out by a complicated, philosophical gospel? We cannot think so. Rather do we bear testimony that we have known many persons strong in faith, giving glory to God, and well instructed in divine doctrine, although in the judgment of boastful wits they have been utterly despised. The gospel of our salvation saves the feeble-minded as well as the clever; it reaches the slow and dull as well as the quick and bright. Is it not well it should be so? The Lord has given a gospel which he may grasp who can scarcely grasp anything else. He has put before us a way of salvation, in which trembling feet may safely tread and find no cause of stumbling. Our gospel needs not that we soar upon wings of imagination up to the heaven of sublimity, nor dive with profound research into the unfathomable sea of mystery; the Lord has brought it near us, put it into our mouths, and laid it near our hearts, that we who are of the common sort may take it to ourselves and enjoy its blessings.

What think you, my friends, would become of the dying if the gospel were intricate and complex? How would even the saints derive consolation in death from a labyrinth of mysteries? We are called at times to visit persons who are in their last hours, passing to judgment without God and without hope. It is a sorrowful business. It is always a cause of trembling with us, when we have to deal with the impenitent upon the borders of the eternal world. But we must never visit another sick bed, for we can never talk with another dying man with any hope, if we have not a gospel to take to such, which can be made plain even to those whose minds are bewildered amid the shadows of the grave. We need a gospel which a man may receive as he takes a draft of medicine, or, better still, as he takes a cup of cold water from the nurse at his bedside. We should expect, therefore, from the design of the gospel to save the many, and to save even the least intelligent of men, that it should be very simple; and so we find it.

Furthermore, dear friends, we see that it is so, if we look at its results. "For ye see your calling, brethren, how that not many wise men after the flesh, not many mighty, not many noble, are called: but God hath chosen the foolish things of the world to confound the wise; and God hath chosen the weak things of the world to confound the things which are mighty; and base things of the world, and things which are despised, hath God chosen, yea, and things which are not, to bring to nought things that are." God's chosen are usually a people of honest and candid mind, who are willing rather to believe than to dispute. The Holy Spirit has opened their hearts; he has not made them subtle and quibbling. He has not put them upon the key of perpetual doubting, and coining at nothing; but he has tuned them to another note, namely, to incline their hearts and come unto the Lord Jesus, and hear that their souls may live. Hence it follows, that the mass of those who follow the Lord Jesus are not anxious to be numbered with the wise and the philosophical; they are content rather to be believers in revelation than proficients in speculation. To us the knowledge of Christ crucified is the most excellent of the sciences, and the doctrine of the cross is the loftiest of all philosophies. We had rather receive the word of our Lord as little children than be held in repute as "men of thought."

You shall find that those who have preached the gospel with the most acceptance, whatever their natural gifts and abilities, have almost always been persons who have preferred to use great plainness of speech. They have felt the gospel to be in itself so beautiful that to adorn it with meretricious ornament would be to dishonor it. They could say with Paul, "If our gospel be hid, it is hid to them that are lost." "We use great plainness of speech." We are not as Moses, who put a veil over his face. True servants of God take away every veil that they can remove, and labor to set forth Christ evidently crucified among the people. The more they have done this, the more has God been pleased to own their message to the conversion of souls.

But, beloved, I need not argue from what we expect or see; I bid you look to the revelation itself, and see if it be not nigh unto us. Even in the days of Moses, how plain some things were! It must have been plain to every Israelite that man is a sinner, else why the sacrifice, why the purgations and the cleansings? The whole Levitical economy proclaimed aloud that man has sinned: all the ten commandments thundered out this truth! They could not avoid knowing it. It was plain also that salvation is by sacrifice. Not a day passed without its morning and evening lambs. All the year round there were special sacrifices by which the doctrine of atonement by blood was clearly declared. It was written clear as a sunbeam, "without shedding of blood there is no remission." Plain enough also was the doctrine of faith; for each bringer of a sacrifice laid his hand upon the victim, confessing his sin, and by that act he transferred his sin to the offering. Thus faith was typically described as that act by which we accept the propitiation prepared of God, and recognize the God-given Substitute. It was also clear to every Israelite that this cleansing was not the effect of the typical sacrifices themselves, otherwise they would not have been repeated year by year and day by day; for as Paul well puts it, the conscience being once purged, there would be no necessity for further sacrifice. The remembrance of sin was made over and over again, to let Israel know that the visible sacrifices pointed to the real way of cleansing, and were meant to set forth that blessed Lamb of God which taketh away the sin of the world. In many ways the Jew was put off from resting in forms and ceremonies, and was directed to the inner truth, the spiritual substance, which is Christ. Equally clear it must have been to every Israelite that the faith which brings the benefit of the great sacrifice is a practical and operative faith which affects the life and character. Continually were they exhorted to serve the Lord with their whole heart. They were exhorted to holiness and warned against transgression, and taught to render hearty obedience to the commandments of the Lord. So that, dim as the dispensation may be considered to have been as compared with the gospel day, yet actually and positively it was sufficiently clear. Even then "the word was nigh" to them, "in their mouth and in their heart."

If I may say thus much of the Mosaic dispensation, I may boldly assert that in the gospel of Christ the truth is now made more abundantly manifest. Moses brought the moonlight, but in Jesus the sun has risen, and we rejoice in his meridian beams. Brethren, blessed are our eyes that we see, and our ears that we hear, things which prophets and kings in vain desired to see and hear. Now our Lord speaketh plainly, and uses no proverb. In our streets we hear the gospel, and have no need to ride the sky or scour the sea to find it. This day we hear every man in his own tongue wherein he was born the wonderful works of God.

II. Secondly, THE WORD HAS COME VERY NEAR TO US. I want your earnest attention to this point. I beg those of you who are unconverted to hear with attention. To us all the gospel has come very near: to the inhabitants of these favored isles it is emphatically so. "The word is very nigh unto thee, in thy mouth." It is a thing which you can speak of; you have talked about it; you still talk of it. It is "familiar in your mouths as household words." Most of you are able to speak it to others, for you learned it in your catechisms, you repeated it to your Sunday-school teachers. You sing it in your hymns; you read it in books, and tracts, and pamphlets; and you write it in letters to your friends. I am glad that you have it upon your tongues: the more it is so, the better: but how near it has come! Oh, that your tongue may also be able to say, "I believe it. I accept Jesus as my Savior. I avow my faith before men"! Then will it be nearer still. Oh, that God the Holy Spirit may graciously lead you so to do! The word of life is not a thing unknowable, and consequently unspeakable: it is a thing that can be spoken of by tongues like ours when we sit in the house or walk by the way. The great thought of God has come very near to us when it can be expressed in the speech of men. I dare humbly, but boldly, to speak of my own ministry, and of you as my hearers, that the word comes very near to you from this pulpit, for I have always aimed at the utmost plainness of speech and directness of address. There is not one among you but what may understand the gospel which you hear from me every Sabbath day. If you perish it is not for want of plain speaking. The word is on your tongue.

Moses also added, "and in thy heart." By the heart, with the Hebrews, is not meant the affections, but the inward parts, including the understanding. My dear hearers, you can understand the gospel. That whosoever believes in the Lord Jesus Christ shall be saved, is not a dark saying. Salvation by grace through faith is a doctrine as plain as the nose on your face. That Jesus Christ gave himself to die in the room and stead of men, that whosoever believeth in him might not perish, but have everlasting life, is a thing to be understood of the least educated under heaven. Moreover, the doctrines of the gospel are such that our inward nature bears witness to the truth of them. When we preach that men are sinners, your conscience says, "That is true." When we declare that there is salvation by sacrifice, your understanding agrees that this is a gracious mode by which God is just, and the justifier of him that believeth. Even if you are not saved by it, you cannot help feeling that it is a system worthy of God, that he should save, through the gift of his only-begotten Son as a sacrifice for sin. If you believe it, this gospel will appear so plainly true that every part of your nature will attest it. Many of us have accepted this way of salvation; now we love it and delight in it, and to us it seems the most simple, and at the same time the most sublime system that could be conceived of. Our heart drinks it in as Gideon's fleece drank in the dew. Our souls live on it, and in it, as the fish lives in the sea. We rejoice in the gospel as the flowers smile in the sun. How glad we are that we have not a gospel wrapped up in hieroglyphics, or entombed in cold metaphysics! It has entered our hearts, it dwells within us, and has become our bosom's Lord.

There are no difficulties and obscurities about the gospel except such as we ourselves create. What we think to be its darkness is really our blindness. If thou dost not believe the gospel, why is it that thou dost not believe it? It is supported by the best of evidence, and it is in itself evidently true. The reason for thine unbelief lies partly in the natural tendency of the human heart towards legalism. Human nature cannot believe in free grace. It is accustomed to buying and selling, and therefore it must bring a price in its hand: to have everything for nothing seems out of the question. The notion of a wage to be earned is natural enough; but that eternal life is the gift of God is not so readily perceived: yet so it is. I have heard that a missionary trying to make an Oriental understand salvation by grace, set it out in many ways to him and failed, until at last he cried, "Salvation is a *backsheesh* of the Almighty." Then the Eastern caught the idea. Eternal life is the free gift of God, which he bestows on men not because of anything in them, or anything that they have done, or felt, or promised, but because of his own infinite bounty, and the delight which he has in showing mercy. You cannot get the idea, of grace into a natural man's head; it requires a divine surgical operation to open a way for this truth into our mercenary minds; yea, it requires that we be made anew before we will see it. That God freely forgives, and that he loves men solely and only because he is love, is a thought divinely simple, but our selfish prejudices refuse to accept it.

In many instances it is pride that makes the gospel appear so difficult. You cannot think that Jesus saves you, and that all you have to do is to accept his finished salvation. Like Naaman, you would prefer to do some great thing. You want to be something, do you not? Human nature craves to have a little hand in salvation—to feel something, to groan a certain time, or despair to a certain length; but when the gospel comes with the one message, "Believe and live," pride will not consent to be saved on such pauperizing terms. Yet so it is; accept it, and you have it; stretch out your hand and take what God most freely gives. The gospel itself is plain enough to a heart humbled by grace. When the scales of pride are removed from the eyes we see well enough. Alas for the unbelief which grows out of this pride, and out of our natural enmity against God! Man will believe anybody but his God. Any lie in the newspaper has legs with which to run round the world; but a grand truth that leaps from the lips of Jehovah himself is made to limp in the presence of ungodly men. Unregenerate men cannot and will not believe their God. This is also caused by the love of sin. Those who do not wish to give up their favorite sins pretend the gospel is very difficult to understand, or quite impossible to accept, and so they excuse themselves for going on in their iniquity. After all, does any man really feel that it is right to throw the blame of his unbelief upon God? Do you dare to make the gospel the cause of your ruin? Do you ask pity for yourself, as if you could not help being an enemy to God, and a rejecter of his way of mercy? Do you murmur that you cannot see? Who has closed your eyes? There are none so blind as those who will not see: your blindness is willful. You do not understand: do you wish to understand? Nothing is so incomprehensible as that which we do not want to comprehend. If you do not desire to be reconciled to God, is it wonderful that you dream that God is unwilling to be reconciled to you? O soul, I beseech you, do not impute your damnation to your God, who in infinite goodness has brought his word so very near to you! Salvation is of the Lord, but damnation is of man only.

There I leave the matter. I can bring you to the water, but I cannot make you drink. May God the Holy Spirit apply to your hearts and consciences the important truth that, whether you enter it or not, "the kingdom of God has come nigh unto you"! O Lord, grant that none of these, my hearers, may put from them thy word, and count themselves unworthy of eternal life!

III. I close with this, that THE DESIGN OF THIS SIMPLICITY AND NEARNESS OF THE GOSPEL IS THAT WE SHOULD RECEIVE IT. Observe how the text expressly words it—"The word is very nigh unto thee, in thy mouth, and in thy heart, that thou mayest do it." "That thou mayest do it." You, who have your Bibles open, will note that the twelfth verse finishes—"That we may hear it, and do it "; the thirteenth verse also says, "That we may hear it, and do it"; that is twice; but when it comes to the third time, in the fourteenth verse, it is not, "That we may hear it, and do it," but, "That we may do it." You have had enough of hearing, some of you; you have heard until your ears must almost ache with hearing. You begin now to say, "It is the old story, we are always hearing that, and nothing else." Will you not go a step further, and be no longer hearers only? "Now, then, do it."

The gospel is not sent to men to gratify their curiosity, by letting them see how other people get to heaven. Christ did not come to amuse us, but to redeem us. His word is not written for our astonishment, but "These are written, that ye may believe that Jesus is the Christ, the Son of God; and that believing, ye may have life through his name." Ever has the gospel a present, urgent, practical errand. It says to each man, "I have a message from God unto thee." It cries, "Today!" and warns men not to harden their hearts. Observe again how the text puts its last address in the singular. You can hear it in the plural—"That we may hear it, and do it"; but the actual doing is always in the singular—"That thou mayest do it." I cannot come round to everybody in the Tabernacle, and take a seat by your side for a minute; but I wish I could do so, and put my hand on every unconverted person and say, "The word is very nigh unto thee, in thy mouth, and in thy heart, that thou mayest do it."

As the word of the Lord is not sent to gratify curiosity, so also it is not sent coolly to inform you of a fact which you may lay by on the shelf for future use. God does not send you an anchor to hang up in your boat-house; but, as you are already at sea, he puts the anchor on board for present use. The gospel is sent us as manna for today, to be eaten at once. It is to be our spending money as well as our treasure.

Oh, my hearer, as thou art a dying man I charge thee to accept at once the present salvation, so that thou mayest at once do what the word requires of thee.

It is not even sent to thee merely to make thee orthodox in opinion as to religious matters, although many persons seem to think that this is the one thing needful. Remember, that perdition for the orthodox will be quite as horrible as eternal ruin for the heterodox. It will be a dreadful thing to go to hell with a sound head and a rotten heart. Alas! I fear that some of you will only increase your own misery as you increase your knowledge of the truth, because you do not practice what you know. God save us from dead knowledge, and give us the gracious action which is the fruit of knowing: "That thou mayest do it"!

Oh, that I could forego language now, and that my heart could speak in some mysterious inward fashion to your hearts! Oh, that the Holy Ghost would now incline each of you to serious personal attention to this matter! Oh, my hearer, thou hast come here to listen to me "that thou mayest do it"! Oh, that it may be done!

What is to be done? There are two things to be done. First, that thou believe in the Lord Jesus Christ as thy Savior. Take him to be thy sacrifice: trust him wholly and alone from this time forth as thy ransom from sin. Take him to be thy Lord as well as thy Savior: yield thyself up to him as thy prophet, priest, and king. Let Jesus be thine all in all, and be thou wholly his. The second thing is that thou confess thy Lord with thy mouth. Avow thyself to be a believer in Jesus, and a follower of him. Do this in his own way; for he hath said, "He that believeth, and is baptized, shall be saved." But let thy confession be sincere; do not lie unto the Lord. Confess that thou art his follower, because thou art indeed so; and henceforth all thy life bear thou his cross and follow him. This is what thou art to do; to yield thyself up to him whom God hath appointed to save his people from their sins.

"But," saith one, "I thought that there was a certain experience." Indeed there is an experience; but all true experience ends in this, in leading the heart to accept Christ as its Savior. "But I thought," says another, "that you -would dwell at length upon the work of the Holy Spirit." I rejoice in that work, and will tell you a great deal about it at another time; but the chief work of the Holy Spirit is to strip you of yourself, and bring you to receive that simple word of God which is the subject of this morning's discourse. "Well," saith one, "I grant you that it is simple: I think it is even too simple." I know it; I know it. And because it is so simple, therefore you kick against it. What folly! Hence you need the Holy Ghost to bring you to accept it. Sometimes you quarrel because it is too hard, and next because it is too easy. This shows how hard and stubborn a thing is the will of man. Almighty grace is required to bring thee to accept thine own salvation. To lead thee to take Christ to be thy Savior needs a miracle of grace! Let him save thee, that is all: but this is too much for our proud self-confidence. Oh, strange resistance, proving the deep depravity of man's nature, that he will not yield even to this! Again I say, the difficulty is not in the gospel, but in the man, whose evil heart will not receive the choicest gift of heaven. If thou art willing to have Christ, Christ is thine. The fact that thou art willing to receive him proves that he has come to thee. Believe that he is thine, and be at peace. If thou wilt now bow before the Christ of God, and take him, henceforth, to be thy Savior, thou art saved. The simple act of trusting Jesus has brought thy justification; and thine open confession of him in his own appointed way shall bring thee a fuller realization of salvation. By coming out on the Lord's side, thou shalt gather strength to overcome the sins which now beset thee, and thou shalt be helped to work out thine own salvation with fear and trembling, because God is working in thee to will and to do of his own good pleasure.

I will preach the gospel once more, and I have done. The apostle Paul, thinking of what Moses said about going up to the sky or down to the sea to find the sacred secret, says in effect, "That is right, Moses; there was a necessity for some one to come down, and an equal necessity for some one to go up: but that necessity exists no longer."

The whole gospel lies in this—there was One in heaven at the right hand of the Father, very God of very God, and in order to save thee, poor lost and ruined sinner, this adorable Son of God came down, down, down to the manger, to the cross, to the grave, to the lowest parts of the earth; and down in grief, in rejection, in agony, in death. Because he came under the weight and curse of sin, he came down indeed! Because Jesus has come down thus, and borne the punishment of sin, he that believes in him is justified. By that coming down of the Lord from heaven the sinner's sin is put away, and the transgression of the believer is forgiven. Believest thou this? Believest thou that Jesus bore thy sins in his own body on the tree? Wilt thou trust to that fact? THOU ART SAVED. Doubt it not.

So far this clears thee of sin. But it was necessary that we should not merely be washed from sin—for that would leave us naked—but that we should be clothed with righteousness. To that end our Lord Jesus rose again, and so came up from the depth. When our Redeemer had finished his going down, and so had made an end of sin, he had yet to bring in everlasting righteousness, and so he returned by the way which he went. He rose from the tomb; he rose from Olivet; he rose until a cloud received him out of his apostles' sight; he rose through the upper regions of the air; he rose to the pearl gate; he rose to the throne of God where he sitteth as one who has accomplished his service, expecting until his enemies are made his footstool. His resurrection has brought to light our righteousness, and has covered us with it; so that at this moment every man that believeth in a risen Savior is robed in the royal robes of the righteousness of God. "If thou believest in thy heart that God hath raised him from the dead, thou shalt be saved." O brothers, live because Jesus lives, rise because he has risen, sit in heaven because he sits in heaven.

"He that believeth is justified": so saith the Scripture. Dost thou see this? I believe it, I believe it with my whole heart, and therefore I confess it before this multitude with my mouth, and I am saved. Wilt thou believe and confess. Oh, that the blessed Spirit may bring thee to this: this is the entrance into the way of eternal life. This is the dawn of a day which shall never die down into darkness. May the blessed Spirit bring thee to this faith, and this confession, for Jesus Christ's sake! Amen.

2

THE HEART OF THE GOSPEL

Preached July 28, 1886
Scripture: 2 Corinthians 5:20-21
From: Metropolitan Tabernacle Pulpit Volume 32

"Now then we are ambassadors for Christ, as though God did beseech you by us: pray you in Christ's stead, be ye reconciled to God. For he hath made him to be sin for us, who knew no sin; that wo might be made the righteousness of God in him."—2 Corinthians v. 20, 21.

THE heart of the gospel is redemption, and the essence of redemption is the substitutionary sacrifice of Christ. They who preach this truth preach the gospel in whatever else they may be mistaken; but they who preach not the atonement, whatever else they declare, have missed the soul and substance of the divine message. In these days I feel bound to go over and over again the elementary truths of the gospel. In peaceful times we may feel free to make excursions into interesting districts of truth which lie far afield; but now we must stay at home, and guard the hearths and homes of the church by defending the first principles of the faith. In this age there have risen up in the church itself men who speak perverse things. There be many that trouble us with their philosophies and novel interpretations, whereby they deny the doctrines they profess to teach, and undermine the faith they are pledged to maintain. It is well that some of us, who know what we believe, and have no secret meanings for our words, should just put our foot down and maintain our standing, holding forth the word of life, and plainly declaring the foundation truths of the gospel of Jesus Christ.

Let me give you a parable. In the days of Nero there was great shortness of food in the city of Rome, although there was abundance of corn to be purchased at Alexandria. A certain man who owned a vessel went down to the sea coast, and there he noticed many hungry people straining their eyes toward the sea, watching for the vessels that were to come from Egypt with corn. When these vessels came to the shore, one by one, the poor people wrung their hands in bitter disappointment, for on board the galleys there was nothing but sand which the tyrant emperor had compelled them to bring for use in the arena. It was infamous cruelty, when men were dying of hunger to command trading vessels to go to and fro, and bring nothing else but sand for gladiatorial shows, when wheat was so greatly needed. Then the merchant whose vessel was moored by the quay said to his shipmaster, "Take thou good heed that thou bring nothing back with thee from Alexandria but corn; and whereas, aforetime thou hast brought in the vessel a measure or two of sand, bring thou not so much as would lie upon a penny this time. Bring thou nothing else, I say, but wheat; for these people are dying, and now we must keep our vessels for this one business of bringing food for them." Alas! I have seen certain mighty galleys of late loaded with nothing but mere sand of philosophy and speculation, and I have said within myself, "Nay, but I will bear nothing in my ship but the revealed truth of God, the bread of life so greatly needed by the people." God grant us this day that our ship may have nothing on board it that may merely gratify the curiosity, or please the taste; but that there may be necessary truths for the salvation of souls. I would have each one of you say: "Well, it was just the old, old story of Jesus and his love, and nothing else." I have no desire to be famous for anything but preaching the old gospel. There are plenty who can fiddle to you the new music; it is for me to have no music at any time but that which is heard in heaven,—"Unto him that loved us, and washed us from our sins in his own blood, to him be glory forever and ever!"

I intend, dear friends, to begin my discourse with the second part of my text, in which the doctrine of Substitution is set forth in these words—"He hath made him to be sin for us, who knew no sin; that we might be made the righteousness of God in him." This is the basis and power of those appeals which it is our duty to make to the consciences of men.

I have found, my brethren, by long experience, that nothing touches the heart like the cross of Christ; and when the heart is touched and wounded by the two-edged sword of the law, nothing heals its wounds like the balm which flows from the pierced heart of Jesus. The cross is life to the spiritually dead. There is an old legend which can have no literal truth in it, but if it be regarded as a parable it is then most instructive. They say that when the Empress Helena was searching for the true cross they digged deep at Jerusalem and found the three crosses of Calvary buried in the soil. Which out of the three crosses was the veritable cross upon which Jesus died they could not tell, except by certain tests. So they brought a corpse and laid it on one of the crosses, but there was neither life nor motion. When the same dead body touched another of the crosses it lived; and then they said, "This is the true cross." When we see men quickened, converted, and sanctified by the doctrine of the substitutionary sacrifice, we may justly conclude that it is the true doctrine of atonement. I have not known men made to live unto God and holiness except by the doctrine of the death of Christ on man's behalf. Hearts of stone that never beat with life before have been turned to flesh through the Holy Spirit causing them to know this truth. A sacred tenderness has visited the obstinate when they have heard of Jesus crucified for them. Those who have lain at hell's dark door, wrapped about with a sevenfold death-shade, even upon them hath a great light shined. The story of the great Lover of the souls of men who gave himself for their salvation is still in the hand of the Holy Ghost the greatest of all forces in the realm of mind.

So this morning I am going to handle, first, the great doctrine, and then afterwards, and secondly, as God shall help me, we shall come to the great argument which is contained in the 20th verse: "Now then we are ambassadors for Christ, as though God did beseech you by us: we pray you in Christ's stead, be ye reconciled to God."

I. First, then, with as much brevity as possible I will speak upon THE GREAT DOCTRINE. The great doctrine, the greatest of all, is this, that God, seeing men to be lost by reason of their sin, hath taken that sin of theirs and laid it upon his only begotten Son, making him to be sin for us, even him who knew no sin; and that in consequence of this transference of sin he that believeth in Christ Jesus is made just and righteous, yea, is made to be the righteousness of God in Christ. Christ was made Bin that sinners might be made righteousness. That is the doctrine of the substitution of our Lord Jesus Christ on the behalf of guilty men.

Now consider, first, who was made sin for us? The description of our great Surety here given is upon one point only, and it may more than suffice us for our present meditation. Our substitute was spotless, innocent, and pure. "He hath made him to be sin for us, who knew no sin," Christ Jesus, the Son of God, became incarnate, and was made flesh, and dwelt here among men; but though he was made in the likeness of sinful flesh, he knew no sin. Though upon him sin was laid, yet not so as to make him guilty. He was not, he could not be, a sinner:

he had no personal knowledge of sin. Throughout the whole of his life he never committed an offence against the great law of truth and right. The law was in his heart; it was his nature to be holy. He could say to all the world, "Which of you convinceth me of sin?" Even his vacillating judge inquired, "Why, what evil hath he done?" When all Jerusalem was challenged and bribed to bear witness against him, no witnesses could be found. It was necessary to misquote and wrest his words before a charge could be trumped up against him by his bitterest enemies. His life brought him in contact with both the tables of the law, but no single command had he transgressed. As the Jews examined the Paschal lamb before they slew it, so did scribes and Pharisees, and doctors of the law, and rulers and princes, examine the Lord Jesus, without finding offence in him. He was the Lamb of God, without blemish and without spot.

As there was no sin of commission, so was there about our Lord no fault of omission. Probably, dear brethren, we that are believers have been enabled by divine grace to escape most sins of commission; but I for one have to mourn daily over sins of omission. If we have spiritual graces, yet they do not reach the point required of us. If we do that which is right in itself, yet we usually mar our work upon the wheel, either in the motive, or in the manner of doing it, or by the self-satisfaction with which we view it when it is done. We come short of the glory of God in some respect or other. We forget to do what we ought to do, or, doing it, we are guilty of lukewarmness, self-reliance, unbelief, or some other grievous error. It was not so with our divine Redeemer. You cannot say that there was any feature deficient in his perfect beauty. He was complete in heart, in purpose, in thought, in word, in deed, in spirit You could not add anything to the life of Christ without its being manifestly an excrescence. He was emphatically an all-round man, as we say in these days. His life is a perfect circle, a complete epitome of virtue. No pearl has dropped from the silver string of his character. No one virtue has overshadowed and dwarfed the rest: all perfections combine in perfect harmony to make in him one surpassing perfection.

Neither did our Lord know a sin of thought. His mind never produced an evil wish or desire. There never was in the heart of our blessed Lord a wish for any evil pleasure, nor a desire to escape any suffering or shame which was involved in his service. When he said, "Father, if it be possible, let this cup pass from me," he never desired to escape the bitter potion at the expense of his perfect lifework. The "if it be possible," meant, "if it be consistent with fall obedience to the Father, and the accomplishment of the divine purpose." We see the weakness of his nature shrinking, and the holiness of his nature resolving and conquering, as he adds, "nevertheless, not as I will, but as thou wilt." He took upon him the likeness of sinful flesh, but though that flesh often caused him weariness of body, it never produced in him the weakness of sin. He took our infirmities, but he never exhibited an infirmity which had the least of blameworthiness attached to it. Never fell there an evil glance from those blessed eyes; never did his lips let drop a hasty word; never did those feet go or. an ill errand, nor those hands move towards a sinful deed; because his heart was filled with holiness and love. Within as well as without our Lord was unblemished. His desires were as perfect as his actions. Searched by the eyes of Omniscience, no shadow of fault could be found in him.

Yea, more, there were no tendencies about our Substitute towards evil in any form. In us there are always those tendencies; for the taint of original sin is upon us. We have to govern ourselves and hold ourselves under stern restraint, or we should rush headlong to destruction. Our carnal nature lusteth to evil, and needs to be held in as with bit and bridle. Happy is that man who can master himself. But with regard to our Lord, it was his nature to be pure, and right, and loving. All his sweet wills were towards goodness. His unconstrained life was holiness itself: he was "the holy child Jesus." The prince of this world found in him no fuel for the flame which he desired to kindle. Not only did no sin flow from him, but there was no sin in him, nor inclination, nor tendency in that direction. Watch him in secret, and you find him in prayer; look into his soul, and you find him eager to do and suffer the Father's will. Oh, the blessed character of Christ! If I had the tongues of men and of angels I could not worthily set forth his absolute perfection. Justly may the Father be well pleased with him! Well may heaven adore him!

Beloved, it was absolutely necessary that any one who should be able to suffer in our stead. should himself be spotless. A sinner obnoxious to punishment by reason of his own offenses, what can he do but bear the wrath which is due to his own sin? Our Lord Jesus Christ as man was made under the law; but he owed nothing to that law, for he perfectly fulfilled it in all respects. He was capable of standing in the room, place, and stead of others, because he was under no obligations of his own He was only under obligations towards God because he had voluntarily undertaken to be the surety and sacrifice for those whom the Father gave him. He was clear himself, or else he could not have entered into bonds for guilty men.

Oh, how I admire him, that being such as he was, spotless and thrice holy, so that even the heavens were not pure in his sight, and he charged his angels with folly, yet he condescended to be made sin for us! How could he endure to be numbered with the transgressors and bear the sin of many? It may be no misery for a sinful man to live with sinful men; but it would be a heavy sorrow for the pure-minded to dwell with a company of abandoned and licentious wretches. What an overwhelming sorrow it must have been to the pure and perfect Christ to tabernacle among the hypocritical, the selfish, and the profane! How much worse that he himself should have to take upon himself the sins of those guilty men. His sensitive and delicate nature must have shrunk from even the shadow of sin, and yet read the words and be astonished: He hath made him to be sin for us, who knew no sin." Our perfect Lord and Master bare our sins in his own body on the tree. He, before whom the sun itself is dim and the pure azure of heaven is defilement, was made sin. I need not put this in fine words: the fact is itself too grand to need any magnifying by human language. To gild refined gold, or paint the lily, were absurd; but much more absurd would it be to try to overlay with flowers of speech the matchless beauties of the cross. It suffices in simple rhyme to say—

"Oh, hear that piercing cry!
What can its meaning be?
'My God! my God! oh! why hast thou
In wrath forsaken me?'

"Oh 'twas because our sins
On him by God were laid;
He who himself had never sinn'd,
For sinners, sin was made."

This leads me on to the second point of the text, which is, what was done with him who knew no sin? He was "made sin." It is a wonderful expression: the more you weigh it the more you will marvel at its singular strength. Only the Holy Ghost might originate such language. It was wise for the divine Teacher to use very strong expressions, for else the thought might not have entered human minds. Even now, despite the emphasis, clearness, and distinctness of the language used here and elsewhere in Scripture there are found men daring enough to deny that substitution is taught in Scripture. With such subtle wits it is useless to argue. It is clear that language has no meaning for them. To read the 53rd chapter of Isaiah, and to accept it as relating to the Messiah, and then to deny his substitutionary sacrifice is simply wickedness. It would be vain to reason with such beings; they are so blind that if they were transported to the sun they could not see. In the church and out of the church there is a deadly animosity to this truth. Modern thought labors to get away from what is obviously the meaning of the Holy Spirit, that sin was lifted from the guilty and laid upon the innocent. It is written, "The Lord hath laid on him the iniquity of us all." This is as plain language as can be used; but if any plainer was required, here it is,—"He hath made him to be sin for us."

The Lord God laid upon Jesus, who voluntarily undertook it, all the weight of human sin. Instead of its resting on the sinner, who did commit it, it was made to rest upon Christ, who did not commit it; while the righteousness which Jesus wrought out was placed to the account of the guilty, who had not worked it out, so that the guilty are treated as righteous. Those who by nature are guilty, are regarded as righteous, while he who by nature knew no sin whatever, was treated as guilty. I think I must have read in scores of books that such a transference is impossible; but the statement has had no effect upon my mind. I do not care whether it is impossible or not with learned unbelievers: it is evidently possible with God, for he has done it. But they say it is contrary to reason. I do not care for that, either: it may be contrary to the reason of those unbelievers, but it is not contrary to mine; and if I am to be guided by reason, I prefer to follow my own. The atonement is a miracle, and miracles are rather to be accepted by faith than measured by calculation. A fact is the best of arguments. It is a fact that the Lord hath laid on Jesus the iniquity of us all. God's revelation proves the fact, and our faith defies human questioning! God saith it, and I believe it; and believing it, I find life and comfort in it. Shall I not preach it? Assuredly I will.

> "E'er since by faith I saw the stream
> His flowing wounds supply,
> Redeeming love has been my theme,
> And shall be till I die."

Christ was not guilty, and could not be made guilty; but he was treated as if he were guilty, because he willed to stand in the place of the guilty. Yea, he was not only treated as a sinner, but he was treated as if he had been sin itself in the abstract. This is an amazing utterance. The sinless one was made to be sin.

Sin pressed our great Substitute very sorely. He felt the weight of it in the Garden of Gethsemane, where he "sweat as it were great drops of blood falling to the ground." The full pressure of it came upon him when he was nailed to the accursed tree. There in the hours of darkness he bore infinitely more than we can tell. We know that he bore condemnation from the mouth of man, so that it is written, "He was numbered with the transgressors." We know that he bore shame for our sakes. Did not your hearts tremble last Sunday evening when our text was, "Then did they spit in his face"? It was a cruel scorn that exhausted itself upon his blessed person. This, I say, we know. We know that he bore pains innumerable of body and of mind: he thirsted, he cried out in the agony of desertion, he bled, he died. We know that he poured out his soul unto death, and yielded up the ghost. But there was at the back, and beyond all this, an immeasurable abyss of suffering. The Greek Liturgy fitly speaks of "Thine unknown sufferings": probably to us they are unknowable sufferings. He was God as well as man, and the Godhead lent an omnipotent power to the manhood, so that there was compressed within his soul, and endured by it, an amount of anguish of which we can form no conception. I will say no more: it is wise to veil what it is impossible to depict. This text both veils and discovers his sorrow, as it says, "He made him to be sin." Look into the words. Perceive their meaning, if you can. The angels desire to look into it. Gaze into this terrible crystal. Let your eyes search deep into this opal, within whose jeweled depth there are flames of fire. The Lord made the perfectly innocent one to be sin for us: that means more of humiliation, darkness, agony, and death than you can conceive. It brought a kind of distraction and well-nigh a destruction to the tender and gentle spirit of our Lord. I do not say that our substitute endured a hell, that were unwarrantable. I will not say that he endured either the exact punishment for sin, or an equivalent for it; but I do say that what he endured rendered to the justice of God a vindication of his law more clear and more effectual than would have been rendered to it by the damnation of the sinners for whom he died. The cross is under many aspects a more full revelation of the wrath of God against human sin than even Tophet, and the smoke of torment which goeth up forever and ever. Who would know God's hate of sin must see the Only Begotten bleeding in body and bleeding in soul even unto death: he must, in fact, spell out each word of my text, and read its innermost meaning. There, my brethren, I am ashamed of the poverty of my explanation, and I will therefore only repeat the full and sublime language of the apostle—"He hath made him to be sin for us." It is more than "He hath put him to grief"; it is more than "God hath forsaken him"; it is more than "The chastisement of our peace was upon him": it is the most suggestive of all descriptions—"He hath made him to be sin for us." Oh depth of terror, and yet height of love!

So I pass on to notice in the third place, who did it? The text saith, "He hath made him to be sin for us"; that is, God himself it was who appointed his dear Son to be made sin for guilty men. The wise ones tell us that this substitution cannot be just. Who made them judges of what is right and just? I ask them whether they believe that Jesus suffered and died at all? If they believe that he did, how do they account for the fact? Do they say that he died as an example?

Then I ask, is it just for God to allow a sinless being to die as an example? The fact of our Lord's death is sure, and it has to be accounted for. Ours is the fullest and truest explanation.

In the appointment of the Lord Jesus Christ to be made sin for us, there was first of all a display of the Divine Sovereignty. God here did what none but he could have done. It would not have been possible for all of us together to have laid sin upon Christ; but it was possible for the great Judge of all, who giveth no account of his matters, to determine that so it should be. He is the fountain of rectitude, and the exercise of his divine prerogative is always unquestionable righteousness. That the Lord Jesus, who offered himself as a willing surety and substitute, should be accepted as surety and substitute for guilty man was in the power of the great Supreme. In his Divine Sovereignty he accepted him, and before that sovereignty we bow. If any question it, our only answer is, "Nay but, O man, who art thou that repliest against God?"

The death of our Lord also displayed divine justice. It pleased God as the Judge of all, that sin should not be forgiven without the exaction of the punishment which had been so righteously threatened to it, or such other display of justice as might vindicate the law. They say that this is not the God of love. I answer, it is the God of love, pre-eminently so. If you had upon the bench today a judge whose nature was kindness itself, it would behove him as a judge to execute justice, and if he did not, he would make his kindness ridiculous; indeed, his kindness to the criminal would be unkindness to society at large. Whatever the judge may be personally, he is officially compelled to do justice. And "shall not the Judge of all the earth do right?" You speak of the Fatherhood of God. Enlarge as you please upon that theme, even till you make a heresy of it; but still God is the great moral Governor of the universe, and it behoves him to deal with sin in such a way that it is seen to be an evil and a bitter thing. God cannot wink at wickedness. I bless his holy name, and adore him that he is not unjust in order to be merciful, that he does not spare the guilty in order to indulge his gentleness. Every transgression and disobedience has its just recompense of reward. But through the sacrifice of Christ he is able justly to pardon. I bless his holy name that to vindicate his justice he determined that, while a free pardon should be provided for believers, it should be grounded upon an atonement which satisfied all the requirements of the law.

Admire also in the substitutionary sacrifice the great grace of God. Never forget that he whom God made to be sin for us was his own Son;—I go further, it was in some sense his own self; for the Son is one with the Father. You may not confound the persons, but you cannot divide the substance of the blessed Trinity in Unity. You may not so divide the Son of God from the Father as to forget that God was in him reconciling the world unto himself. It is the Father's other self who on the cross in human form doth bleed and die. "Light of light, very God of very God": it is this Light that was eclipsed, that Godhead which purchased the church with his own blood. Herein is infinite love! You tell me that God might have pardoned without atonement. I answer, that finite and fallible love might have done so, and thus have wounded itself by killing justice; but the love which both required and provided the atonement is indeed infinite. God himself provided the atonement by freely and fully giving up himself in the person of his Son to suffer in consequence of human sin.

What I want you to notice here is this, if ever your mind should be troubled about the propriety or rightness of a substitutionary sacrifice, you may at once settle the matter by remembering that God himself "hath made him to be sin for us who knew no sin." If God did it, it is well done. I am not careful to defend an act of God: let the man who dares accuse his Maker think what he is at. If God himself provided the sacrifice, be you sure that he has accepted it. There can be no question ever raised about it, since Jehovah made to meet on him our iniquities. He that made Christ to be sin for us, knew what he did, and it is not for us to begin to say, "Is this right, or is this not right?" The thrice holy God hath done this, and it must be right. That which satisfies God may well satisfy us. If God is pleased with the sacrifice of Christ, shall not we be much more than pleased? Shall we not be delighted, entranced, emparadised, to be saved by such a sacrifice as God himself appoints, provides, and accepts? "He hath made him to be sin for us."

The last point is, what happens to us inconsequence? "That we might be made the righteousness of God in him." Oh this weighty text! No man living can exhaust it. No theologian lived, even in the palmiest days of theology, who could ever get to the bottom of this statement.

Every man that believes in Jesus is through Christ having taken his sin made to be righteous before God. We are righteous through faith in Christ Jesus, "justified by faith." More than this, we are made not only to have the character of "righteous," but to become the substance called "righteousness." I cannot explain this, but it is no small matter. It means no inconsiderable thing when we are said to be "made righteousness." What is more, we are not only made righteousness, but we are made "the righteousness of God." Herein is a great mystery. The righteousness which Adam had in the garden was perfect, but it was the righteousness of man: ours is the righteousness of God. Human righteousness failed; but the believer has a divine righteousness which can never fail. He not only has it, but he is it: he is "made the righteousness of God in Christ." We can now sing,

"With my Savior's vesture on,
Holy as the Holy One."

How acceptable with God must those be who are made by God himself to be "the righteousness of God in him"! I cannot conceive of anything more complete.

As Christ was made sin, and yet never sinned, so are we made righteousness, though we cannot claim to have been righteous in and of ourselves. Sinners though we be, and forced to confess it with grief, yet the Lord doth cover us so completely with the righteousness of Christ, that only his righteousness is seen, and we are made the righteousness of God in him. This is true of all the saints, even of as many as believe on his name. Oh, the splendor of this doctrine! Canst thou see it, my friend? Sinner though thou be, and in thyself defiled, deformed, and debased, yet if thou wilt accept the great Substitute which God provides for thee in the person of his dear Son, thy sins are gone from thee, and righteousness has come to thee. Thy sins were laid on Jesus, the scapegoat; they are thine no longer, he has put them away. I may say that his righteousness is imputed unto thee; but I go further, and say with the text, "Thou art made the righteousness of God in him." No doctrine can be more sweet than this to those who feel the weight of sin and the burden of its curse.

II. So now, gathering all up, I have to close with the second part of the text, which is not teaching, but the application of teaching,—A GREAT ARGUMENT. "Now then we are ambassadors for Christ, as though God did beseech you by us: we pray you in Christ's stead, be ye reconciled to God."

Oh, that these lips had language, or that this heart could speak without them! Then would I plead with every unconverted, unbelieving soul within this place, and plead as for my life. Friend, you are at enmity with God, and God is angry with you; but on his part there is every readiness for reconciliation. He has made a way by which you can become his friend—a very costly way to himself, but free to you. He could not give up his justice, and so destroy the honor of his own character; but he did give up his Son, his Only Begotten, and his Well-Beloved; and that Son of his has been made sin for us, though he knew no sin. See how God meets you! See how willing, how anxious he is that there should be reconciliation between himself and guilty men. O sirs, if you are not saved it is not because God will not or cannot save you; it is because you and refuse to accept his mercy in Christ. If there is any difference between you and God today it is not from want of kindness on his part; it is from want of willingness on yours. The burden of your ruin must lie at your own door: your blood must be on your own skirts.

Now observe what we have to say to you today is this: we are anxious that you should be at peace with God, and therefore we act as ambassadors for Christ. I am not going to lay any stress upon the office of ambassador as honorable or authoritative, for I do not feel that this would have weight with you: but I lay all the stress upon the peace to which we would bring you. God has reconciled me to himself, and I would fain have you reconciled also. I once knew him not, neither did I care for him. I lived well enough without him, and sported with the trifles of a day, so as to forget him. He brought me to seek his face, and seeking his face I found him. He has blotted out my sins and removed my enmity. I know that I am his servant, and that he is my Friend, my Father, my All. And now I cannot help trying in my poor way to be an ambassador for him with you. I do not like that any of you should live at enmity with my Father who made you; and that you should be wantonly provoking him by preferring evil to good. Why should you not be at peace with one who so much wants to be at peace with you? Why should you not love the God of love, and delight in him who is so kind to you? What he hath done for me he is quite willing to do for you: he is a God ready to pardon. I have preached his gospel now for many years, but I never met with a sinner yet that Christ refused to cleanse when he came to him. I never knew a single case of a man who trusted Jesus, and asked to be forgiven, confessing his sin and forsaking it, who was cast out. I say I never met with one man whom Jesus refused; nor shall I ever do so. I have spoken with harlots whom he has restored to purity, and drunkards whom he has delivered from their evil habit, and with men guilty of foul sins who have become pure and chaste through the grace of our Lord Jesus. They have always told me the same story—"I sought the Lord, and he heard me; he hath washed me in his blood, and I am whiter than snow." Why should you not be saved as well as these?

Dear friend, perhaps you have never thought of this matter, and this morning you did not come here with any idea of thinking of it; but why should you not begin? You came just to hear a well-known preacher; I pray you forget the preacher, and think only of yourself, your God and your Savior. It must be wrong for you to live without a thought of your Maker. To forget him is to despise him. It must be wrong for you to refuse the great atonement: you do refuse it if you do not accept it at once. It must be wrong for you to stand out against your God; and you do stand out against him if you will not be reconciled to him. Therefore I humbly play the part of an ambassador for Christ, and I beseech you believe in him and live.

Notice how the text puts it: "We are ambassadors for Christ, as though God did beseech you by us." This thought staggers me. As I came along this morning I felt as if I could bury my head in my hands and weep as I thought of God beseeching anybody. He speaks, and it is done; myriads of angels count themselves happy to fly at his command; and yet man has so become God's enemy that he will not be reconciled to him. God would make him his friend, and spends the blood of his dear Son to cement that friendship; but man will not have it. See the great God turns to beseeching his obstinate creature! his foolish creature! In this I feel a reverent compassion for God. Must he beseech a rebel to be forgiven? Do you hear it? Angels, do you hear it? He who is the King of kings veils his sovereignty, and stoops to beseeching his creature to be reconciled to him! I wonder not that some of my brethren start back from such an idea, and cannot believe that it could be so: it seems so derogatory to the glorious God. Yet my text saith it, and it must be true—"As though God did beseech you by us." This makes it awful work to preach, does it not? I ought to beseech you as though God spoke to you through me, looking at you through these eyes, and stretching out his hands through these hands. He saith, "All day long I have stretched forth my hands unto a disobedient and gainsaying people." He speaks softly, and tenderly, and with paternal affection through these poor lips of mine, "as though God did beseech you by us."

Furthermore notice that next line, which if possible has even more force in it: "We pray you in Christ' s stead." Since Jesus died in our stead we, his redeemed ones, are to pray others in his stead; and as he poured out his heart for sinners in their stead, we must in another way pour out our hearts for sinners in his stead. "We pray you in Christ's stead." Now if my Lord were here this morning how would he pray you to come to him? I wish, my Master, I were more fit to stand in thy place at this time. Forgive me that I am so incapable. Help me to break my heart, to think that it does not break as it ought to do, for these men and women who are determined to destroy themselves, and, therefore, pass thee by, my Lord, as though thou wert but a common felon, hanging on a gibbet! Omen, how can you think so little of the death of the Son of God? It is the wonder of time, the admiration of eternity. O souls, why will you refuse eternal life? Why will ye die? Why will ye despise him by whom alone you can live? There is but one gate of life, that gate is the open side of Christ; why will ye not enter, and live? "Come unto me," saith he; "Come unto me." I think I hear him say it: "Come unto me, all ye that labor and are heavy laden, and I will give you rest. Take my yoke upon you, and learn of me; for I am meek and lowly in heart: and ye shall find rest unto your souls." I think I see him on that last day, that great day of the feast, standing and crying, "If any man thirst, let him come unto me, and drink." I hear him sweetly declare, "Him that cometh to me I will in no wise cast out." I am not fit to pray you in Christ's stead, but I do pray you with all my heart You that hear my voice from Sunday to Sunday, do come and accept the great sacrifice, and be reconciled to God. You that hear me but this once, I would like you to go away with this ringing in your ears, "Be ye reconciled to God." I have nothing pretty to say to you; I have only to declare that God has prepared a propitiation, and that now he entreats sinners to come to Jesus, that through him they may be reconciled to God.

We do not exhort you to some impossible effort. We do not bid you do some great thing; we do not ask you for money or price; neither do we demand of you years of miserable feeling; but only this—be ye reconciled. It is not so much reconcile yourselves as "be reconciled." Yield yourselves to him who round you now the bands of a man would cast, drawing you with cords of love because he was given for you. His spirit strives with you, yield to his striving. With Jacob you know there wrestled a man till the breaking of the day; let that man, that God-man, overcome you. Submit yourselves. Yield to the grasp of those hands which were nailed to the cross for you. Will you not yield to your best friend? He that doth embrace you now presses you to a heart that was pierced with the spear on your behalf. Oh, yield thee! Yield thee, man! Dost thou not feel some softness stealing over thee? Steel not thine heart against it. He saith, with a tone most still and sweet, "Today if ye will hear his voice, harden not your hearts." Believe and live! Quit the arch-enemy who has held thee in his grip. Escape for thy life, look not behind thee, stay not in all the plain, but flee where thou seest the open door of the great Father's house. At the gate the bleeding Savior is waiting to receive thee, and to say, "I was made sin for thee, and thou art made the righteousness of God in me." Father, draw them! Father, draw them! Eternal Spirit, draw them, for Jesus Christ thy Son's sake! Amen.

3

FOR WHOM IS THE GOSPEL MEANT?

Preached on March 25, 1877
Scripture: Mark 2:17
From: Metropolitan Tabernacle Pulpit Volume 23

"They that are whole have no need of the physician, but they that are sick: I came not to call the righteous, but sinners to repentance."—Mark ii. 17.
Christ died for the ungodly."—Romans v. 6.
"God commendeth his love toward us, in that, while we were yet sinners, Christ died for us."—Romans v. 8.
"This is a faithful saying, and worthy of all acceptation, that Christ Jesus came into the world to save sinners."
—1 Timothy i. 15.

LAST Thursday evening, with considerable difficulty, I stood here to preach the gospel of Jesus Christ, and I handled one of the simplest imaginable texts full of nothing but the very plainest elements of the gospel. Within a very few minutes I had a harvest for the sermon. The congregation was slender, for you know how ill a night it was, and how little you expected that your pastor would be able to preach, but three souls came forward uninvited to acknowledge that they had found peace with God. How many more there were I do not know, but these three sought out the brethren, and bore a good and hearty confession to the blessed fact that for the first time in their lives they had understood the plan of salvation. Now, it seemed to me that if a plain gospel theme was so promptly profitable, I had better keep to the like subjects. If a farmer finds that a certain seed has paid him so well that he never had a better crop before, then he will keep to that seed, and sow more of it. Those processes of husbandry which have been successful should be persevered in, and even used upon a larger scale. So this morning I shall just preach the A B C of the gospel, the first rudiments of the art of salvation, and I thank God this will be no new thing to me. May God the Holy Spirit, in answer to your prayers, grant us a reward this morning after the same proportion as last Thursday, and, if so, our heart will be exceeding glad.

Out of a very great number I have selected the four texts which I have read just to set forth the truth that the mission of our Lord related to sinners. What did Christ come into the world for? For whom did he come? These are questions of the greatest importance, and they are clearly answered in Scripture. When the children of Israel first found manna outside the camp they said to one another, "Manna?" or, what is it? for they wist not what it was. There it lay, a small round thing, as small as the hoar frost upon the ground. No doubt they looked at it and rubbed it m their hands, and smelt it, but how glad they were when Moses said, "This is the bread which the Lord has given you to eat." They were not long before they put the good news to the test, for each man gathered his omer full and took it home, and prepared it according to his liking. Now, concerning the gospel, there are many who might call out "Manna?" for they know not what it is. Very frequently, too they make a mistake as to its bearings and its objects, dreaming that it is a kind of improved law, or an easier system of salvation by works; and hence they err also in their idea of the persons for whom it is designed. They imagine that surely the blessings of salvation must be meant for deserving persons, and Christ must be the Redeemer of the meritorious. On the principle of "good for the good" they infer that grace is for the excellent and Christ for the virtuous. Hence it is a most useful thing for us continually to be reminding men what the gospel is, and for whom it is sent into the world; for, though the great mass of you know full well, and do not need to be told, yet there are multitudes around us who persist in grave mistakes, and need to be instructed over and over again in the very simplest of the doctrines of grace. There is less need for laborious explanations of profound mysteries than for simple explanations of plain truths. Many men need only a simple latchkey to lift the latch and open the door of faith, and such a key I hope God's infinite mercy may put into their hands this morning. Our business is to show that the gospel is intended for sinners, that it has an eye to guilty persons; that it is not sent into the world as a reward for the good and for the excellent, or for those who think they have any measure of fitness or preparation for the divine favor; but that it is intended for law breakers, for the undeserving, for the ungodly, for those who. have gone astray like lost sheep, or left their father's house like the prodigal. Christ died to save sinners, and he justifieth the ungodly; The truth is plain enough in the Word, but since the human heart kicks against it we will the more earnestly insist upon it.

First, EVEN A SUPERFICIAL GLANCE AT OUR LORD'S MISSION SUFFICES TO SHOW THAT HIS WORK WAS FOR THE SINFUL. For, dear brethren, the descent of the Son of God into this world as a Savior implied that men needed to be delivered from a great evil by a divine hand. The coming of a Savior who should by his death provide pardon for human sin supposed men to be greatly guilty, and to be incapable of procuring pardon by any doings of their own. Yon would never have seen a Savior if there had not been a fall Eden's withering was a necessary preface to Gethsemane's groaning. Yon would never have heard of a cross and a bleeding Savior on it if you had. not first heard of the tree of the- knowledge of good and evil, and of a disobedient hand which plucked the forbidden fruit. If the mission of our Lord did not refer to the guilty it was- an unnecessary errand altogether, so far as we can see. What justifies the incarnation except man's ruin? What explains our Lord's suffering life but man's guilt? Above all, what explains his death and the cloud, under which he died but human sin? "All we like sheep have gone astray, and the Lord hath laid on him the iniquity of us all"—that is the answer to an otherwise unanswerable riddle.

If we give a glance at the covenant under which our Lord came we soon perceive that its bearing is towards guilty men. The blessing of the covenant of works has to do with men who are innocent, and to them it promises great blessings. If there had been salvation by works it would have been by the law, for the law is upright and just and good; but the new covenant evidently deals with sinners, for it does not speak of the reward of merit, but it freely promises, "I will be merciful to their unrighteousness, and their sins and their iniquities will I remember no more." If there had been no sins and iniquities, and no unrighteousness, then there had been no need of the covenant of grace, of which Christ is the messenger and the ambassador. The slightest glimpse at our Lord's official character as the Adam of a new covenant should suffice to convince us that his errand is to guilty men. Moses comes to show how the holy should behave, hut Jesus comes to reveal how the unholy may be cleansed.

Whenever we hear the mission of Christ spoken of it is described as one of mercy and of grace. In the redemption which is in Christ Jesus it is always the mercy of God that is extolled—according to his mercy he saved us. He for Christ's sake, according to his abundant mercy, forgiveth us our trespasses. "The law was given by Moses, but grace and truth by Jesus Christ." "The grace of God, and the gift by grace, which is by one man Jesus Christ, hath abounded unto many." The apostle Paul, who most fully expoundeth the gospel, makes grace to be the one word upon which he rings the changes: "where sin abounded grace did much more abound." "By grace are ye saved, through faith, and that not of yourselves, it is the gift of God." "Grace reigns through righteousness unto eternal life, by Jesus Christ our Lord." But, brethren, mercy implies sinfulness: there can be no mercy extended to the just, for justice itself secures every good thing to them. Grace, too, can only be for offenders. What grace is wanted by those who have kept the law, and deserved well at Jehovah's hands? To them eternal life would be a matter of debt, a fairly earned reward; but when you talk of grace you at once shut out merit and introduce another principle. Mercy can only he exercised where there is sin and grace cannot be manifested except to the undeserving. This is plain enough, and yet the whole tenor of some men's religion is based on another theory.

The fact is, when we begin to study the gospel of the grace of God we see that it turns its face always towards sin, even as a physician looks towards disease, or as charity looks towards distress. The gospel issues its invitations; but what are the invitations? Are they not addressed to those who are burdened with a load of sin, and laboring to escape from its consequences? It invites every creature because every creature has its needs, but it specially says "Let the wicked forsake his way and the unrighteous man his thoughts." It invites the man who has no money, or, in other words, no merit. It calls to those who are needy, and thirsty, and poor, and naked, and all these are but used as figures of states produced by sin. The very gifts of the gospel imply sin; life is for the dead, sight is for the blind, liberty is for the captives, cleansing is for the filthy, absolution is for the sinful. No gospel blessing is proposed as a reward, and no invitation is issued to those who claim the blessings of grace as a matter of right; men are invited to come and receive them freely according to the grace of God. And what are the commands of the gospel? Repent. But who repenteth save a sinner? Believe. But believing is not according to the law; the law speaks only of doing. Believing has to do with sinners, and with the method of salvation by grace.

The gospel representations of itself usually look sinner-ward. The great king who makes a feast finds not a guest to sit at the table among those who were naturally expected to come, but from the highways and hedges men are compelled to come in. If the gospel describes itself as a feast it is a great feast for the blind, the halt, and the lame; if it describes itself as a fountain it is a fountain opened for sin and for uncleanness. Everywhere, in all that it does and says and provides to men, the gospel proves itself to be the sinner's friend. The motto of its

Founder and Lord still is "this man receiveth sinners." The gospel is an hospital for the sick, none but the guilty will ever accept its benefits; it is medicine for the diseased, the whole and the self-righteous will never relish its saving drafts. Those who imagine that they have some excellence before God will never care to be saved by sovereign grace. The gospel, I say, looks sinner-ward. That way and that way only doth it cast its blessings.

And brethren, ye know that the gospel has always found its greatest trophies amongst the most sinful: it enlists its best soldiers not only from amongst the guilty but from amongst the most guilty. "Simon," said our Lord, "I have somewhat to say unto thee—A certain man had two debtors, the one owed him five hundred pence, and the other fifty, and when they had nothing to pay he frankly forgave them both. Tell me therefore, which of them will love him most?" The gospel goes upon the principle that he who has had much forgiven the same loveth much, and so its gracious Lord delights to seek out the most guilty and to manifest himself to them with abundant and overflowing love, saying "I have blotted out thy sing like a cloud, and like a thick cloud thy transgressions." Among great transgressors it finds its warmest lovers when once it has saved them, from these it receives the heartiest welcome and in them it obtains the most enthusiastic adherents. Great sinners when saved crown free grace with its most illustrious diadems. Well may we be sure that it has its eye towards sinners, since it is amongst the chief of sinners that it finds its highest glory.

There is one other reflection which also lies very near the surface, namely, that if the gospel do not look towards sinners, to whom else could it look? There seems to have been a revival lately of the old cavilling spirit, so that proud Pharisees constantly tell us that the preaching of justification by faith is overdone, and that we are leading people to think less of morality by preaching up the grace of God. This oft refuted objection is coming forth again, because Protestantism is losing its sap and soul. The very force and backbone of the Reformers' teaching was that great doctrine of grace, that salvation is not of works but of the grace of God alone; and because men are getting away from the Reformation, and drifting into Romanism, they are casting into the background this grand truth of justification by faith alone, and pretending to be afraid of it. But O, knaves and fools that most men are upon this matter! I put to all such this one question—To whom, sirs, would the gospel look if mot towards sinners, for what are you but sinners? You who talk about morality being injured, about holiness being ignored, what have you to do with either? The people who usually urge these objections, as a rule, had better be quiet on such topics. In general these fierce defenders of morality and holiness are exceedingly lax, while believers in the grace of God are frequently charged with Puritanism and rigidity. He who stands out most to speak against the doctrines of grace is frequently the man who needs grace most, while the very man who cries down good works as a ground of trust is just the person whose life is carefully directed by the statutes of the Lord. Know ye, O men, that there lives not on the face of the earth a man upon whom God can look with pleasure if he consider that man on the ground of his law. "They are all gone out of the way, they are altogether become unprofitable; there is none that doeth good, no not one,"—not one is sound and right before God by nature, not one life is pure and clean when the Lord comes to examine it with his all-searching eye. We are shut up in the same prison as all guilty: if not alike guilty, yet guilty according to the proportion of our light and knowledge, and each one justly condemned, for we have erred in heart and have not loved the Lord. To whom, then, could the gospel look if it did not cast its eyes sinner-ward? For whom else could the Savior have died? Who is there in the world for whom the benefits of grace could be designed?

II. Secondly, THE MORE CLOSELY WE LOOK THE MORE CLEAR THIS FACT BECOMES, for, brethren, the work of salvation was certainly not performed for any one of us who are saved on account of any goodness in us. If there be any goodness in us, it was put there by the grace of God and it certainly was not there when first the bowels of Jehovah's love began to move towards us. If you take the first ensign of salvation that was actually visible on earth, namely, the coming of Christ, we are told concerning it that "when we were yet without strength, in due time Christ died for the ungodly. For scarcely for a righteous man will one die: yet peradventure for a good man some would even dare to die. But God commendeth his love toward us, in that, while we were yet sinners, Christ died for us." So that our redemption, my brother, was effected before we were born. This was the fruit of the Father's great love "wherewith he loved us, even when we were dead in sins." There was nothing in us going before which could have merited that redemption, indeed the very idea of meriting the death of Jesus is absurd and blasphemous. Yes, and when we were living in sin and loving it, there were preparations made for our salvation j divine love was busy on our behalf when we were busy in rebellion. The gospel was brought near to us, earnest hearts were set a praying for us, the text was written which would convert us; and as I have already said, the blood was spilt which cleanses us, and the Spirit of God was given, who should renew us. All this was done while as yet we had no breathings of soul after God. Is not that a wonderful passage in Ezekiel, where the Lord passed by and saw the helpless infant cast out in the open field while it was yet unswaddled and unwashed, but was foul and polluted in its own blood? He says that it was a time of love, and yet it was a time of pollution and loathing. He did not love the chosen babe because it was well washed and fitly clad, but he loved it when it was foul and naked. Let every believing heart admire the freeness and compassion of divine love.

> *"He saw me ruin'd in the fall.*
> *Yet loved me, notwithstanding all;*
> *He saved me from my lost estate,*
> *His loving-kindness, oh, how great!"*

When thy heart was hard, when thy neck was obstinate, when thou wouldst not repent nor yield to him but rebelled yet more and more, he loved thee, even thee, with supreme affection. Why such grace? Why indeed, but because his nature is full of goodness and he delighteth in mercy. Is not mercy seen to be evidently extended towards the sinful and not exerted because of some goodness moving thereto?

Look a little closer still. What did our Lord come into the world to do? Here is the answer. "He was wounded for our transgressions, he was bruised for our iniquities: the chastisement of our peace was upon him; and with his stripes we are healed." He came that he might be a sin-bearer: and do you think he came to bear only the little, trifling sins of the best sort of men, if such sins there 'be? Do you suppose that he is a little Savior, who came to save us from little offenses? Beloved, it is Jehovah's darling Son that comes to earth and bears the load of sin, a load which, when he bears it, he finds to be no fictitious burden, for it forces from him the bloody sweat. So heavy is that load that he bows his head to the grave, and even unto death, beneath it. That stupendous load which lay on Christ was the heap of our sins; and hence as we look into the subject we perceive that the gospel must have to do with sinners. No sin! Then is the cross a mistake. No sin! Then the *lama sahachthani* was a just complaint against unnecessary cruelty. No sin! Then, O Redeemer, what are those glories which we have so eagerly ascribed to thee? How canst thou put away sin which does not exist? The existence of great sin is implied in the coming of Christ, and that coming was occasioned and rendered necessary by sin, against which Jesus comes as our Deliverer. He declares that he has opened a fountain, filled with the blood of his own veins. But what for? A cleansing fountain implies filth. It must be, sinner, that somewhere or other there are filthy people, or else there had not been such an amazing fountain as this, filled from the heart of Christ. If thou be guilty thou art one who needs the fountain, and it is opened for thee. Come thou with all thy sin and foulness about thee and wash this morning, and be clean.

> *"'Twas for sinners that he suffer'd*
> *Agonies unspeakable;*
> *Canst thou doubt thou art a sinner?*
> *If thou canst—then hope farewell.*
> *"But, believing what is written—*
> *'All are guilty'—'dead in sin,'*
> *Looking to the Crucified One*
> *Hope shall rise thy soul within."*

Brethren, all the gifts which Jesus Christ came to give, or at least most of them, imply that there is sin. What is his first gift but pardon? How can he pardon a man who has not transgressed? With all reverence do I speak, there can be no such thing as pardon where there is no offence committed. Propitiation for sin and blotting out of iniquity both require that there must be sin to be blotted out, or what is there real about them? Christ comes to bring justification, and this shows that there must be a lack of natural holiness in men, for if not they would be justified by themselves and by their own works. And why all this outcry about justification by the righteousness of the Son of God if men are already justified by a righteousness of their own? Those two blessings, and others of the same kind, are clearly applicable only to sinful men. To no other men can they be of any use.

Our Lord Jesus Christ came girded also with divine power. He says, "The Spirit of the Lord is upon me." To what end was he girded with divine power unless it be because sin had taken all power and strength from man, and man was in a condition out of which he could not be lifted except by the energy of the eternal Spirit? And what does this imply but that Christ's errand bears upon those who through sin are without strength and without merit before God? The Holy Spirit is given because man's spirit has failed: because sin has taken the life out of man, and made him dead in trespasses and sins, therefore comes the Holy Spirit to quicken him into newness of life, and that Spirit comes by Jesus Christ. Therefore the errand of Jesus Christ is manifestly to the guilty.

I will not omit to say that the great deeds of our Lord, if you look at them carefully, all bear upon sinners. Jesus lives; it is that he may seek and save that which is lost. Jesus dies; it is that he may make a propitiation for the sins of guilty men. Jesus rises; he rises again for our justification, and as I have shown, we should not want justification unless we had been naturally guilty. Jesus ascends on high, and he receives gifts for men; but note that special word, "Yea, for the rebellious also, that the Lord God may dwell among them." Jesus lives in heaven, but he lives there to intercede. "Wherefore he is able also to save them to the uttermost that come unto God by him, seeing he ever liveth to make intercession for them." So take whatever part of his glorious achievements you please you will find that there is a distinct bearing towards those who are immersed in guilt.

And beloved, all the gifts and blessings that Jesus Christ has brought to us derive much of their radiance from their bearing upon sinners. It is in Christ Jesus that we are elect, and to my mind the glory of electing love lies in this, that it pitched upon such undeserving objects. How had there been any election had it been according to merit? Then men would have taken rank by right according to their own deeds, but election's glories are brilliant with grace, and grace always has for its foil and background the unworthiness of the objects towards whom it is manifested. The election of God is not according to our works, but it is a gracious election of sinners. Adore and wonder.

Turn you to effectual calling, and see how delightful it is to view that calling as a calling from among the dead, as a calling of the things that are not as though they were, as a calling of condemned ones into forgiveness and favor. Turn ye next to adoption. What is the glory of adoption, but that God has adopted those who were strangers and rebels to make them his children? What is the peculiar beauty of regeneration, but that he has been able of these stones to raise up children unto Abraham? What is the beauty of sanctification, but that he has taken such unholy creatures as we are to make us kings and priests unto God, and to sanctify us wholly—spirit, soul, and body? To my mind it is the glory of heaven to think that yonder white-robed choristers were once foully defiled; those happy worshippers were once rebels against God. It is a happy sight to see the unfallen angels who have kept their first estate, perfectly pure and forever praising God; but the vision of fallen -men divinely restored is more full of the glory of God. Lift as they may their joyful voices in perpetual chorales the angels can never reach the special sweetness of that song—"We have washed our robes and made them white in the blood of the Lamb." They cannot experimentally enter into that truth which is of Jehovah's name its crowning glory—"Thou wast slain and hast redeemed us to God by thy blood."

Thus I have abundantly shown that the further we look the more clear it is that the gospel is aimed at sinners and especially intended for their benefit.

III. Now, thirdly, it is evident that IT IS OUR WISDOM TO ACCEPT THE SITUATION. I know that to many this is very UDPALATABLE doctrine. Well, friend, you had better have your palate altered, for you will never be able to alter the doctrine. It is the truth of the everlasting God, and cannot be changed. The very best thing you can do, since the gospel looks towards sinners, is to get where the gospel looks; and I can recommend this to you, not merely on the ground of policy, but on the ground of honesty, because you will be only in your right place when you get there. I think I hear you raising objections. "I do not admire this system. Am I to be saved in the same way as the dying thief?" Precisely so, sir, unless there should happen to be even more grace shown towards you than to him. "But you do not mean to assert that in the matter of salvation I am to be put on a level with the woman that was a sinner? I have been pure and chaste, and am I to owe my salvation just as much to the absolute mercy of God as she did?" Yes, sir, I do say that, exactly as it stands. There is but one principle upon which the Lord saves men, and it is that of pure grace. I want you to understand this. Even if it grinds like grit between your teeth, and makes you angry; I shall not regret it so long as you know what I mean; for the truth may yet find entrance into your soul, and you may yet bow before its power. Oh, you children of godly parents, you young people of excellent morals and delicate consciences, to you I speak, even to you. Rejoice in your privileges, but do not boast in them, for you too have sinned, you have sinned against light and knowledge, you know you have. If you have not plunged into the grosser sins in act and deed, yet in desire and in imagination you have gone far enough astray, and in many things you have offended grievously against God. If, with these considerations before you, you take your place as a sinner you will not be disgraced, but be merely standing where you certainly are.

And then remember, if you get the blessing this way, you will have obtained, it in the safest possible way. Suppose there are a number of guest chambers, and I have my seat in one of the best of them, I may have no right to be there. I am eating and drinking of what is provided for superior guests, but my ticket does not mark me out as one of these, and therefore I am ill at ease. Every mouthful that I eat I think to myself, "I do not know whether I shall be allowed to remain here, perhaps the Lord of the feast will come in and say to me, 'Friend how earnest thou in hither?' and I must begin with shame to take the lowest room." Brethren, when we begin at the bottom, and sit in the lowest room we feel safe, we are satisfied that what we do get is meant for us, and will not be taken away from us. Perhaps, also, when the king comes he may take us up to a higher room. There is nothing like beginning, in the lowliest place. When I lay hold of the promise as a saint I have my doubts about it, but when I grasp it as a sinner I can have no question. If the Lord bid me feed on his mercy as his child I do it, but the devil whispers that I am presuming, for I never was really adopted by grace; but when I come to Jesus as a guilty, undeserving sinner, and take what the Lord freely presents to me upon believing, the devil himself cannot tell me that I am not a sinner, or if he does the lie is too transparent, and causes me no distress. There is nothing like having an indefeasible title, and if the description given to you in the title is that you are a sinner, it is an indisputable one, for depend upon it a sinner you are. So the sinner's place is your true place and your safest place.

Another blessing is, it is a place into which you can get directly, even at this very moment. If the gospel looks towards men in a certain state of heart in which there are commendable virtues, then how long will it take me to raise my heart to that state? If Jesus Christ comes into the world to save men who have a certain measure of excellence, then how long will it take me to obtain that excellence? I may be taken sick and die within half-an-hour, and hear the sentence of eternal judgment, and it would be poor gospel to tell me that I might possibly obtain salvation if I attained a state which would take me several months to reach. At this hour I, a dying man, do know that I may be gone out of this world and beyond the reach of mercy within an hour; what a comfort it is that the gospel comes to me and gives itself to me just now, even as it finds me! I am already in that position in which grace begins with men, for I am a sinner, and I have only to own that I am so. Now then, poor soul, just sit thee down before the Lord and say, "Lord, does thy Son come to save the guilty? I am such, and I trust him to save me. Did he die for the ungodly? L am such, Lord, I trust in his blood to cleanse me. Was his death for sinners? Lord, I take up the position. I plead guilty. I accept the sentence of thy law as being just, but save me, Lord, for Jesus died." It is done; you are saved. Go in peace, my son; thy sins, which are many, are forgiven thee. Go, my daughter, go thy way, and rejoice: the Lord hath put away thy sin; thou shalt not die, for he that believeth is justified from all sin. Blessed is the man to whom the Lord imputeth not iniquity, and in whose spirit there is no guile. Get, then, into your true position, accept the situation in which grace considers you to be; Do not talk of justice and merit; but appeal to pity and love. A certain man had several times plotted against the first Napoleon, and eventually, being entirely in the emperor's hands, sentence of death was pronounced upon him. His daughter earnestly pleaded for his life, and at last, having obtained an audience with the emperor, she fell upon her knees before him. "My girl," said the emperor, "it is of no use to plead for your father, for I have the clearest evidence of his repeated crimes, and it is but justice that he should die." The girl replied, "Sire, I do not ask for justice, I beg for mercy. It is upon the mercifulness of your heart and not upon the justice of the case that I rely." She was heard patiently, and her father's life was spared at her request. Imitate this appeal, and cry, "Have mercy upon me, O God, according to thy lovingkindness." Justice owes you nothing but death, mercy alone can spare you. Have done with every idea of making out a good case: admit it to be a bad one and plead guilty. Cast yourself upon the mercy of the court and ask for mercy, free mercy, undeserved mercy, gratuitous favor: this is what you must ask for, and as in law they have a form of suing called in *forma pauperis*, that is, in the form of a pauper, do you adopt the method, and as a man full of necessities do you beg for favor at the hands of God, in *forma pauperis*, and it shall be bestowed upon you.

IV. Now I close this discourse with the next point, which is, THIS DOCTRINE HAS A GREAT SANCTIFYING INFLUENCE. "There," Says One, "I do not believe that. Surely you have been holding out a premium to sin by saying that Christ came to save nobody but sinners, and does not call anybody to repentance but the sinful." My dear sirs, I have heard all that sort of talk so many times that I know it by heart; the same objections were raised against this doctrine in Luther's day by the Papists, and since then by workmongers of all classes. There is nothing substantial in their notion that free grace is opposed to morality: it is only their fancy. They dream that the doctrine of justification by faith will lead to sin, but it can be proved by history that whenever this doctrine has been best preached men have become most holy, and whenever this truth has been darkened, all manner of corruption has abounded. Gracious, doctrine and gracious living fitly go together, and legal teaching and unlawful living are generally found associated.

Let us show you the sanctifying power of this gospel. Its first operation in that direction is this: when the Holy Spirit brings the truth of free pardon home to a man it completely changes his thoughts concerning God. "What," says he, "has God freely forgiven me all my offenses for Christ's sake? And does he love me notwithstanding all my sin? I did not know he was such an one as this, so gracious and kind! I thought he was hard; I called him a tyrant, gathering where he had not strewed; but does he feel towards me like this?" "Then," saith the soul, "I love him in return." There is a complete revulsion of feeling; the man is turned right round as soon as ever he understands redeeming grace and dying love. Conversion follows on a sight of grace.

Moreover, this grand truth does more than turn a man, it inspires, melts, enlivens, and inflames him. This is a truth which stirs the deeps of the heart, and fills the man with lively emotions. You talked to him about doing good, and about right, and justice, and reward, and punishment, and he heard it all, and it may have it had a measure of influence over him, but he did not deeply feel it. Such teaching is too cold to warm the heart. The truth which comes home to the man appears to him to be new and exciting. It runs like this,—God out of his free mercy forgives the guilty, and he has forgiven you. Why, this awakens him, stirs him up, touches the fountain of his tears, and moves his whole being. Perhaps at the first hearing of the gospel he does not care for it, and even hates it, but when it comes with power it obtains a wonderful mastery over him. When he really receives its message as his own, then his cold heart of stone is turned to flesh; warm emotion, tender love, humble desire, and a sacred longing after the Lord are all excited in his bosom. The quickening power of this divine truth, as well as the converting power of it, can never be too much admired.

Besides, this truth when it enters the heart deals a deadly blow at the man's self-conceit Many a man would have become wise only he thought he was so already; and many a mam would have been virtuous only he concluded that he had already attained thereto. Behold, this doctrine smites upon the skull all confidence in your own goodness, and makes you feel your guilt; and in so doing it removes the great evil of pride. A sense of sin is the very threshold of mercy. A consciousness of shortcoming, a grief because of past offenses, is a necessary preparation for a higher and a nobler life. The gospel digs out the foundation, makes a great vacuum, and so makes room to lay in their places the glorious stones of a noble spiritual character.

Moreover, where this truth is received there is sure to spring up in the soul a sense of gratitude. The man who has had much forgiven will be sure to love much in return. Gratitude to God is a grand mainspring for holy action. Those who do right in order to be rewarded for it are acting selfishly. Selfishness is at the bottom of their character, they abstain from sin only lest self should suffer, and they obey only that self may be safe and happy. The man who does right, not because of heaven or hell but because God has saved him, and he loves the God who saved him, is the truly right-loving man. He who loves right because God loves it has risen out of the bog of selfishness and is capable of the loftiest virtue, yea, he has in him a living spring, which will well up and flow forth in holy living so long as he exists.

And, dear brethren, I think: you will all see that free forgiveness to sinners is very conducive towards one part of a true character, namely, readiness to forgive others, for he who has been forgiven much himself is the very man who finds it easy to pass by the transgressions of others. If he do not so he may well doubt whether he has been himself forgiven; but if the Lord has blotted out his debt of a thousand talents he will readily enough forgive the hundred pence which his brother owes him.

Last of all, some of us know, and we wish that all knew by personal experience, that a sense of undeserved favor and free forgiveness is the very soul of enthusiasm, and enthusiasm is to Christianity what the lifeblood is to the body. Were you ever made enthusiastic by a cold discourse upon the excellence of morality? Did you ever feel your soul stirred within you by listening to a sermon upon the rewards of virtue? Were you ever made enthusiastic by being told of the punishments of the law? No, sirs; but preach up the doctrines of grace, let the free favor of God be extolled, and mark the consequences. There are people who will walk for many miles and stand without weariness by the hour together to hear this. I have known them labor many a weary mile to listen to this doctrine. What for? Because the man was eloquent, or because he put it well? Not so: it has sometimes been badly spoken, and in uncouth language, and yet this doctrine has always aroused the people. There is something in the soul of man that is looking out for the gospel of grace, and when it comes there is a hungering to hear about it. Look at the Reforming times, when death was the penalty of listening to a sermon: how the people crowded at midnight; how they journeyed into the deserts and the caves to listen to the teaching of these grand old truths. There is sweetness about mercy, divine mercy, freely given, which holds the ear of man and stirs his heart. When this truth enters the soul it breeds zealots, martyrs, confessors, missionaries, saints. If any Christians are in earnest, and full of love to God and man, they are those who know what grace has done for them. If any remain under reproaches faithful, under losses and crosses joyful, they are those who are conscious of their indebtedness to divine love. If any delight in God while they live, and rest in him as they die, they are the men who know that they are justified by faith in Jesus Christ who justifieth the ungodly. All glory be to the Lord, who lifteth the beggar from the dunghill and setteth him among princes, even the princes of his people. He takes the very cast-offs of the world and adopts them into his family, and makes them heirs of God by Jesus Christ. The Lord give us all to know the power of the gospel upon our sinful selves. The Lord endear to us the name, work, and person of the Sinner's Friend. May we never forget the hole of the pit whence we were drawn, nor the hand which rescued us, nor the undeserved kindness which moved that hand. Henceforth let us have more and more to say of infinite grace. "Free grace and dying love." Well does the old song say, "Ring those charming bells." Free grace and dying love—the sinner's windows of hope! Our hearts exult in the very words. Glory be unto thee, O Lord Jesus, ever full of compassion. Amen.

4

THE TRUE GOSPEL, NO HIDDEN GOSPEL

Preached on June 4, 1882
Scripture: 2 Corinthians 4:3-4
From: Metropolitan Tabernacle Pulpit Volume 28

"But if our gospel be hid, it is hid to them that are lost: in whom the God of this world hath blinded the minds of them which believe not, lest the light of the glorious gospel of Christ, who is the image of God, should shine unto them." —2 Cor. iv. 3, 4.

I THINK in this case the Revised New Testament gives a better translation than does the Authorized Version, and I will therefore read it:—"But and if our gospel is veiled, it is veiled in them that are perishing in whom the God of this world hath blinded the minds of the unbelieving, that the light of the gospel of the glory of Christ, who is the image of God, should not dawn upon them." Paul had been speaking of Moses with the veil over his face, and we lose the track of his thought if we use the word "hid" instead of veiled. Our gospel wears no veil, but exhibits all the glory of its countenance to the sons of men. Oh that they may be able steadfastly to behold it, and see in it their own salvation and the glory of the Lord.

Observe at the outset the confidence with which Paul speaks. It is abundantly evident that he has no doubt whatever that the gospel which he proclaims is assuredly true; nay, that it is so manifestly time that if those who have heard it do not accept it, it must be because the God of this world hath blinded their minds. The accent of conviction makes every word emphatic. He believes and is sure, and he is convinced that those who do not believe must be under the thraldom of the devil. This is not the ordinary style in which the gospel is preached nowadays. We hear men courteously apologize for stating anything as certain, for they are fearful of being thought narrow-minded and bigoted: we hear them prove what is clear as noonday, and back up with arguments what God himself has said; as if the sun needed candles to exhibit it, or as if God's word wanted the support of human reasoning. The apostle did not take the defensive ground at all: he carried the war across the border and assailed the unbelievers. He came forth fresh from God with a revelation, and his every word seemed to challenge men with,—"This is God's word, believe it; for if you do not you will incur sin, and prove that you are lost, and are under the influence of the devil." When the gospel was preached in that royal style it mightily prevailed, and annihilated opposition. Cavillers came, of course. "What will this babbler say?" was a common question; but the heralds of the cross made short work of all cavillers, for they simply went on declaring the glorious gospel. Their one word was, "This is from God: if you believe it you shall be saved, if you reject it you shall be damned." They made no bones about it, but spoke like men who believed in their message, and judged that it left unbelievers without excuse. They never altered their doctrine or softened the penalty of refusing it. Like fire among stubble, the gospel consumed all before it when it was preached as God's revelation. It does not spread today with equal rapidity because many of its teachers have adopted what they fancy are wiser methods: they have become less certain and more indifferent, and therefore they reason and argue where they should proclaim and assert. Some preachers rake up all the nonsense that any scientific or unscientific man likes to bring forward, and spend half their time in trying to answer it. What can be the use of untying the knots which are tied by sceptics? They only tie more. It is not for my servant to dispute about my message, but to deliver it correctly as mine, and there leave it. If we get back again to the old platform, and speak as from God, we shall not speak in vain, for he will surely honor his own word. The preacher should either speak in God's name or hold his tongue. My brother, if the Lord has not sent you with a message, go to bed, or to school, or mind your farm; for what does it matter what you have to say of your own? If heaven has given you a message, speak it out as he ought to speak who is called to be the mouth for God. If we are to make up our gospel as we go along, out of our own heads, and compound our own theology, as chemists make up mixtures of drugs, we have an endless task before us, and failure stares us in the face. Alas for the weakness of human wit and the fallacy of mortal reasoning! But if we have to deliver what God declares we have a simple task, and one which must lead to grand results, for the Lord has said, "My word shall not return unto me void."

Where did the apostle learn to speak thus positively? He tells us in the first verse of the chapter," Therefore seeing we have this ministry, as we have received mercy, we faint not." He had himself been once a persecutor; and he had been convinced of his error by the appearance of the Lord Jesus to him. This was a great deed of mercy. He now knew that his sins were forgiven him; he felt in his own heart that he was a regenerated man, changed, cleansed, new created, and this was to him overwhelming evidence that the gospel was from God. To himself at any rate the gospel was a truth past argument, needing no other demonstration than its marvelous effect upon himself. Having received mercy for himself he judged that other men were in need of mercy even as he was, and that the same gospel which had brought light and comfort to his own soul would bring salvation to them also. This braced him to his work. By this consciousness he was made to speak as one having authority. There was no hesitancy about him, for he spoke what he had felt. Ah, friends, we not only deliver a message which we believe to be from God, but we tell out that which we have tested and tried within our own souls. An unconverted preacher must be in a sorry plight, for he lacks evidence of the truth which he proclaims. A man who is not familiar with the effect of the gospel upon his own heart must endure much disquietude when he stands up to preach upon it. What does he really know about it if he has never felt its power? But if he has been converted by its means then he is confident, and is not to be moved by the questions and quibbles of those who oppose him. His inner consciousness strengthens him in the delivery of his message. We also must feel the influence of the word that we may speak what we do know, and testify what we have seen. Having received mercy we cannot but speak of that mercy positively as of a thing which we have tested and handled: and knowing that it is God who has given us the mercy we cannot but speak with anxious desire that others may partake of divine grace.

Come we now to consider our text. Our first observation shall be: the gospel is in itself a glorious light, for in the fourth verse Paul speaks of the light of the glorious gospel of Christ; secondly, this gospel is in itself plain and simple; thirdly, if we preach it as we ought to preach it we keep it plain, and do not muddle it up by worldly wisdom; and fourthly, therefore, it being in itself a great light, and in itself clear, and the preaching being clear, if men do not see it is because they are lost: it is a fatal sign when men are unable to perceive the light of the gospel of the glory of Jesus Christ.

I. First, then, THE GOSPEL IS IN ITSELF A GLORIOUS LIGHT. In countless places it is so described in the New Testament. This is the light which has come into the world. "The darkness is past, and the true light now shineth." Observe that this light reveals the glory of Christ. This is the new translation, and it is a valuable one—"The light of the gospel of the glory of Christ." You know the Hebrews had a different mode of expression from the Greek, and if we are to read the Greek as though Paul Hebraized it, then we read it according to the version we have here,—"the glorious gospel of Christ"; but if we read the Greek as Greek, then it runs, u the light of the gospel of the glory of Christ." The renderings are equally true, but the second one has a fullness and freshness of sense about it worthy of special note. The gospel reveals the glory of Christ. It tells us that he is the eternal Son of the Father, by whom all things were made, for whom all things were created, and by whom they continue to exist. This might not have been good news to us if it had stood alone, though it ought always to be good to the creature to be informed of his Creator; but the gospel further reveals to us that this ever-blessed Son of the Highest came down to earth in infinite pity, espoused our nature, and was born at Bethlehem, and became as truly man as he was assuredly God. This was the first note of the gospel, and there was so much of delight in it that it set all the angels in heaven singing, and the shepherds who kept watch over their flocks by night heard the chorales of the first Christmas rung out from the midnight sky,—"Glory to God in the highest, and on earth peace, and good will toward men." It could not but mean peace to man that God should become man; it could not but mean mercy to the guilty that the heir of glory should be born into their race; it must be good news to us that the offended One should take upon himself the nature of the offender. So outrang the first pure gospel music that made glad the ear of mankind. The Lord God omnipotent became Immanuel—God with us: "Unto us a child is born, unto us a son is given, and his name shall be called Wonderful." This is the beginning of the gospel of the glory of Christ: he gained a greater glory by laying aside his divine glory. Furthermore the gospel tells us that this same mighty God, the everlasting Father, the Prince of Peace, dwelt here among men, preaching and teaching, and working miracles of matchless mercy; everywhere proving himself to be man's brother, sympathetic and tender and gentle, receiving to himself even the lowest of the people, and bowing himself to the least of the race. It is written, "Then drew near unto him the publicans and sinners for to hear him"; and again he took little children into his arms, and blessed them, and said, "Suffer the little children to come unto me, and forbid them not." There was a gospel about all that he did, and a glory which men who are pure in heart both see and admire. His life was good news: it was a new and a glad thing that God should dwell among men, and be found in fashion as a man. The God that hateth sin, and whose wrath burns against iniquity, tabernacled among sinners, and saw and felt their evil ways, and prayed for them, "Father, forgive them." His glory lay in his being so patient, gentle, and self-sacrificing, and yet so just and true. Well did John say, "The Word was made flesh, and dwelt among us, (and we beheld his glory, the glory as of the only begotten of the Father,) full of grace and truth."

But the gospel's biggest bell, which rings out with clearest note, is that this Son of God in due time gave himself for our sins, making an offering of his whole human nature as a propitiation for the guilt of men. Herein is an excessive glory of love. What a sight it was to see him in the garden oppressed with our load of guilt till the bloody sweat was forced from him; to see him bearing that stupendous weight up to the tree, and there hanging in agonies of death, bearing the desertion of his Father, and all the thick clouds of darkness that came of it: dying the "just for the unjust to bring us to God"! It was the glory of Christ that he was there bereft of all glory. Never can a more glorious thing be said of him than that he for our sakes was obedient to death, even the death of the cross. And this is the gospel we preach, the gospel of substitution, that Jesus stood in the sinner's place and bore in the sinner's stead what was due to the law of God on account of man's transgression. Tell it out among the heathen that the Lord reigneth from the tree.

> "Fling out the banner! Let it float
> Skyward and seaward, high and wide;
> Our glory only in the cross,
> Our only hope, the Crucified."

No gladder news could come to man than that the incarnate God had borne man's sins and died in man's stead. Yet there is another note, for he that died and was buried is risen from the dead, and has borne our nature up into the glory, and there he wears it at the Father's right hand. His loving heart is still occupied with the same divine errand that brought him down below; he is by his intercession saving sinners whom he purchased with his blood. He is able to save them to the uttermost who come unto God by him, seeing he ever liveth to make intercession for them. This is the gospel of the glory of Christ. It is our Lord's glory that he mediates between man and God, pleading for the unjust ones, using as his all-prevailing argument the blood which he hath shed.

But I must not leave out the fact that he who now in glory pleads for sinners will speedily come again to gather all his own unto himself, to shed abroad on them the fullness of his own glory, and to take them up to be with him where he is. There is wondrous light in the gospel, both for the future and the present. It sets forth to us the glory of Christ, the glory of love, the glory of mercy, the glory of a blood which can wash the blackest white, the glory of a plea which can make the poorest prayer acceptable, the glory of a living and triumphant Savior, who having put his hand to the work will not fail nor be discouraged till all the purposes of infinite love shall be achieved by him. This is "the gospel of the glory of Christ," and the light of it is exceeding clear and bright.

We are now called to a second truth: the gospel is a light which reveals God himself, for according to our text the Lord Jesus is the image of God. Did not Jesus say, "He that hath seen me hath seen the Father"? For, first, our Lord Jesus is the image of God in this sense, that he is essentially one with God. He is "the brightness of the Father's glory and the express image of his person." He is "very God of very God," as the creed hath it, and I know not how better to express the idea. Our Lord himself said, "I and my Father are one." But the text means more than that. Christ is the image of God in this sense, that he shows us what God is. If you know the character of Jesus you know the character of God. God himself is invisible, and is not seen of mortal eye, neither can he be comprehended of finite mind. He cannot, indeed, be truly known at all except by the teaching of the Holy Spirit. But all that can be known of God is fairly writ in capital letters in the person of Jesus. What higher conception of God can you have? Even those who have denied our Lord's deity have yet been subdued into admiration by his matchless character. Read his life through, and see if you could improve it. Can you suggest anything that should be left out, or anything that could be added? He is God, and in him we see God as far as it is possible for us to discern that matchless Father of our spirits. Thus the gospel is full of light, revealing first the Mediator and then the Lord God himself.

Now, dear friends, this gospel of the glory of Christ is really light to tis, that is to say, it brings with it all that the metaphor of light sets forth. First of all it brings illumination. It is a lighting up of the soul "to know thee, the only true God, and Jesus Christ whom thou hast sent." It is light to the understanding to be able to see that the Only Begotten has revealed the Father. Man feels after God if haply he may find him, and the heathen stumbles upon this and that in his blind gropings. Perhaps the world was nearest the truth when it called him "the unknown God." When the wisdom of this world once began to define and to describe the Deity, then it proved its own folly. "The world by wisdom knew not God," but in the person of the Lord Jesus we have the true icon, the image and representation of the Godhead. It cannot be said of true Christians, "Ye worship ye know not what," for we know what we worship. Each one of us can affirm, "I know whom I have believed." We have no question about who is our God, or what he is. There is a knowledge given by the gospel to men, which creates daylight in the understanding.

But it is light in another sense, namely, that of comfort. Let a man see God in Jesus Christ, and he cannot be unhappy. Is it sin that burdened him? Let him see Jesus Christ bearing sin in his own body on the tree, and let him believe in this same sin-bearer, and that burden is gone. Let him be fretting under the cares and trials of life, and let him get a view by faith of Jesus, an infinitely greater sufferer, sympathizing with him in his sorrow, and surely the sting of his grief is removed. Is he afraid to die? Let him hear Jesus say, "I am the resurrection and the life," and he shall be taught rather to long for death than to dread it. Is he troubled about the things to come? Does the awful future lower darkly before him? Let him only hear Jesus say, "I am he that liveth and was dead, and am alive forevermore, amen, and hold the keys of hell and death," and he will no longer be afraid of the separate world of spirits of which Christ hath the key; nor will he tremble at the burning of the world, and the ruin of creation, for he has a hold upon One who has said, "Because I live ye shall live also." Never did another such a light ever shine upon the sons of men: neither for instruction nor for comfort can this eternal truth be rivaled. It were not in the power of an archangel to tell you the joy which this "gospel of the glory of Christ" has given to the sons and daughters of affliction. Wherever it comes it liberates the captive mind, and removes the pains of remorse. At the very sight of it tearful eyes are brightened till they flash with delight. Oh, the joy unspeakable of having Christ to be our Savior, and the glorious God to be our Father. He is rich to all the intents of bliss who knoweth this. This is light, and all else is darkness. We now advance a seep, and observe that—

II. THIS GOSPEL IS IN ITSELF MOST PLAIN AND CLEAR. The gospel contains nothing which can perplex anybody unless he wishes to be perplexed. There is nothing in the gospel which a man may not apprehend if he desires to apprehend it. It is all plain to the man who yields his understanding to his God. Whenever I get a book which puzzles me very much to make out its meaning, I wish I could send it back to the author, and tell him to write it over again, because I am sure he is not very clear about his own meaning, or else he could easily make me know what he meant. A man has never fairly mastered a subject until he is able to communicate his thoughts on that subject, so that persons of ordinary intelligence can tell what he is at. Now, the Lord has in his own mind a clearly-defined way of salvation for men, and he has expressed himself without ambiguity. Certain divines like to preach an incomprehensible gospel, for it gives them the air of wisdom in the judgment of the foolish. Certain hearers prefer sermons which they cannot understand. To them the difficult and intricate are as marrow and fatness. I heard of one who said he liked a bit of gristle in the sermons, or a bone to try his teeth upon. We could easily gratify such friends, but we see no authority in Scripture for gratifying this longing. I carefully endeavor to take the stones out of the fruit before preparing the dish. When we are eating it is by no means a good thing to swallow the bones, for our digestion might not master them, and we might be injured by their presence within. Souls want spiritual nutriment, not problems and riddles. So, when a man preaches the gospel so that you cannot make head or tail of it, you need not fret, for what he has to say is not worth your trouble in listening to it. If it be the Lord's own gospel, you who are doers of the Lord's will can understand it; and if you cannot it is not the gospel of the glory of Christ, but a gospel of human inventing. The true gospel is simplicity itself.

Listen! That God should come among men and espouse our nature is so far a great mystery that we do not know how it could be. Blessed be God, we do not want to know how it was done; we only know that it was done, and that fact is enough for us. We understand that the Word was made flesh and dwelt among us, and we rejoice therein. Observe the doctrine of the atonement— this also as a fact is plain enough. How it became right for Christ to suffer in our stead, and for his sufferings to be an expiation for our sins, may be a very deep question, but the fact is clearly revealed. I do not think substitution to be a bewildering mystery, but some do. What if it is? The secret reason of it is nothing to us. If God has set forth Christ to be a propitiation for our sins our most reasonable course is to accept him. We need not quarrel with grace because we cannot understand everything about it. It is wiser to eat that which is set before us than to die of hunger because we do not know all the secrets of cookery. I am not asked to understand how God justifies us in Christ, but I am asked to believe that he does so. The fact is plain enough, and the fact is the object of faith. That Jesus should suffer in my stead is a simple matter of truth, and in it there is no darkness at all. That precious doctrine that we are justified by faith, that all the merit of Christ's glorious work comes to us simply by our believing: is there any difficulty about that? I know that men may cavil till they are black in the face, but the doctrine is plain as a pikestaff. At times persons inquire, "What is believing?" Well, it is trusting, depending, leaning upon, relying upon—that is all. Is there anything hard about that? Do you want to put on your spectacles to see through it? Will it require a week to work your way into the idea? No, the fact that God was made flesh and dwelt among us, and that being found in fashion as a man he became obedient to death for our sakes, and that he now bids us simply trust him and we shall live, is as simple as any truth within the sphere of knowledge. Some people would like a gospel of puzzlement; they prefer a little confusion of the intellect; they love to wander in a luminous haze, in which nothing is clearly defined. They feel that they are getting on when they are leaving others behind, and rising into sublime absurdity. Now, suppose the gospel consisted in terrible mysteries, bristling with matters hard to be understood; suppose it required eighteen volumes to be read through before you could see it; suppose it needed mathematical precision and classical elegance before you could see it,—millions would never get, to heaven, for they have never read through a single volume, and therefore they are not likely to digest a library. Some men are so busy, and some have their brains so constituted, that they never will be deep students, and if the gospel required of them deep thought and long research they might give themselves up for lost. If men needed to be philosophers in order to be Christians, the majority of men would be out of the pale of hope. If the masses of the people must read hard before they can catch the idea of salvation by faith in Christ Jesus, they will never catch the idea; they must inevitably perish. And would you, learned men, like them to perish? I fear that some of you have less concern about that than about your own credit for talent and thought. For the sake of getting a profound little gospel all to yourselves you would dig a moat around the cross to keep the vulgar crowd from intruding. That is not the gospel, nor the spirit of the Lord Jesus. Take care lest you miss the truth yourselves. I fear that while you are fumbling for the latch of heaven's gate, the people whom you despise will get inside the door and be singing, "Glory, hallelujah, we have found the Savior." The Lord permits the disputer of this world to stumble, while those who receive the kingdom of God as little children find out the great secret, and rejoice in it. Suppose the gospel had been such a difficult thing to explain, and such a very hard matter to understand, what would become of the many who are now rejoicing in Christ, and yet have by birth and constitution the most shallow capacities? It is wonderful how one but little raised above an idiot can yet grasp the gospel. What a blessing that it is so! I have heard of a poor boy whom his teachers had been instructing for years, and one day they said to him, "Well, Jack, have you a soul?" "No, I've got no soul." They feared that they had lost their labor; but their minds were changed when he added, "I had a soul once, and I lost it, and Jesus Christ came and found it, and so I let him keep it." That was better gospel than we get from many a learned divine. He had the whole thing at his fingers' ends. Christ had found his soul, and was keeping it for him; even he who will not fail to keep that which we have committed to his charge. We clap our hands for joy because the gospel reveals the plain man's pathway to heaven, and makes the most illiterate wise unto salvation. The shepherd on Salisbury Plain can understand the gospel as well as the Bishop in Salisbury Cathedral; and the Dairyman's Daughter can feel its power as fully as a Princess.

Suppose the gospel were hard to be understood, what should we do at the death-bed? We are sent for all in a hurry to see persons who have neglected attendance upon the means of grace, and are dying in ignorance. It is our sorrowful task to explain the path of life to them, when they are entering upon the dark descent of death. While the lamp continues to burn we have hope, and therefore we proceed to state the way by which a sinner may return to God. Is it not well to have it packed away in a small compass, and expressed in common words? We tell them that Jesus Christ came into the world to save sinners, and that whosoever believeth in him shall not perish, but have everlasting life. What could we do if the gospel were not thus plain? Must I have a handcart, and wheel it about with me, so as to carry to each dying man half-a-dozen folios in Latin? Nothing of the kind. Right well do Cowper's often-quoted lines set forth the plainness of the gospel, and rebuke those who reject it on that account.

> *"Oh how unlike the complex work of man,*
> *Heaven's easy, artless, unencumber'd plan!*
> *No meretricious graces to beguile,*
> *No clustering ornaments to clog the pile:*
> *From ostentation as from weakness free,*
> *It stands like the cerulean arch we see,*
> *Majestic in its own simplicity.*
> *Inscribed above the portal from afar*
> *Conspicuous as the brightness of a star,*
> *Legible only by the light they give,*
> *Stand the soul-quickening words—BELIEVE, AND LIVE.*
> *Too many, shock'd at what should charm them most,*
> *Despise the plain direction, and are lost.*
> *Heaven on such terms! (they cry with proud disdain)—*
> *Incredible, impossible, and vain!—*
> *Rebel because 'tis easy to obey,*
> *And scorn, for its own sake, the gracious way."*

III. Thirdly, IN THE TRUE PREACHING OF THE GOSPEL THIS SIMPLICITY IS PRESERVED. Paul expressly said,—"Having this hope in us we use great plainness of speech," and yet again, "My speech and my preaching was not with enticing words of man's wisdom, but in demonstration of the Spirit and of power." The apostle Paul was a deep thinker, a man of profound insight and subtle mind. The bent of his mind was such that he would have made a meta-physician of supreme rank, or a mystic of the deepest darkness; but he went against his natural inclination, and devoted all his energies to the unveiling of the gospel. It was a sublime self-denial for him to put on one side all his logic among the other things which he counted loss for Christ; for says he, "I determined not to know anything among men save Jesus Christ and him crucified." He "determined," he was resolute, and had made up his mind to it, or he would not have accomplished it. He was the man who wrote some things hard to be understood, which Peter mentions, but when he came to the gospel he would have nothing but simplicity there. He was tender among them as a nurse with her child, and made himself an instructor of babes, dealing out the word with such plainness as children would require. The true man of God will not veil the gospel beneath performances and ceremonies. Mark those who do this, and avoid them. We see his reverence walking with clasped hands to the right and to the left, repeating Latin sentences unknown by the people. He turns, and bobs, and turns again. We see his face for a moment and then his back. I suppose it is all meant for edification; but I, poor creature, cannot find the least instruction in it, nor, as far as I can discover, do the people who are looking on. What mean these little boys in pretty gowns, making such a smoke? And what are these flowers and images on the altar? What a splendid cross is that which adorns the priest's back! It seems to be made of roses. The folks look on, and some are wondering where he buys his lace, while others are speculating as to the quantity of wax which will be consumed in those candles every hour; and there is the end of it. Christ is veiled behind the millinery, if he is there at all. I know numbers who would disdain to do that, and yet they hide their Lord under finery of language. It is a grand thing to mount aloft upon the wings of eloquence and display the glory of speech, till you ascend in a splendid peroration, as many another exhibition closes, with fireworks. But this is not becoming in preachers of the Lord Jesus. I always tell our young men that one of their commandments should be, "Thou shalt not perorate." To attempt anything grand in language when we are preaching salvation is to leave our proper work. Our one business is to tell out the gospel plainly. We deal in bread, not in flowers. Let tawdry ornaments be left to the stage or to the bar, where men amuse themselves, or dispute for gain; or let these poor gewgaws be reserved for the Senate, where men will defend or denounce according as it suits their party. It is not ours to make the worse appear the better reason, or to hide truth under floods of words. As for us, we are to hide ourselves behind the cross, and make men know that Jesus Christ came to save the lost, and that if they believe in him they shall be saved at once and forever. If we do not make them know this we have missed our mark, however grandly we have performed. What, shall we become acrobats with words, or jugglers displaying wonders? Then God is insulted, his gospel is degraded, and souls are left to perish.

I venture to put in a word for myself, and then leave this point. I can say with the apostle, "I have used great plainness of speech," and therefore if the gospel which I have preached be hidden, I have not produced the veil. I have used vulgar words when I thought that they would be better understood, and I have told all sorts of simple stories when I thought I could make the gospel known. I have never used a hard word where I could help it. My one desire has been by manifesting the truth to touch your consciences and win your hearts. If you see not the light it is not because I have hidden it from you.

IV. With this we close. IF THE GOSPEL BE VEILED TO OUR HEARERS IT IS A FATAL SIGN. "If our gospel be hid it is hid to them that are lost": the god of this world has blinded their unbelieving eyes lest the light of the glorious gospel of Christ should dawn upon them. Not to believe, understand, appreciate, and accept the gospel is a sign of perishing. I want to put this very plainly to any here who say that they have not received the gospel, for they cannot understand it, and they see nothing remarkable in it. If you have heard it plainly preached, it is so plain in itself that if it is hid from your eyes it is because you are still in the gall of bitterness and in the bonds of iniquity. You who receive the gospel are saved; faith is the saving token. If you believe that Jesus is the Christ you are born of God: if you have accepted him as your Savior whom God sets forth as such, then you are saved; but if you say, "No, I cannot see it," then your eyes are blinded and you are lost. The sun is bright enough, but those who have no sight are not enlightened. Do you say, I cannot receive the gospel: I want something more difficult? By sinful pride your judgment is perverted and your heart is hardened. While you are among the unbelieving you are still among the perishing, and the god of this world blindfolds you. O Spirit of God, convince men of this sin, that they believe not on Jesus Christ. This work is out of thy servant's power, but, oh, do thou perform it. Oh that our text, like a sharp lancet, may cut deep and reach the conscience. May this truth pierce between the joints and marrow, and discern the thoughts and intents of your hearts.

According to the text, he that believes not on Jesus Christ is a lost man. God has lost you; you are not his servant. The church has lost you; you are not working for the truth. The world has lost you really; you yield no lasting service to it. You have lost yourself to right, to joy, to heaven. You are lost, lost, lost, like the prodigal son when he was away from his father's house, and like the sheep that went astray from the fold. It is not only that you will be lost, but that you are lost; for "he that believeth not is condemned already, because he hath not believed on the Son of God." Press those two words upon your conscience,—"Condemned already":—lost even now. You are perishing; that is to say, you are gradually passing into that condition in which you must abide forever, as one that has perished before God, and become utterly useless and dead. It is an appalling truth that this is proved by the fact that you do not understand the gospel, or if you understand it you do not appreciate it; you do not see beauty or glory in it; or if you do in a measure appreciate it, and see some glory in it, yet it has never stirred your affection, or drawn your heart towards its great subject. In a word, you have not come to trust in Jesus. He is the only one that you can trust to, and yet you reject him. It must be the simplest thing in all world to trust in Christ, and yet you will not do that simple thing. Trust in him should be attended to at once, and ought not to be delayed, and yet you have delayed for years. If faith brings salvation, why not have salvation? Why abide still in unbelief—in unbelief of the most glorious truth that not God himself ever revealed to men;—in unbelief of that which you dare not deny? Oh, what a condition to be in; willfully in darkness, shutting your eyes to the light. You are certainly lost.

The apostle explains how a man gets into that condition. He says that Satan, the god of this world, hath blinded his mind. What a thought it is that Satan should set up to be a god. Christ is the image of God; Satan is the ape of God: he mimics God, and holds an usurped power over men's minds and thoughts. To maintain his power he takes great care that his dupes should not see the light of the gospel. The veils he uses are such as men's selfish hearts approve; for he speaks thus: "If you were to become a Christian, you would never get on in the world." He claps a sovereign on each eye, and then you cannot see, though the sun shine at midday. Pride binds a silken band across the eyes, and thus again the light is excluded. Satan whispers, "If you become a Christian, you will be laughed at": thus he hoodwinks his victim with fear of ridicule. He has many a crafty device by which he perverts the human judgment till they cannot see that which is self-evident, and will not believe that which is unquestionable. He makes the gain of heaven to seem inconsiderable when weighed with the little loss which religion may involve. He hides from the soul the bliss of sin forgiven, of adoption into God's family, and the certainty of eternal glory, by throwing dust into the eyes, so that the mind cannot look at things truthfully.

What shall I say in closing but this: are you lost, any of you? Upon the showing of the text all of you are to whom the gospel is hidden. Well, but thank God you may be found yet: lost today, but you need not be lost tomorrow: lost while sitting in these pews, but you may be found before you leave the Tabernacle. The Good Shepherd has come out to find the lost sheep. Have you any desire after him, any wish to return to him? Then look to him with trustful glance. You are not lost if so you look, nor shall you ever be. He that believes in Jesus is saved, and saved eternally. Are any of you blinded? You must so be if the gospel is hid from you, so that you cannot see its brightness. Ah, but you need not remain in the dark. There is One abroad today who opens blind eyes. Cry to him as did the two blind men, "Thou Son of David, have mercy on me! Thou Son of David, have mercy on me!" The Messiah came on purpose to give sight to the blind: it was a part of his commission when he came forth from the Father's glory. He will give sight to you. Oh seek it.

Is the god of this world your master? He must be if you do not see the glory of the gospel; but he need not be your god any longer. I pray the Holy Spirit to help you to dethrone this intruder. Why should you adore him? What good has he ever done to you? What is there about his character that makes him worthy to be your god? Break off the yoke; burst the fetters which now hold you his slave. The true God has come in the flesh to set you free, and to destroy all the works of the devil. Whatsoever keeps you from beholding the glory of God in the face of Jesus Christ can be removed. I am sent to say in my Master's name, "Whosoever believeth in him is not condemned: he that believeth and is baptized shall be saved." "Come now, and let us reason together, saith the Lord: though your sins be as scarlet, they shall be as white as snow; though they be red like crimson, they shall be as wool." Trust the Savior, trust the incarnate God; trust him now and trust him at once, and though a moment ago you were black as hell's midnight you shall be clean and bright as heaven's eternal noon. In one instant sins that have taken you fifty years to accumulate shall disappear; the transgressions of all your days shall be plunged beneath the sea, and shall be found no more. Only be willing and obedient, and yield yourselves up to the incarnate God, who ever liveth to take care of those who put their trust in him. May the Lord bless you, dear friends, evermore. Amen and amen.

5

THE ESSENCE OF THE GOSPEL

Preached on December 4, 1870
Scripture: John 3:18
From: Metropolitan Tabernacle Pulpit Volume 16

"He that believeth on him is not condemned: but he that believeth not is condemned already, because he hath not believed in the name of the only begotten Son of God." —John iii. 18.

I MAY have preached from this text before, I may have done so several times; if I have not, I ought to have done. It is the whole Bible in miniature. We may say of it so many words so many volumes, for every single syllable here is charged to the full with meaning. We may read it, and re-read it, and continue still to read it day and night, yet ever find some fresh instruction in it. It is the essence of the gospel. The good news in brief.

When our Lord Jesus Christ shall come a second time, before him shall be gathered all nations, and he shall separate them one from another, as the shepherd divideth the sheep from the goats. That will not, however, be the first time in which the presence of the Lord Jesus has acted as a separator. It is always so wherever he comes. Men are as one body in their fallen condition, all alike estranged from God until he appears, but his coming finds out the chosen and calls them apart, and on the other hand, the unbelievers are discovered. Two camps are formed out of the once mingled multitude. Each goes to each, each one after its own kind finds its fellow, and between the two fellowships there is a deep gulf, which divides them as clearly as light is distinct from the darkness, or death is divided from life. Other distinctions sink into insignificance in the presence of Jesus; riches or wealth, learning or ignorance, power or weakness, are matters of too small account to divine mankind in the presence of the great Discerner of spirits. Only these two characters, believers and unbelievers, stand out in clear relief. As it is in our text, so is it as a matter of fact in the entire universe; the only two really vital distinctions for time and for eternity, are just these, believers and unbelievers, receivers of Christ and rejectors of him. Furthermore, as today the presence of Christ divides the mass, and gathers men into assorted companies, so also does that presence ensure a present judgment. It is written, that he shall say to them on his right hand, "Come, ye blessed," and to those on his left, "Depart, ye cursed," and even so at this moment his presence with equal certainty produces a judging; for here in the text we find believers not condemned, or in other words, acquitted, and we find unbelievers condemned already. The "Come, ye blessed," is anticipated in the non-condemnation, and the "Depart, ye cursed," is as it were already heard in the verdict, "Condemned already." I charge you, therefore, this morning, while the word is preached in your hearing, to remember that a clear and all-important division will be wrought while this sermon is being delivered. This day the Son of David holds his throne, and in this house he sits in judgment. In the preaching of the gospel at this moment his majestic voice divides the sinners from the saints, and if sensitive to his presence, we shall either tremble or rejoice. God grant that while this division shall go on, as it must go on, for he will be this day a savor of death unto death or a life unto life to every one of our souls, we may all be found amongst believers, and none of us shut out as condemned already by being unbelievers.

I. I shall ask you, this morning, first, to CONSIDER TO WHICH OF THE TWO CLASSES MENTIONED IN THE TEXT WE BELONG.

"He that believeth on him is not condemned." Have we a share in that character? Let us see to it.

What is meant by believing on him, or rather in him, for the word "eis" is rather in him than on him. If I mistake not, the word "believeth in him" means a great deal more than most of us have seen in it. I think I see many shades of believing. There are some who believe concerning Christ, that is to say, they believe that he is the Messiah and is the Savior of men. Many accept this for truth because their fathers did so, and it is to them a matter of unquestioned tradition. They are born in what is commonly thought to be a Christian country, and therefore have they taken up with the Christian faith, and theoretically and notionally they believe that Jesus is the Son of God and the Redeemer of the world. They would not hesitate to stand up and say, "I believe in Jesus Christ his only Son, our Lord, who was begotten of the Holy Ghost, born of the Virgin Mary, suffered under Pontius Pilate, was crucified, dead and buried," and so on. But remember, you may believe all that is orthodox concerning the Lord Jesus, and yet it will be no token that you are justified in him. No one may dare to say that a belief in the Athanasian creed will ensure us of salvation. If you reject his Deity, if you deny his atonement, such errors will be conclusive evidence that you are not a believer in him, because you are not a believer of the truth concerning him, and therefore you must take your place among unbelievers who are condemned already; but on the other hand, if you hold the scriptural truth, and believe accurately concerning the Lord Jesus, yet if you go no further, your mere faith about him, or concerning him, will not bring you salvation. To know Christ is of no avail, unless it can be said, "Flesh and blood hath not revealed this unto thee."

It is a step further when we have come to believing him. This is sometimes mentioned in Scripture—believing him. "I know whom I have believed." Believing concerning him that he is God's Christ, his Anointed, his sent One, his Messiah, we therefore should, as a matter of course, accept whatever he says as being true; and if with our hearts we do this, I trow we are saved. But we may think we do this, and notionally may give our assent to his teaching, and yet, notwithstanding, we may not have attained unto his salvation; we may still be condemned unbelievers, though we may think, and say, and profess that we believe him.

Frequently in Scripture there is another form of the believing which clusters about the Greek word, *"epi"* believing upon him. Our translators seem to have placed the -word "on" here as though it were in our text, but it is hardly so in the Greek. There is a difference between believing on him and believing in him. To believe on Jesus is indeed a saving faith, for he that believeth on him shall not be confounded. To believe on him is, as it were, to lean upon him, to receive him as God has set him forth, and in consequence to make him the foundation of our hope. Believing concerning him, and believing him, we then come to repose upon him, and to make him our confidence. We believe that he can save us, we trust in him to save us, and this is the essence of saving faith—to believe upon the appointed Redeemer. But in this- particular case our text speaks of believing in him, and this is something more than believing upon him. Every man who really believes upon Christ will ere long come to believe in him; but there is a growth—believing in him is more than believing upon him. How is that? If I thoroughly believe in a man, what is the result of it? Is he an advocate, and am I immersed in law? Then I trust my case to him; I leave the affair in his hands without fear, for

I believe in my advocate. Very good, so far that may be believing upon him. But now he gives me directions and rules of action. If I believe in him I shall certainly follow those rules to the letter, being fully convinced that they will lead me to a right issue. I commit the matter practically as well as theoretically to the man whom I have chosen to represent me, and I do so cheerfully, for I believe in him. I am like a man on board a vessel: I believe in him who is the captain. What then? If he bids me do this, or that, or the other, I may hear some one call his orders foolish, but I believe in him, and I do at once whatever he bids me. His bidding may appear absurd to one who has no faith in him, but to me it is wise and right. Suppose there should be raised up at this juncture for poor unhappy France, a man of high military genius, a man who shall be capable with such material as may come to hand to meet the terrible foe, and to disperse the cloud which now hangs over the capital city. If the people shall believe in the man, what then? Why they will surrender the direction of affairs to him. They will implicitly follow his lead. Does he command a sortie, does he bid the army advance? They believe in him, and the sortie is made, and the troops advance gallantly to the conflict. Should he counsel delay, and the avoidance of a great battle, those who believe in him will entrench themselves, or retire before the foe. If they are absolutely sure in their hearts that he is the man who guarantees victory, they will be certain to obey his orders; he will be their oracle, their dictator, and that most joyfully on their parts. So that to believe in our Lord means this, that I believe him to be the Son of God, and believe all other truths concerning him; that I also believe whatever he says to be the truth, in other words, I believe him; yet more than this, I cast my soul upon his atoning merits that he may save it, and so believe upon him; and furthermore, having so done I give myself up entirely to the Savior's holy guidance; I believe him to be infallible as the director of my spirit; I feel a union with him; I come to be in him, his cause is my cause, my cause his cause—I believe into him. Now this is the man of whom the text says, "He that believeth in him is not condemned," and the question I put this morning to myself and to you is, Have we believed in Jesus? Do we really take him to be our all in all? Do we consent that he should guide and lead us till he brings us to eternal felicity?

The connection of our text will help us to form a judgment as to whether we are indeed believers in Jesus. Brethren and sisters, have you realized, by a true exercise of faith, what is meant by the fourteenth and fifteenth verses of the present chapter? "As Moses lifted up the serpent in the wilderness, even so must the Son of man be lifted up: that whosoever believeth in him should not perish, but have eternal life." As the serpent-bitten Israelite looked to the brazen serpent when it was uplifted, have you in the same way looked to Jesus and found healing through looking to him? By this ye may judge yourselves. Have ye been healed of the wounds of sin and quickened into a new and heavenly life? Have you in very deed made the crucified Savior your soul's resting-place? In the verses which follow the text, you find such words as these, "He that doeth truth cometh to the light." Do you, my brethren, as the result of having trusted in Christ come to the light? Is it your desire to know God's truth, God's will, God's law, God's word? Are you seeking after the light, and are you desirous that the works wrought in you should be seen to be the fruit of God's own Spirit? By this also can you judge yourself? It is vain to say, "I trust in Christ," if thou hast never looked to him with that same childlike look with which the Israelite looked to the brazen serpent: and equally vain for thee to profess to be a believer in him, unless thou desirest the light. Thou mayst be in partial darkness still, as doubtless thou art, but art thou seeking more light, seeking God, seeking truth, seeking right? By this shalt thou know whether the Father has begotten thee unto a new birth, whether thou art to a certainty a new man, no longer a light-shunner but a light-seeker; no longer, because thy deeds are evil, seeking to conceal thyself from the convincing word of God, but because thy deeds are truthful, seeking to receive more light, that thy works may be made manifest to thine own conscience as being truly wrought of God in thy soul.

The consideration which I proposed just now has to be taken up with regard to the second class. Are we unbelievers? It is to be feared that there are some such here. If that be so, it may be of some service to them to know where they are, and what they are. "He that believeth not is condemned already." Some of you here are very inconsistent, because though you believe not in Christ Jesus, that is to say, do not trust your souls with him, nor give yourselves up obediently to serve him, yet you believe concerning him that he is the Christ of God, and if he were here today and spoke to you, you would believe his words, though I cannot say you would so believe them as to act upon them. It is so very strange that you should believe him to be the Son of God and yet should not trust him; that you should know that what he speaks is true, and that after he has warned you of the wrath to come, you should yet sit down in stolid indifference, and not seek the salvation which he provides. Instead of looking to the brazen serpent, you act as the Israelites would have done had they sought out another remedy. You have not believed in Christ, but if you have any belief that you need a Savior, I suppose your own common reason makes you seek one. You are evidently, therefore, seeking another salvation than that which God provides. You are refusing what God has ordained that you may find something of your own. There is but one Savior, that Savior this day you will not trust in—you are refusing him to your own destruction. You are this day shutting your eyes to the one only light, and though you have some desire towards light at times, yet you love darkness rather than light, and still continue as you were—dark, dark, dark, for you do not like to be reproved, you cannot bear that the gospel should come too cuttingly home to touch you in your conscience and rebuke you for your sins. To this day you remain an unbeliever and a lover of the darkness. Search, I pray you, and look. While this heart which now addresses you will pity you, I trust God's heart may pity you too, and may you yet escape out of the condition of the unbeliever, and yet be numbered with the believers in Christ.

Thus much on our first point, which I leave to your earnest self-examination, hoping that it may not be treated slightingly.

II. Now, secondly, and for a very short time, let us CONSIDER THE CONDITION OF THE BELIEVER. "He that believeth on him is not condemned." What a joyful sentence is this! Provided you have ascertained that you do believe in Jesus, turn this sweet word over and over in your souls, my brethren. Is it not delightful to think that you have it from God's own mouth by inspiration, and to note that the inspiration is of a remarkable kind, for you have it not only by the Spirit of God, but you have from Jesus Christ himself the sweet assurance that you are not condemned! What joy, what peace this word should speak unto your soul!

Let me show you for a minute how the believer escapes condemnation. "He that believeth on him is not condemned." One reason is because he does not offer himself for judgment. He that believes in Christ does not present himself to be tried. He says, "Nay, my Lord, I have no argument with thee, I plead guilty, I confess the condemnation. There is no need of trial, thou art justified when thou speakest, and clear when thou condemnest." There sits the judge, and the prisoner should stand opposite to him, for they are two parties; but behold, in this case the prisoner leaves the place, declines a trial, falls at the judge's feet, acknowledges that the sentence if carried out would be just, and pleads guilty. Having done this the believer sees that the sentence which he acknowledges and confesses to be right has been already laid upon his Surety, and in that Surety he believes. What does he believe about him? Why, that God, that he might magnify his justice and his grace, was in Christ Jesus, and that the Son of God did hang upon the cross, and bleed and die, the just for the unjust that he might bring us to God. The believer confesses the justice of the sentence, and therefore is at one with God. He comes to the light, and his deeds are reproved, and he accepts the reproof, and acknowledges it to be true. Then he looks to the cross, and he says,

"This very sentence to which I do subscribe with mine own hand that it is just, has been laid upon my ever glorious and blessed Surety, the only begotten of the Father, and he has been punished instead of me, and I am therefore clear, since Christ my ransom died." This is the way in which the believer comes not to be condemned: he accepts the condemnation, and then sees it laid upon his Surety. This brings him peace. The justice of God would have disturbed his mind; he sees that justice satisfied, and he declares in his own heart that if God be satisfied he is satisfied; if God's justice be honored then conscience feels that all is well. And now what happens? Why this believer in Christ not being condemned seeks the light; from this day forward he desires more and more to walk in the light of knowledge, the light of the divine presence, the light of divine holiness. O my brethren, there was a time when our souls inclined after sin, but now though we sin we mourn over it, and because we mourn it we have evidence that "it is no longer I," as the apostle saith, "but sin that dwelleth in me." The veriest inmost I, the truest, reallest ego within our soul desires holiness. If we could be as we would, we would be pure as God is pure, for our heart hungers and thirsts after righteousness. We come to the light, and now having believed, we are in such a condition that our deeds when we come to the light, though discovered, do not bring us shame and confusion of face, for in that very light our works are made manifest that they are wrought in God, and we rejoice that God is working in us by his Spirit all holy desires, emotions, and actions, which shall go on increasing until we shall be perfectly delivered from sin. This is the condition of the man who believeth in Christ, a very happy condition, a very hopeful condition, a very heavenly condition, who would not desire to be in it? It all hinges upon the believing, for with the believing in Jesus there comes the new birth, with the new birth there comes the desire after light, with the desire after light there arises a progress towards it, and a manifestation of the secret working of the Holy Spirit within the soul. Happy believers, thrice happy in what you are as well as in what you shall be.

III. And now, thirdly, and here comes our most solemn work—may God's Holy Spirit help us in it. CONSIDER THE CONDITION OF THE UNBELIEVER. "He that believeth not is condemned already, because he hath not believed on the name of the only-begotten Son of God." Observe the fact itself which is here stated! "He that believeth not is condemned already." Let me enlarge upon this very solemn truth.

First, he offers himself for judgment. "He hath not believed on the name "—what is the name? It is the Savior, Jesus. He who believes on Jesus, the Savior, confesses that he needs saving, and declines to stand on the footing of law; but he who refuses the Savior does in effect say, "I do not require a Savior, I am willing to stand my trial by the law." I tell you every soul that declines a Savior does in effect ask to be judged by the law. There stands the alternative; are you guilty, will you confess it?" If so, accept the Savior. But if on the other hand you say, "I will not accept the Savior," in the bottom of your soul there lies the presumptuous conceit, "I can stand the judgment; I do not want pardon and grace." Then, sir, if you ask for judgment you shall have it, and behold the result of it: God declares you to be condemned already. You have not believed, you have asked for judgment, you shall have it, but it is your ruin.

The unbeliever himself gives personal evidence to his own condemnation. Do you inquire how he does this? The text points us to his not believing. Is yonder person a condemned or uncondemned man? Ask him what he thinks of Christ. If he replies honestly, he says, "I do not accept God's testimony about Jesus Christ; I do not receive Jesus as my Savior." Either he claims that he does not need a Savior or else he does not feel that Jesus is the Savior he needs. He rejects the testimony of God concerning Christ—is not that enough to condemn a man? If a man in the very presence of the judge committed theft or murder, he would condemn himself; but is it not a still higher offence than this, in the very presence of God to do despite to his Son, by practically declaring his work and blood to have been unnecessary? Is it not the height of daring that a soul should stand in the presence of the God of mercy and hear him say in his word, "Behold the Lamb of God, which taketh away the sin of the world," and that the soul should reply, "I have nothing to do with the Lamb of God"? What further witness do we want with regard to your enmity to God? He that will not believe in Christ would murder God if he could. His not believing in Christ is virtually to make God a liar.

Still further, he that believes not in Christ gives evidence against himself, for he rejects "the name." Observe the text, "He hath not believed on the name." As I had already hinted, that name is Jesus, the Savior. The man says, "I will not have the Savior." Many of you have not said so much in words, but you practically say it; for you do not believe in the Savior, you remain at this moment Savior-less, out of Christ, without hope, without pardon, without mercy; and you have continued to do so under the preaching of the gospel now for many years. What more evidence do you want? If a man will reject God, even as a Savior, there must be a dreadful venom in his heart against God. If God appoints Christ to be King, and I reject him, that rejection shows that I dislike God; but when he appoints him to be a Savior, the errand being one entirely of mercy and goodness, if I reject him I must in my soul have an amazing depth of enmity against God. By this clear proof I condemn myself.

My brother, if you look at the text again you will see that he who believes not, rejects a most exalted person; for he hath not believed on the name "of the only-begotten Son of God." What a word is that, "On the Jesus, who is God's only-begotten Son." I wish I had language suitable for the utterance of a thought which presses down my very spirit, as it did last Sabbath evening; that God should send a Savior, and for a Savior the Only-begotten, the Lord of heaven and earth, without whom was not anything made that is made, and that he should come with testimony of love, the love of God to sinners, and seal that testimony with his blood; and that men should refuse to believe in him, is the most monstrous iniquity that could be imagined. I cannot see that Satan himself, with all his blasphemy, has ever gone this length; he was never placed where he could reject, as a Savior, the only-begotten Son of God. When men rejected Moses they perished without mercy, for he was sent of God; but when a man despises the Only-begotten, in whom dwelleth the fullness of the Godhead bodily, we may well say, call no witnesses against the man, rake up none of the details of his past life, this is quite evidence enough. If he hath not believed on such a one as this, he is condemned already. There is no need of trial, unbelief itself is the vilest of all treason; out of his own mouth the sinner is condemned.

Do you not see, O sinner, how the matter stands? The infinite Lord of mercy, that you. might not perish, has devised a wondrous way of salvation, which has astonished cherubim and seraphim, and made heaven ring with song, and this you utterly reject. The plan so stupendous in conception is briefly this, that the Creator should suffer that the created rebel might escape: that the Infinite should come into this world and be put to shame that the guilty might be clear; and all you are asked to do, all that is demanded of you is that you submit to be saved by this plan, that you do but trust in the Jesus who is divine, who is also man, do but trust him to save you. Will you not? Oh, will you not? Sirs, will you spurn almighty love? Can you turn away from boundless mercy? Then what shall I say of you, but just what the text says—you condemn yourselves, you are "condemned already"? You must be infinitely wicked, you must be enormously, monstrously, diabolically at enmity with God, or else surely a boon so precious you would not slight, a plan of mercy so adapted to your condition you could not have the impertinence to reject. "Condemned already because he hath not believed on the name of the only-begotten Son of God." Solemn words! Hear ye them and tremble!

From the verses following the text we gather that you unbelievers go on to give further evidence against yourselves, for every man who rejects Christ, the true light, always goes-on to reject other forms of the light of God's word, God's Spirit, and his conscience. He loves darkness rather than light, and comes not to the light lest his deeds should be reproved. You quench the Spirit, I know you do, if you reject the Savior. You turn a deaf ear to your conscience, you do violence to your own judgment. The truth of God you do not wish to learn. It is not possible that you can be a candid seeker after light if you refuse to receive him who is truth's central Sun. Your further rejection of light is confirmatory evidence that you are condemned already though your not believing is in itself evidence enough.

And now solemnly, and in the name of him that liveth, and was dead, and is alive forevermore, speaking for that Christ who though once he was slain now sitteth at the right hand of God, I ask those who are under this second character to listen to these simple but weighty words of admonition.

Consider, I pray you, O unbeliever, that the condemnation which is pronounced upon you already is no matter of form. Our judges sometimes read out sentence of death upon a certain order of criminals, and the sentence is recorded, though it is never intended that the sentence shall be executed; but from God's bar there never proceeds a sentence that is meant needlessly to alarm. You are condemned already, and as surely as you live, and as surely as God lives, he will not let his word remain a dead letter. That sentence shall be no idle threat, but in your proper person you shall be made to know what the power of his wrath is. "Who knoweth the power of thine anger?" saith the psalmist; they only know it who feel it, and you will feel it ere long, for the sentence will assuredly be fulfilled.

The Lord has power at this or any moment to fulfill his sentence. What power have you to resist it? Who is there that can help you to withstand him? You are utterly in his hands, you cannot break prison and escape. If you climbed up to heaven he is there; if you dived to hell he is there; the whole universe is but one great prison for an enemy of God. You cannot escape him neither can you resist him. If your bones were granite and your heart were steel, his fires would melt down your spirit. Against him thou canst no more stand than the chaff against the fire or the dust against the whirlwind. O that thou wouldst feel this and desist from thine insane rebellion!

Remember, there is no promise given to you that he will not execute the sentence of his wrath this very day. You have no warrant either from his word or from his angels to assure you that God has suspended spared the sentence even for the next hour. You are living by his forbearance, spared by the divine sovereignty. Some rave against sovereignty, but in his case it is not justice that spares you, it is the mere will of God that for awhile keeps you out of hell. You tell me that nothing endangers your life at this moment, how know you that? The arrows of death often fly imperceptibly. I have stood in congregations preaching on two occasions when the unseen darts of death struck one of my hearers, so that one died on each occasion while listening to the word of the gospel. God needs no miracle to put his sentence into execution at this moment. He need not disturb the natural order of affairs for you to die instantly; and if he so willed it, your soul's destruction would, without the slightest effort on his part, take place at this very moment, even where you are.

Remember with deep concern that God is angry with you now. This statement is no invention of mine, it is written by the pen of inspiration that "God is angry with the wicked every day: if he turn not he will whet his sword: he hath bent his bow, and made it ready." God is more angry with some of you than he is with some in hell. Are you startled by the assertion? "It shall be more tolerable for Sodom and Gomorrha in the day of judgment than for you." The sins you have already committed are greater than those of Sodom and Gomorrha, and the anger is in proportion to the guilt. An angry God holds you over the gulf of hell, justice demands that you fall into it, and it is nothing but his merciful will that keeps you out of it. He has but to will it, and you who are condemned already, would be forever where the worm dieth not and the fire is not quenched, ere next time the clock shall tick.

Up to this time, let me remind you, you have done nothing to appease the divine wrath. You have gone on sinning; or if you tell me you have reformed, that you have thought of these things, that you have prayed, do you think that such things will remove the divine wrath? The Lord has told you that the only way of salvation is to believe in Jesus, but you try to find another. Do you think that such conduct will please him, that such a procedure will make him less angry with you? You insult his Son when you suppose that you can save yourself by your tears and prayers—will this turn away the Lord's anger? When you imagine that your church-goings and chapel-goings will save you, you set a low estimate upon what Jesus did. You do despite to the cross as long as you remain unbelievers. You say, "We are doing what we can." You are doing nothing, I tell you, that can appease the anger of God, you are rather by these very actions of yours, which you think to be good, setting up in opposition to him an Antichrist upon which he will look with abhorrence. He saith he will save by Christ, and no how else, and so long as you seek another way, you do as it were spit into the very face of the Only-begotten by the insolence of your self-righteousness.

Meanwhile, let me remind you that God's wrath, though it come not on you yet, is like a stream that is dammed up. Every moment it gathers force, if it burst not the dyke, yet every hour is swelling it. Each day, and each moment of each day in which you remain an unbeliever, you are treasuring up wrath against the day of wrath when the measure of your iniquity is full. How earnestly would I persuade you to escape from condemnation! If you dream that to be condemned of God is a trifle, undeceive your souls, for those who have passed where the sentence is executed, could they come back to you need not tell the tale of woe, the very sight of them would convince you that to be lost is an awful thing. On their heads must fall the wrath of God, who, by softening down the punishment, become the means of hardening sinners in their sins. It is not within the power of thought to conceive what God's wrath is. No language, even though it should make both the ears to tingle, can ever fully express it. I am not one of those who would so delude your poor souls, O unbelievers, as to make you think it a light thing to fall into the hands of the living God. O turn ye, turn ye, turn ye! Why will ye die? Why will ye reject him whom you have such reasons to receive? Concerning whom his very person is the best argument for love? The Christ of God must be worthy of our hearts' affections: his very errand to earth, as it seems to me, would, if we were not mad, ensure our confidence; for he came to save, to pardon, to pass by the sin of the past. Oh, wherefore do ye stand out against him, and in this way pull down upon your heads the wrath of an angry God? Let me point out to you the way to escape. The only way of escape for any man or woman here is to believe in Jesus Christ. "I am praying about it," says one. My text saith nothing of the sort. "I will think of it." Think of it; you will think yourself into hell before long. Immediate faith is what I, as God's ambassador, demand of you in the name of the Christ of God—immediate, instantaneous faith in Jesus. Behold the emblem of the gospel minister and of his message! Moses lifted up the brazen serpent in the wilderness upon the great central standard in the very midst of the camp, where men were dying all around him. They are bitten with the serpent, and what has Moses to declare to them as a remedy? He bids them look and live. Some of them will think of it, some of them will consider it, others of them will pray about it; but he has no commission to console any of these: his one command is an immediate look, he has no promise to those who will not look. Even thus is Jesus lifted up among you; there is life in a look, life now, life at this moment. I cannot guarantee you that the serpent's bite shall not be your eternal ruin if you linger for a single hour. The prophet's one word is, "Look now." Today, God in mercy sends to everyone in this house this message. "The times of your ignorance God winked at," but now commandeth all men everywhere to repent. He sends his gospel message, "Believe in the Lord Jesus Christ, and thou shalt be saved." That message I cannot be certain will ever come to you again. "Now is the accepted time, now is the day of salvation." Every moment you are an unbeliever, you are sinning against God by that unbelief. I cannot therefore tolerate that you should wait a moment. Jesus is God; he became man, he died, he lives, and bids you trust him, promising that you shall live. Trust him now, then. He is worthy of your confidence. Sin not against him; sin not against your own souls by rejecting him. Remember what it was which Moses lifted up, it was a serpent, the image of that same serpent which bit them. Were they healed by looking to that which poisoned them? Assuredly they were. What is that which has poisoned you, sinner? It is the curse of sin. What is that which I hold up today in the gospel? It is Christ made a curse for us. He takes upon himself our sin; though in him was no sin, yet he was made sin for us—and if you trust him to be the sin-offering for you, to suffer for you, to bleed for you, and so trust in him as to take him henceforth as your standard, resolving to follow the uplifted Crucified One throughout life, even until he brings you to Christ himself in heaven, you are not condemned. But if Jesus be lifted up, and you refuse to believe, on your heads be your guilt, I say, with trembling solemnity, on your own heads be your guilt. Those words of mine, O unbelievers, will be swift witnesses against you at the last great day. As truly as ever Christ came to Jerusalem, so truly does he come to you this morning in the preaching of the word. I am a poor feeble man, but I speak to you as best I can; nevertheless if you refuse my word it is not me you reject, that were nothing, you reject the gospel which I preach to you. In the name of him that made heaven and earth, that made you, and holds you in life, against whom you have sinned, these terms of mercy are presented to you—will you have them? This grace is brought home to you, and I am bidden to press it upon you, even as the word saith, to "compel them to come in." If you reject the only begotten Son of God there must still abide against you this solemn sentence, "He that believeth not is condemned already, because he hath not believed." Did I hear you say, "I hope I shall believe." Sir, I have nothing to do with that, and I have no hope of you. "I hope I shall repent one day." I despair of you while you talk so. It is today that God separates this congregation into the two parts, the believer and the unbeliever. Today he blessed the believer and testifies that he is not condemned; today he curses the unbeliever and tells him he is condemned already. My business is not with tomorrows, nor can I promise that the white flag of mercy will be hung out tomorrow. Today the cross is the banner of grace. Look to it and live. It is the ladder which reaches to heaven; the crucified Savior is the gate of salvation. O that you would receive him! May God grant you may, and he shall be glorified by you in this life and in the world to come. God bless you. Amen.

6

THE PARABLE OF THE SOWER

Preached on April 15, 1860
Scripture: Luke 8:4-8
From: New Park Street Pulpit Volume 6

"And when much people were gathered together, and were come to him out of every city, he spake by a parable: a sower went out to sow his seed: and as he sowed, some fell by the way side; and it was trodden down, and the fowls of the air devoured it. And some fell upon a rock; and as soon as it was sprung up, it withered away, because it lacked moisture. And some fell among thorns; and the thorns sprang up with it, and choked it. And other fell on good ground, and sprang up, and bare fruit an hundredfold. And when he had said these things, he cried, He that hath ears to hear, let him hear."—Luke 8:4-8

In Our country, when a sower goes forth to his work, he generally enters into an enclosed field, and scatters the seed from his basket along every ridge and furrow; but in the East, the corn-growing country, hard by a small town, is usually an open area. It is divided into different properties, but there are no visible divisions, except the ancient landmarks, or perhaps ridges of stones. Through these open lands there are footpaths, the most frequented being called the highways. You must not imagine these highways to be like our macadamized roads; they are merely paths, trodden tolerably hard. Here and there you notice bye-ways, along which travelers who wish to avoid the public road may journey with a little more safety when the main road is infested with robbers: hasty travelers also strike out short cuts for themselves, and so open fresh tracks for others. When the sower goes forth to sow he finds a plot of round scratched over with the primitive Eastern plow; he aims at scattering his seed there most plentifully; but a path runs through the center of his field, and unless he is willing to leave a broad headland, he must throw a handful upon it. Yonder, a rock crops out in the midst of the plowed land, and the seed falls on its shallow soil. Here is a corner full of the roots of nettles and thistles, and he flings a little here; the corn and the nettles come up together, and the thorns being the stronger soon choke the seed, so that it brings forth no fruit unto perfection. The recollection that the Bible was written in the East, and that its metaphors and allusions must be explained to us by Eastern travelers, will often help us to understand a passage far better than if we think of English customs.

The preacher of the gospel is like the sower. He does not make his seed; it is given him by his divine Master. No man could create the smallest grain that ever grew upon the earth, much less the celestial seed of eternal life. The minister goes to his Master in secret, and asks him to teach him his gospel, and thus he fills his basket with the good seed of the kingdom. He then goes forth in his Master's name and scatters precious truth. If he knew where the best soil was to be found, perhaps he might limit himself to that which had been prepared by the plow of conviction; but not knowing men's hearts, it is his business to preach the gospel to every creature—to throw a handful on the hardened heart, and another on the mind which is overgrown with the cares and pleasures of the world. He has to leave the seed in the care of the Lord who gave it to him, for he is not responsible for the harvest, he is only accountable for the care and industry with which he does his work. If no single ear should ever make glad the reaper, the sower will be rewarded by His Master if he had planted the right seed with careful hand. If it were not for this fact with what despairing agony should we utter the cry of Esaias, "Who hath believed our report? And to whom is the arm of the Lord revealed?" Our duty is not measured by the character of our hearers, but by the command of our God. We are bound to preach the gospel, whether men will hear, or whether they will forbear. It is ours to sow beside all waters. Let men's hearts be what they may the minister must preach the gospel to them; he must sow the seed on the rock as well as in the furrow, on the highway as well as in the plowed field. I shall now address myself to the four classes of hearers mentioned in our Lord's parable. We have, first of all, those who are represented by the way-side, those who are "hearers only"; then those represented by the stony-ground; these are transiently impressed, but the word produces no lasting fruit; then, those among thorns, on whom a good impression is produced, but the cares of this life, and the deceitfulness of riches, and the pleasures of the world choke the seed; and lastly, that small class—God be pleased to multiply it exceedingly—that small class of good-ground hearers, in whom the Word brings forth abundant fruit.

I. First of all, I address myself to those hearts which are like the Way-Side—"Some fell by the wayside; and it was trodden down, and the fowls of the air devoured it." Many of you do not go to the place of worship desiring a blessing. You do not intend to worship God, or to be affected by anything that you hear. You are like the highway, which was never intended to be a cornfield. If a single grain of truth should fall into your heart and grow it would be as great a wonder as for corn to grow up in the street. If the seed shall be dexterously scattered, some of it will fall upon you, and rest for a while upon your thoughts. 'Tis true you will not understand it; but, nevertheless, if it be placed before you in an interesting style, you will talk about it till some more congenial entertainment shall attract you. Even this slender benefit is brief, for in a little season you will forget all that you have heard. Would to God we could hope that our words would tarry with you, but we cannot hope it, for the soil of your heart is so hard beaten by continual traffic, that there is no hope of the seed finding a living root-hold. Satan is constantly passing over your heart with his company of blasphemies, lusts, lies, and vanities. The chariots of pride roll along it, and the feet of greedy mammon tread it till it is hard as adamant. Alas! For the good seed, it finds not a moment's respite; crowds pass and repass; in fact, your soul is an exchange, across which continually hurry the busy feet of those who make merchandise of the souls of men. You are buying and selling, but you little think that you are selling the truth, and that you are buying your soul's destruction. You have no time, you say, to think of religion. No, the road of your heart is such a crowded thoroughfare, that there is no room for the wheat to spring up. If it did begin to germinate, some rough foot would crush the green blade ere it could come to perfection. The seed has occasionally lain long enough to begin to sprout, but just then a new place of amusement has been opened, and you have entered there, and as with an iron heel, the germ of life that was in the seed was crushed out. Corn could not grow in Cornhill or Cheapside, however excellent the seed might be: your heart is just like those crowded thoroughfares; for so many cares and sins throng it, and so many proud, vain, evil, rebellious thoughts against God pass through it, that the seed of truth cannot grow. We have looked at this hard road-side, let us now describe what becomes of the good word, when it falls upon such a heart. It would have grown if it had fallen on right soil, but it has dropped into the wrong place, and it remains as dry as when it fell from the sower's hand. The word of the gospel lies upon the surface of such a heart, but never enters it. Like the snow, which sometimes falls upon our streets, drops upon the wet pavement, melts, and is gone at once, so is it with this man. The word has not time to quicken in his soul: it lies there an instant, but it never strikes root, or takes the slightest effect. Why do men come to hear if the word never enters their hearts? That has often puzzled us. Some hearers would not be absent on the Sunday on any account; they are delighted to come up with us to worship, but yet the tear never trickles down their cheek, their soul never mounts up to heaven on the wings of praise, nor do they truly join in our confessions of sin. They do not think of the wrath to come, nor of the future state of their souls. Their heart is as iron; the minister might as well speak to a heap of stones as preach to them. What brings these senseless sinners here? Surely we are as hopeful of converting lions and leopards as these untamed, insensible hearts. Oh feeling! Thou art fled to brutish beasts, and men have lost their reason! Do these people come to our assemblies because it is respectable to attend a place of worship? Or is it that their coming helps to make them comfortable in their sins? If they stopped away conscience would prick them; but they come hither that they may flatter themselves with the notion that they are religious. Oh! My hearers, your case is one that might make an angel weep! How sad to have the sun of the gospel shining on your faces, and yet to have blind eyes that never see the light. The music of heaven is lost upon you, for you have no ears to hear. You can catch the turn of a phrase, you can appreciate the poetry of an illustration, but the hidden meaning, the divine life you do not perceive. You sit at the marriage-feast, but you eat not of the dainties; the bells of heaven ring with joy over ransomed spirits, but you live unransomed, without God, and without Christ. Though we plead with you, and pray for you, and weep over you, you still remain as hardened, as careless, and as thoughtless as ever you were. May God have mercy on you, and break up your hard hearts, that his word may abide in you. We have not, however, completed the picture. The passage tells us that the fowls of the air devoured the seed. Is there here a way-side hearer? Perhaps he did not mean to hear this sermon, and when he has heard it he will be asked by one of the wicked to come into company. He will go with the tempter, and the good seed will be devoured by the fowls of the air. Plenty of evil ones are ready to take away the gospel from the heart. The devil himself, that prince of the air, is eager at any time to snatch away a good thought. And then the devil is not alone—he has legions of helpers. He can set a man's wife, children, friends, enemies, customers, or creditors, to eat up the good seed, and they will do it effectually. Oh, sorrow upon sorrow, that heavenly seed should become devil's meat; that God's corn should feed foul birds! O my hearers, if you have heard the gospel from your youth, what wagon-loads of sermons have been wasted on you! In your younger days, you heard old Dr. So-and-so, and the dear old man was wont to pray for his hearers till his eyes were red with tears! Do you recollect those many Sundays when you said to yourself, "Let me go to my chamber and fall on my knees and pray"? But you did not: the fowls of the air ate up the seed, and you went on to sin as you had sinned before. Since then, by some strange impulse, you are very rarely absent from God's house; but now the seed of the gospel falls into your soul as if it dropped upon an iron floor, and nothing comes of it. The law may be thundered at you; you do not sneer at it, but it never affects you. Jesus Christ may be lifted up; his dear wounds may be exhibited; his streaming blood may flow before your very eyes, and you may be bidden with all earnestness to look to him and live; but it is as if one should sow the sea-shore. What shall I do for you? Shall I stand here and rain tears upon this hard highway? Alas! My tears will not break it up; it is trodden too hard for that. Shall I bring the gospel plow? Alas! The plowshare will not enter ground so solid. What shall we do? O God, thou knowest how to melt the hardest heart with the precious blood of Jesus. Do it now, we beseech thee, and thus magnify thy grace, by causing the good seed to live, and to produce a heavenly harvest.

II. I shall now turn to the second class of hearers:—"And some fell upon a Rock; and as soon as it was sprung up, it withered away, because it lacked moisture." You can easily picture to yourselves that piece of rock in the midst of the field thinly veiled with soil; and of course the seed falls there as it does everywhere else. It springs up, it hastens to grow, it withers, it dies. None but those who love the souls of men can tell what hopes, what joys, and what bitter disappointments these stony places have caused us. We have a class of hearers whose hearts are hard, and yet they are apparently the softest and most impressible of men. While other men see nothing in the sermon, these men weep. Whether you preach the terrors of the law or the love of Calvary, they are alike stirred in their souls, and the liveliest impressions are apparently produced. Such may be listening now. They have resolved, but they have procrastinated. They are not the sturdy enemies of God who clothe themselves in steel, but they seem to bare their breasts, and lay them open to the minister. Rejoiced in heart, we shoot our arrows there, and they appear to penetrate; but, alas, a secret armor blunts every dart, and no wound is felt. The parable speaks of this character thus—"Some fell upon stony places, where they had not much earth: and forthwith they sprung up, because they had no deepness of earth." Or as another passage explains it: "And these are they likewise which are sown on stony ground; who, when they have heard the word, immediately receive it with gladness; and have no root in themselves, and so endure but for a time: afterward, when affliction or persecution ariseth for the word's sake, immediately they are offended." Have we not thousands of hearers who receive the word with joy? They have no deep convictions, but they leap into Christ on a sudden, and profess an instantaneous faith in him, and that faith has all the appearance of being genuine. When we look at it, the seed has really sprouted. There is a kind of life in it, there is apparently a green blade. We thank God that a sinner is brought back, a soul is born to God. But our joy is premature: they sprang up on a sudden, and received the word with joy, because they had no depth of earth, and the self-same cause which hastened their reception of the seed also causes them, when the sun is risen with his fervent heat, to wither away. These men we see every day in the week. They come to join the church; they tell us a story of how they heard us preach on such-and-such an occasion, and, oh, the word was so blessed to them, they never felt so happy in their lives! "Oh sir, I thought I must leap from my seat when I heard about a precious Christ, and I believed on him there and then; I am sure I did." We question them as to whether they were ever convinced of sin. They think they were; but one thing they know, they feel a great pleasure in religion. We put it to them, "Do you think you will hold on?" They are confident that they shall. They hate the things they once loved, they are sure they do. Everything has become new to them. And all this is on a sudden. We inquire when the good work began. We find it began when it ended, that is to say, there was no previous work, no plowing of the soil, but on a sudden they sprang from death to life, as if a field should be covered with wheat by magic. Perhaps we receive them into the church; but in a week or two they are not so regular as they used to be. We gently reprove them, and they explain that they meet with such opposition in religion, that they are obliged to yield a little. Another month and we lose them altogether. The reason is that they have been laughed at or exposed to a little opposition, and they have gone back. And what, think you, are the feelings of the minister? He is like the husbandman, who sees his field all green and flourishing, but at night a frost nips every shoot, and his hoped-for gains are gone. The minister goes to his chamber, and casts himself on his face before God, and cries, "I have been deceived; my converts are fickle, their religion has withered as the green herb." In the ancient story Orpheus is said to have had such skill upon the lyre, that he made the oaks and stones to dance around him. It is a poetical fiction, and yet hath it sometimes happened to the minister, that not only have the godly rejoiced, but men, like oaks and stones, have danced from their places. Alas! They have been oaks and stones still. Hushed is the lyre. The oak returns to its rooting-place, and the stone casts itself heavily to the earth. The sinner, who, like Saul, was among the prophets, goes back to plan mischief against the Most High. If it is bad to be a wayside hearer, I cannot think it is much better to be like the rock. This second class of hearers certainly gives us more joy than the first. A certain company always comes round a new minister; and I have often thought it is an act of God's kindness that he allows these people to gather at the first, while the minister is young, and has but few to stand by him: these persons are easily moved, and if the minister preaches earnestly they feel it, and they love him, and rally round him, much to his comfort. But time, that proves all things, proves them. They seemed to be made of true metal; but when they are put into the fire to be tested, they are consumed in the furnace. Some of the shallow kind are here now. I have looked at you when I have been preaching, and I have often thought, "That man one of these days will come out from the world, I am sure he will." I have thanked God for him. Alas, he is the same as ever. Years and years have we sowed him in vain, and it is to be feared it will be so to the end, for he is without depth, and without the moisture of the Spirit. Shall it be so? Must I stand over the mouth of your open sepulcher, and thin, "Here lies a shoot which never became an ear, a man in whom grace struggled but never reigned, who gave some hopeful spasms of life and then subsided into eternal death"? God save you! Oh! May the Spirit deal with you effectually, and may you, even you, yet bring forth fruit unto God, that Jesus may have a reward for his sufferings.

III. I shall briefly treat of the third class, and may the Spirit of God assist me to deal faithfully with you. "And some fell among Thorns; and the thorns sprang up with it, and choked it." Now, this was good soil. The two first characters were bad: the wayside was not the proper place, the rock was not a congenial situation for the growth of any plant; but this is good soil, for it grows thorns. Wherever a thistle will spring up and flourish, there would wheat flourish too. This was fat, fertile soil; it was no marvel therefore that the husbandman dealt largely there, and threw handful after handful upon that corner of the field. See how happy he is when in a month or two he visits the spot. The seed has sprung up. True, there's a suspicious little plant down there of about the same size as the wheat. "Oh!" he thinks, "that's not much, the corn will out-grow that. When it is stronger it will choke these few thistles that have unfortunately mixed with it." Ay, Mr. Husbandman, you do not understand the force of evil, or you would not thus dream! He comes again, and the seed has grown, there is even the corn in the ear; but the thistles, the thorns, and the briars have become intertwisted with one another, and the poor wheat can hardly get a ray of sunshine. It is so choked with thorns every way, that it looks quite yellow: the plant is starved. Still it perseveres in growing, and it does seem as if it would bring forth a little fruit. Alas, it never comes to anything. With it the reaper never fills his arm. We have this class very largely among us. These hear the word and understand what they hear. They take the truth home; they think it over; they even go the length of making a profession of religion. The wheat seems to spring and ear; it will soon come to perfection. Be in no hurry, these men and women have a great deal to see after; they have the cares of a large concern; their establishment employs so many hundred hands; do not be deceived as to their godliness—they have no time for it. They will tell you that they must live; that they cannot neglect this world; that they must anyhow look out for the present, and as for the future, they will render it all due attention by-and-by. They continue to attend gospel-preaching, and the poor little stunted blade of religion keeps on growing after a fashion. Meanwhile they have grown rich, they come to the place of worship in a carriage, they have all that heart can wish. Ah! Now the seed will grow, will it not? No, no. They have no cares now; the shop is given up, they live in the country; they have not to ask, "Where shall the money come from to meet the next bill?" or "how shall they be able to provide for an increasing family." Now they have too much instead of too little, for they have riches, and they are too wealthy to be gracious. "But," says one, "they might spend their riches for God." Certainly they might, but they do not, for riches are deceitful. They have to entertain much company, and chime in with the world, and so Christ and his church are left in the lurch. Yes, but they begin to spend their riches, and they have surely got over that difficulty, for they give largely to the cause of Christ, and they are munificent in charity; the little blade will grow, will it not? No, for now behold the thorns of pleasure. Their liberality to others involves liberality to themselves; their pleasures, amusements, and vanities choke the wheat of true religion: the good grains of gospel truth cannot grow because they have to attend that musical party, that ball, and that soiree, and so they cannot think of the things of God. I know several specimens of this class. I knew one, high in court circles, who has confessed to me that he wished he were poor, for then he might enter the kingdom of heaven. He has said to me, "Ah! Sir, these politics, these politics, I wish I were rid of them, they are eating the life out of my heart; I cannot serve God as I would." I know of another, overloaded with riches, who has said to me, "Ah! Sir, it is an awful thing to be rich; one cannot keep close to the Savior with all this earth about him." Ah! My dear readers, I will not ask for you that God may lay you on a bed of sickness, that he may strip you of all your wealth, and bring you to beggary; but, oh, if he were to do it, and you were to save your souls, it would be the best bargain you could ever make. If those mighty ones who now complain that the thorns choke the seed could give up all their riches and pleasures, if they that fare sumptuously every day could take the place of Lazarus at the gate, it were a happy change for them if their souls might be saved. A man may be honorable and rich, and yet go to heaven; but it will be hard work, for "It is easier for a camel to go through the eye of a needle, than for a rich man to enter into the kingdom of heaven." God does make some rich men enter the kingdom of heaven, but hard is their struggle. Steady, young man, steady! Hurry not to climb to wealth! It is a place where many heads are turned. Do not ask God to make you popular; they that have popularity are wearied by it. Cry with Agur—"Give me neither poverty nor riches." God give me to tread the golden mean, and may I ever have in my heart that good seed, which shall bring forth fruit a hundredfold to his own glory.

IV. I now close with the last character, namely, the Good Ground. Of the good soil, as you will mark, we have but one in four. Will one in four of our hearers, with well-prepared heart, receive the Word? The ground is described as "good": not that it was good by nature, but it had been made good by grace. God had plowed it; he had stirred it up with the plow of conviction, and there it lay in ridge and furrow as it should lie. When the gospel was preached, the heart received it, for the man said, "That is just the blessing I want. Mercy is what a needy sinner requires." So that the preaching of the gospel was THE thing to give comfort to this disturbed and plowed soil. Down fell the seed to take good root. In some cases it produced fervency of love, largeness of heart, devotedness of purpose of a noble kind, like seed which produces a hundredfold. The man became a mighty servant for God, he spent himself and was spent. He took his place in the vanguard of Christ's army, stood in the hottest of the battle, and did deeds of daring which few could accomplish—the seed produced a hundredfold. It fell into another heart of like character;—the man could not do the most, but still he did much. He gave himself to God, and in his business he had a word to say for his Lord; in his daily walk he quietly adorned the doctrine of God his Savior,—he brought forth sixty-fold. Then it fell on another, whose abilities and talents were but small; he could not be a star, but he would be a glow-worm; he could not do as the greatest, but he was content to do something, however humble. The seed had brought forth in him tenfold, perhaps twenty-fold. How many are there of this sort here? Is there one who prays within himself, "God be merciful to me a sinner"? The seed has fallen in the right spot. Soul, thy prayer shall be heard. God never sets a man longing for mercy without intending to give it. Does another whisper, "Oh that I might be saved"? Believe on the Lord Jesus Christ, and thou, even thou, shalt be saved. Hast thou been the chief of sinners? Trust Christ, and thy enormous sins shall vanish as the millstone sinks beneath the flood. Is there no one here that will trust the Savior? Can it be possible that the Spirit is entirely absent? That he is not moving in one soul? Not begetting life in one spirit? We will pray that he may now descend, that the word may not be in vain.

7

THE GLORIOUS GOSPEL OF THE BLESSED GOD

Preached on June 30, 1867
Scripture: 1 Timothy 1:11
From: Metropolitan Tabernacle Pulpit Volume 13

"According to the glorious gospel of the blessed God, which was committed to my trust."—1 Timothy 1:11

THIS verse occurs just after a long list of sins, which the apostle declares to be contrary to sound doctrine; from which we gather that one test of sound doctrine is its opposition to every form of sin. That doctrine which in any way palliates sin may be popular, but is not sound doctrine: those who talk much of their soundness, but yet by their lives betray the rottenness of their hearts, need far rather to be ashamed of their hypocrisy than to be proud of their orthodoxy. The apostle offers us in the verse before us another standard by which to test the doctrines which we hear; he tells us that sound doctrine is always evangelical—"sound doctrine according to the glorious gospel." Any doctrine which sets up the will or the merit of man, any doctrine which exalts priestcraft and ceremonial, any doctrine, in fact, which does not put salvation upon the sole footing of free grace, is unsound. These two points are absolutely needful in every teaching which professes to come from God; it must commend, and foster holiness of life; and, at the same time, it must, beyond all question, be a declaration of grace and mercy through the Mediator.

Our apostle was, by the drift of his letter, led incidentally to make mention of the gospel; and then, in a moment, taking to himself wings of fire, he mounts into a transport of praise, and calls it "the glorious gospel of the blessed God." Such is his mode of writing generally, that if he comes across a favorite thought, he is away at a tangent from the subject that he was aiming at, and does not return until his ardent spirit cools again. In this case, or ever he was aware, his soul made him like the chariots of Ammi-nadib. His glowing heart poured forth the warmest eulogium upon that hidden treasure, that pearl of price immense, which he prized beyond all price, and guarded with a sacred jealousy of care. I think I see the radiant countenance of the apostle of the Lord, as with flashing eye he dictates the words, "The glorious gospel of the blessed God, which was committed to my trust."

Our subject affords us fine sea-room, but our time is short, our boat is small, and the atmosphere is so hot and heavy that scarcely a breath of air is to be had, and therefore I will keep to one straightforward track, and not distract you with many topics. To open up the text in all its length and breadth would be fit exercise for the loftiest intellect, but we must be content with a few experimental and practical remarks, and may the Lord enable us to weave them into a heart searching discourse.

I. In the first place, then, Paul praises the gospel to the utmost by calling it "the glorious gospel of the blessed God:" HAVE WE EXPERIENCED ITS EXCELLENCE?

It is needful to ask the question even in this congregation; for even to great multitudes who attend our houses of prayer, the gospel is a dry, uninteresting subject. They hear the word because it is their duty; they sit in the pew because custom requires an outward respect to religion; but they never dream of the gospel having anything glorious in it, anything that can stir the heart or make the pulse beat at a faster rate. The sermon is slow, the service is dull, the whole affair is a weariness to which nothing but propriety makes men submit. Some people do their religion as a matter of necessity, as a horse drags a wagon ; but if that necessity of respectability did not exist, they would be as glad to escape from it as the horse is to leave the shafts and to miss the rumbling of the wheels. It is necessary, then, to ask the question; and I shall put it before you in three or four ways. Paul calls the sacred message of mercy the gospel. Has it been the gospel to us? The word is plain, and I hardly need remind you that it means "good news." Now, has the gospel been "good news" to us? Has it ever been "news" to you? "We have heard it so often," says one," that we cannot expect it to be news to us. We were trained by godly parents; we were taken to the Sunday-school; we have learned the gospel from our youth up; it cannot be news to us." Let me say to you, then, that you do not know the word of reconciliation unless it has been, and still is, news to you. To every man who is ever saved by the gospel, it comes as a piece of news as novel, fresh, and startling, as if he had never heard it before. The letter may be old, but the inward meaning is as new as though the ink were not yet dry In the pen of revelation. I confess to have been tutored in piety, put into my cradle by prayerful hands, and lulled to sleep by songs concerning Jesus; but after having heard the gospel continually, with line upon line, precept upon precept, here much and there much, yet when the word of the Lord came to me with power, it was as new as if I had lived among the unvisited tribes of central Africa, and had never heard the tidings of the cleansing fountain filled with blood from the Savior's veins. The gospel in its spirit and power always wears the dew of its youth; it glitters with morning's freshness—its strength and its glory abide forever. Ah! my dear hearer, if thou hast ever felt thy guilt, if thou has been burdened under a sense of it, if thou hast looked into thine own heart to find some good thing, and been bitterly disappointed, if thou hast gone up and down through the world to try this and that scheme of getting relief, and found them all fail thee like dry wells in the desert which mock the traveler, it will be a sweet piece of news to thy heart that there is present salvation in the Savior. It is a most refreshing novelty to near the voice of Jesus say, "Come unto me and rest." Though thou hast heard the invitation outwardly thousands of times, yet Jesus' own voice, when he speaks to thy heart, will be as surprisingly fresh to thee as if these dumb walls should suddenly find a tongue, and reveal the mysteries which have been hidden from the foundation of the world. To every believer the gospel comes as news from the land beyond the river, God's mind revealed by God's Spirit to his chosen.

It is good news too. Now, has the gospel ever been experimentally good to you, my hearer? Good in the best sense, good emphatically, good without any admixture of evil, the gospel is to those who know it: is it so to you? Have you ever been deeply sensible of your overwhelming debt to the justice of God, and then gladly received the gracious information that your debts are all discharged? Have you trembled beneath the thunder-charged cloud of Jehovah's wrath, which was ready to pour forth its tempest upon you, and have you heard the gentle voice of mercy saying, "I have blotted out, as a thick cloud, thy transgressions, and, as a cloud, thy sins"? Hast thou ever known what it is to be fully absolved, to stand before God without fear, accepted in the Beloved, received as a dear child, covered with the righteousness of Christ? If so, the gospel has been "good" indeed to thee. Grasping it by the hand of faith, and feeling the power of it in thy soul, thou countest it to be the best tidings that ever came from God to man.

I shall now ask you earnestly to answer my question as in the Sight of God; let no man escape from this most vital inquiry, Has that which Paul calls the gospel, proved itself to be gospel to you? Did it ever make your heart leap, just as some highly gratifying information excites and charms you? Has it ever seemed to you an all-important thing? If not, thou knowest not what the gospel means. O let my anxious questions tenderly quicken thee to be concerned about thy soul's affairs, and to seek unto the Lord Jesus for eternal life.

Paul having called the message of mercy "the gospel," then adds an adjective—"the glorious gospel," and as glorious gospel it is for a thousand reasons: glorious in its antiquity; for before the beams of the first morning drove away primeval shades, this gospel of our salvation was ordained in the mind of the Eternal. It is glorious because it is everlasting—when all things shall have passed away as the hoar frost of the morning dissolve before the rising sun, this gospel shall still exist in all its power and grace. It is glorious because it reveals the glory of God more fully than all the universe beside. Not all the innumerable worlds that God has ever fashioned, though they speak to us in loftiest eloquence from their celestial spheres, can proclaim to us the character of our heavenly Father as the gospel does. "The heavens are telling the glory of God," but the gospel which tells of Jesus has a sweeter and a clearer speech. The poet talks of the great and wide sea wherein the almighty form mirrors itself in tempest; so, indeed, the finger of God may mirror itself, but a thousand oceans could not mirror the Infinite himself—the gospel of Jesus Christ is the only molten looking-glass in which Jehovah can be seen. In Jesus we see not only God's train, such as Moses saw when he beheld the skirts of Jehovah's robe in the cleft of the rock, but the whole of God is revealed in the gospel of Jesus, so that our Lord could say, "He that hath seen me, hath seen the Father." If the Lord be glorious in holiness, such the gospel reveals him. Is his right hand glorious in power? so the gospel speaks of him. Is the Lord the Goa of love? Is not this the genius of the gospel? The gospel is glorious because every attribute of Deity is manifested in it with unrivaled splendor.

But I desire to come home to your consciences by asking, Is the gospel to you a glorious gospel? Beloved friends, we may know our state very much by what answer we shall give to that question. The gospel, seen with these eyes and heard With these external ears, will be like the Lord himself, "A root out of a dry ground, having no form nor comeliness;" but the gospel understood by the renewed heart, will be quite a different thing. Oh, it will be a glorious gospel indeed, if you are raised up in newness of life, to enjoy the blessings which it brings to you. So, I beseech you, answer the question: and to help you, let me remind the people of God how glorious the gospel has been to them. Do you recollect the day when the gospel carried your heart by storm? You never can forget when the great battering-ram of truth began to beat against the gates of Mansoul. You recollect how you strengthened the posts and bars, and stood out against the gospel resolving not to yield. You were at times compelled to weep under impressions, but you wiped away your transient tears—your emotions was "as the morning cloud, and as the early dew." But eternal love would not relinquish its gracious assaults, for it was determined to save. Providence and grace together besieged the city of your soul and brought divine artillery to bear upon it. You were straightly shut up till—as it was with Samaria, so it was with you—there was a great famine in your soul. You recollect how, Sabbath after Sabbath, every sermon was a fresh assault from the hosts of heaven from the celestial battering-ram. How often, when the—gates a new of your blow prejudice were dashed to shivers, did you set Up fresh barricades! Your heart trembled beneath the terrible strokes of justice, but, by the gospel battering-ram gave—the effectual blow of grace, the gates flew the wide open, and in rode the Prince of Peace, Immanuel, like a conqueror, riding in the chariots of salvation. Our will was subdued, our affections were overcome, our whole soul was brought into subjection to the sway of mercy. Jesus was glorious in our eyes that day, "the chief among ten thousand, and the altogether lovely." That day of days we have registered upon the tablets of our heart: it was the true coronation-day of Jesus in us, and our birthday for eternity. When our glorious Lord entered into Our souls, wearing his vesture dipped in blood, pardoning and blessing in the plenitude of his grace, then the bells of our heart rang merry peals; the streamers of our joy floated in the fragrant air; the streets of our soul were strewn with roses ; the fountains of our love ran with rich red wine, and our soul was as full of bliss as a heart could be this side of heaven ; for salvation had come to our house, and mercy's King had deigned to visit us. Oh, the sweet perfume of the spikenard, when, for the first time, the King sat at our table to sup with us! how the savor of his presence filled every chamber of our inner man! That day When grace redeemed us from our fears, the gospel was a glorious gospel indeed! Ah! dear hearer, you stood in the crowded aisle to hear the sermon, but you did not grow weary, the lips of the preacher refreshed you, for the truth dropped like sweet smelling myrrh. You could have gone over hedge and ditch to hear the gospel at that season of first love; no matter how roughly it might have been served up by the preacher, you rolled the bread of heaven under your tongue as a sweet morsel, for it was the gospel of your salvation.

Christian, I will refresh your memory' farther. Do not forget the after conquests of that gospel. If you have made any advance in the divine life, it has been by the power of the gospel of Jesus Christ applied by the Holy Ghost. We make mistakes sometimes, for, having began in the Spirit we hope to be made perfect in the flesh. I mean that frequently we try to battle with our inbred sins by smiting them with legal reasonings. No believer ever conquered sin by being afraid of the punishment of it—this is a weapon fit only for sons of the bondwoman. It is the blood of Jesus which is the conquering weapon in the holy war against natural corruption. "They overcame by the blood of the Lamb." Knowing that I am dead to sin and risen with Christ, it is in the power of resurrection life that I wrestle against the old man, and overcome him. Beloved, recollect that you are always weak when you get away from the cross, that it is only as a sinner saved by blood that you can hope to make any advance in sanctification. Do not attempt to flog yourself into grace, the new life must not be touched with the whip of bondage. Go to the cross for motive and energy as to holiness. Look to Jesus in the gospel as you did in the beginning of your new life. Know yourself to be saved in him, and then go forth to battle with temptation, with the gospel as the standard of your lifelong warfare. If any of you have tried to make war with sin apart from the Captain of your salvation, you have either been wounded to your hurt already, or you will be; but if Judah's Lion shall go up before you, and you follow with the gospel as your war-cry, your victory is sure, and you shall have another wreath to lay at the feet of Jesus and his glorious gospel.

Beloved, let me say that all true saints have found it to be a glorious gospel from its comforting us in our darkest hours. We are not without our troubles, for which we would be grateful; they are flinty rocks which flow with oil. The roots of our soul might take too firm a hold upon this poor clay soil, if they were not Roughly loosened by affliction; this is not our rest, it is polluted, and our sorrows are useful because they remind us of this. But what has such power to calm the troubled spirit as the gospel? Go ye to the Lord Jesus, ye daughters of grief; know and understand once more your union with him, and your acceptance in him, and you will repine no more: you will bow your shoulder and cheerfully take up your cross when you have found out in your hour of need that the gospel has a glorious power to sustain those who are ready to sink. Did you never perceive the glory of the gospel in its power to resist the attacks of the great enemy? The soul has been beleaguered by a thousand temptations; Satan, has howled, and all the fiends of hell have joined in horrible chorus, and your own poor distracted thoughts have said, "I shall perish notwithstanding all my high enjoyments and confidence." Have you never gathered, as John Bunyan would picture it, all your forces to the top of the wall to Bling the great stones against the enemy? Have you not felt that the castle would be taken, till, as a last resort, yon ran up the blood-red flag of the cross, seized the sword of the Spirit, and went to the rampart determined to hold the wall against the enemy? Then when the scaling ladder touched the wall, and the foe leaped on the bulwarks, you dashed him down again in the name of Jesus by the power of the cross, and as often as he came up, so often did you hurl him down again, always overcoming in the power of the gospel; keeping your ground against temptation from without, and corruption from within, by the energy which the gospel of Jesus Christ alone could give you.

One point may help us to see the glory of the gospel, namely, that it has saved us from tremendous ills. The ills which are to come upon the unbeliever, who shall describe them? If a spirit could cross the bridge-less gulf which parts us from the land of darkness and the shadow of death, if he could tell us what are the pangs unutterable which are endured by guilty souls, then might we say, "Glorious indeed is that gospel which can lift us from the gates of hell, and preserve us from going down to the pit." Think, my brethren, of what the joys are for which the gospel is preparing us! It is by the Holy Ghost, through the preaching of the word, that we are ripening for those joys which "eye hath not seen," and which "ear hath not heard." Meetness for heaven will not come to us by the law, but by the gospel. Not so much as one of the celestials came there by the deeds of the flesh, but altogether by the sovereign grace of God revealed to them in the gospel of Jesus Christ. A glorious gospel it is, for it brings its disciples to glory!

Let me ask you whether it is glorious to you at this hour? I think I can say it is to me. I wish it were in my power to make it more glorious in my ministry; but it is glorious to my own heart. After some years of experience; the Christian comes to know better than he did at first how much the gospel suits him. He finds that its simplicity suits his bewilderment; its grace suits his sinfulness; its power is suitable to his weakness; its comfort is suitable to his despondency; and the older he grows the more he loves the gospel of the grace of God. Give it up? Ah! never; we will hold Christ the more firmly because men despise him. To whom or whither should we go if we should turn aside from our Lord Jesus?

Now, dear hearers, before I leave this point, I want to put it to you again, with much loving solicitude. Is the gospel glorious to you? Remember, if it be not, there can be no hope for you. There is no way of salvation except by the good news that "Jesus Christ came into the world to save sinners," and if that news should sound in your ears as a dry, dull thing, rest assured you are not on the way to heaven, for the gospel to every saved soul is sweeter than the sound of the best earthly music. Is it so to you? God is pleased today to put up before your eyes the white flag of mercy, calling you to come to Jesus and live. But recollect if you do not yield to it, he will run up the red flag of threatening, and then the black flag of execution will not be far off. Perhaps some of you have been suffering under bodily disease, take that as a warning. When our vessels of war would stop a suspicious vessel, they fire a shot athwart her bows as a warning. If she does not haul to, perhaps they give another, and if no notice is taken of this, the gunners go to their business in real earnest, and woe to the offender. Your affliction is the gospel's warning gun. Pause awhile, I beseech you, ask the Lora in mercy to look upon you that you may be saved! As I think upon some of you here who are not saved, I feel something like the boy I read of yesterday in the newspapers. Last week there were two lads on the great rocks of Lundy Island, in the Bristol Channel, looking for sea-gull's eggs; one of them went far down the cliff, and lost his footing, and when his brother, hearing a faint voice, looked down, he saw him clinging to a jutting crag, and striving in vain to find a place for his feet. There stood the anxious brother, alarmed and paralyzed with dread, quite unable to help the younger one in so much peril below, who soon relaxed his hold and was dashed to pieces far beneath. I feel somewhat like that alarmed brother, only there is this happy difference: I can hope for you, and bid you hope for yourselves. You are clinging now, perhaps, to some false hope, and striving to find a rest where rest is not to be found; but the strong-winged angel of the everlasting gospel is just underneath you this morning, crying, Drop now; simply drop into my arms; I will take you and bear you aloft in safety." That angel is the Angel of the Covenant, the Lord Jesus Christ. You must be dashed to pieces forever unless you rest in him; but cast yourself upon him, I pray you, and then, as you are carried in safety far off from every fear, you will magnify the grace of God, and extol the glorious gospel.

I must leave that point, and observe that Paul recognized the gospel as being the gospel of God. Here arises another inquiry, by which we may know whether we are saved or not. Has the gospel been the gospel of God to you, my friends? It is easy to receive the gospel as the gospel of "my minister." I am afraid there is a good deal of that sort of thing among us. We have great faith in our religious teachers, and very properly so, if we have received benefit from them; but if the gospel only comes to us as the gospel of such-and-such a preacher, it will not save us; it must come distinctly and directly as God's gospel, and we must receive it so. It is in solemn silence of the mind our privilege to hear the voice of God speaking to us, and to receive the truth in the love of it as coming with divine authority directly from God. Recollect that all religion which is not the work of the Holy Spirit in the heart will have to be unraveled, let it be woven ever so cunningly. We may build, as our little children do on the sea-shore, our sand houses, and we may pile them up very quickly too, and be very pleased with them, but they will all come down as the tide of time advances; only that which God the Holy Ghost builds upon the foundation of Christ's finished work will stand the test of time and eternity. How is it with you? If the Spirit of Christ be not in you ye are dead. If the gospel itself should come to you in a sort of power, but only because of the pathos of the preacher, or the eloquent manner of his speech, it has not brought eternal life to you.

If the gospel be indeed the gospel of God to us, it will exalt God in our estimation. The Father we shall love and adore, having chosen us to eternal life. The Son we shall love with warmest affection, having redeemed us with his precious blood. The Holy Spirit we shall constantly reverence, and we shall cherish him as dwelling a welcome guest within these bodies of ours. By this we may tell whether we have received the truth of God, by its bringing us consciously into connection with God. Does God dwell in you, my hearer? for, if not, you will not dwell where God is. You must know the Holy Spirit, not as an influence to be poured out as some pray, but as dwelling within you, resting in your heart. I put that as a very important question, but I will not pause over it, for I have to close our first head by noticing that the gospel was to Paul the "gospel of the blessed God." I believe William Knibb used to read this passage, "The gospel of the happy God," and it was not a mistake—it is the very gist of the matter. "The gospel of the happy God." Have you ever considered how happy God must be! how supremely happy? No care, no sorrow, can ever pass across his infinite mind. He is serenely blessed evermore. Now, when a man is miserable, and of a miserable turn of mind, he as naturally makes people miserable, as a foul fountain pours out foul water; but when a good man is superlatively happy, he imparts happiness. A happy face attracts many of us, and a happy temperament, a quiet mind, a serene disposition, why, a man who has these, inevitably tries to make others happy; and it is, I suppose, because God is infinitely happy, that he delights in the happiness of his creatures. The fabled gods of the heathen were vexed with all sorts of ambitions, longings, and cravings, which they could not gratify, or which, when gratified, only made them crave the more, consequently they are pictured as revengeful and cruel, delighting in the miseries of men; but our God is so perfectly blessed, that he has no motive for causing needless sorrow to his creatures. He has all perfection within himself; and, consequently, he delights to make us happy. How much satisfaction God finds in the happiness of Creatures that are devoid of intellect? You may have seen sometimes when the sea is going down, a little fringe at the edge of the wave which looks like mist; but if you were carefully to examine it, you would find that there were countless multitudes of very tiny shrimps, all leaping up and casting themselves into all manner of forms of intense delight. Look again at the gnats, as you walk in your gardens in the summer evenings—how they dance up and down—these little mirthful beings are all exhibiting to us the perfect blessedness that God would have to be manifested by all his creatures. He would have his people supremely blest, he would have every vessel of mercy full to the, brim with the oil of joy; and the war to make us so is to give us the gospel. The gospel is sent, to use our Savior's words, "that his joy may be in us, and that our joy may be full." We enjoy heaven upon earth as we sit at the feast of fat things on earth—what will be our glory when the gospel of the blessed God shall have turned out all our sin; when we shall swim in the gospel as the fish swims in the sea; when the gospel shall become our element in the next world. Oh I the happiness of the creatures that are full of the gospel spirit before the throne of God I Dear hearer, did the gospel ever come to you in that shape ? I am afraid that to most people the gospel is a bondage, because they do not know it in very deed. I am afraid that to many, gospel emotion is a sort of spasm; they are satisfied with the truth sometimes, and at other times when they feel they must have a treat, they go into the world for it. Where you get your treats there your heart is; whatever it is that gives you the most happiness, that is the master of your spirit. The Christian feels that he can sing with old Mason: —

> *"I need not go abroad for joys, I have a feast at home;*
> *My sighs are turned into songs, my heart has ceased to roam.*
> *Down from above the bless'd Dove is come into my breast,*
> *To witness God's eternal love, and give my spirit rest*
> *My God, I'll praise thee while I live, and praise thee when I die;*
> *And praise thee when I rise again, and to eternity."*

The religion of the genuine Christian is calculated to impart perfect delight; the truly regenerated man desires to have more and more of it, that his soul may be baptized in heavenly joy.

"The gospel of the happy God," also means the gospel of the God whom we must bless in return. As being happy, he makes us happy; so we, being happy, desire to ascribe to him all the glory of our happiness. Now, is the gospel to you, my dear young friend over there, the gospel of a God whom you bless from all your heart, because he has sent it to you, and made you willing to receive it? If so, you are saved. But if not?, if no emotions of Sincere gratitude stir the deeps of your soul, then the gospel has been to you no more than a sounding brass and a tinkling cymbal.

II. The apostle says, "The glorious gospel of the blessed God, which is committed to my TRUST" DO YOU RECOGNIZE YOUR RESPONSIBILITY?

Paul speaks not here of himself alone; he might have said, "which is committed to the trust of every believer in Christ" The gospel is a priceless treasure, and the saints ate the bankers of it. It is committed to our trust as men commit business to their agents.

First, we are bound to believe it all. Take heed of receiving a divided and maimed gospel. It- has been said that "only half the truth is a lie," and so it is. Most of the ill reports which distress the world have truth at the foundation of them, but they become false through the exaggeration of one part, and the omission of the next. It should be the duty Of every enlightened Christian to labor to master the whole compass of truth so far as possible. I suppose none but the Infinite mind can know all the lengths and breadths of truth, but still we should not be warped by education, nor be kept from receiving truth by prejudice. We should strive against all partiality, and it Should be, whenever we open this Book, one of our prayers, "Open thou mine eyes, that I may behold wondrous things out of thy law." To have a mind like molten metal, ready to be run into the mold of the truth; to have a soul like the photographer's sensitive plate, ready to receive the light-writing of God at once, so that the truth may be there In its entirety; to be willing to give up the most cherished dogma, the most flesh-pleasing form of teaching, when we find it to be contrary to Scripture, this is to be a true disciple. To sit at Jesus' feet and learn of him, is the life-business of the Christian in this house of his pilgrimage. The gospel is in this sense committed to our trust, for we are to lay it up in our hearts. But some one demands, "How am I to know which is the gospel?" You may know it by searching the Scriptures. "But one sect says this, and another sect says the reverse; what have you to do with the sects ? Read the Book of God for yourself. "But some men do read it and arrive at one opinion, and some maintain the opposite, and thus they Contradict themselves, and yet ate equally right." Who told you that? That is impossible Men cannot be equally right when they contradict each other. There is a truth and there is a falsehood; if yes be true, no is false. It may be true that good men have held different opinions, but are you responsible for what they may have held, or are you to gather that because they were good personally, therefore everything they believed was true?

No, but this Book is plain enough; it is no nose of wax that everybody may shape to what form he likes. There is something taught here plainly and positively, and if a man will but give his mind to it, by God's grace he may find it out. I do not believe that this Book is so dark and mysterious as some suppose, or, if it were, the Holy Spirit who wrote it still lives, and the Author always knows his own meaning: you have only to go to him in prayer, and he will tell you what it means. You will not become infallible, I trust you will not think yourself to be so, but you will learn doctrines which are infallibly true, and upon which you may put down your foot and say, "Now, I know this, and am not to be duped out of it." It is a grand thing to have the truth burnt into you, as with a hot iron, so that there is no getting it out of you. The priest, when he took away the Testament from the boy, thought he had done the work; "But," said the boy, "six, what will you do with the six-and-twenty chapters which I learned by heart? You cannot take them away." Yet memory might fail, and, as the lad grew into an old man, he might forget the six-and-twenty chapters; but suppose they changed his heart and made him a new creature in Christ, there would be no getting that away, even though Satan himself should attempt the task. Seek to carry out the sacred trust committed to you by believing it, and believing it all. Search the word to find out what the gospel is, and endeavor to receive it into your inmost heart, that it may be in your heart's core forever.

Next, as good stewards we must maintain the cause of truth against all comers. "Never get into religious controversies," says one; that is to say, being interpreted, be a Christian soldier, but let your sword rust in its scabbard, and sneak into heaven like a coward. Such advice I cannot endorse. If God has called you by the truth, maintain the truth which has been the means of your salvation. We are not to be pugnacious, always contending for every crotchet of our own; but wherein, we have learned the truth of the Holy Spirit, we are not tamely to see that standard torn down which our fathers upheld at peril of their blood. This is an age in which truth must be maintained zealously, vehemently, continually. Playing fast and loose as many do, believing this today and that tomorrow, is the sure mark of children of wrath; but having received the truth, to hold fast the very form of it, as Paul bids Timothy to do, is one of the duties of heirs of heaven. Stand fast for truth, and may Cod give the victory to the faithful.

We must believe the gospel and maintain it, for it, is committed to our trust. It seems to me, however, that the most of us may best fulfill our responsibility to the gospel by adorning it in our lives. Men give jewels to those whom they love; and so, if we love the gospel, let our virtues be the jewels which shall display our love. A servant girl may adorn the gospel. She goes to a place of worship, and perhaps her irreligious mistress may object to her going. I remember Mr. Jay telling a story of such a case, where the master and mistress had forbidden the girl to attend a Dissenting place of worship. She pleaded very hard, and at last determined to leave the house. The master said to his wife, "Well, you see our servant is a very excellent servant; we never had such an industrious girl as she is. Everything, in the house is kept so orderly, and she is so obedient, and so on. Now, she does not interfere with our consciences, it is a pity we should interfere with hers. Wherever she goes, it certainly does her no hurt—why not let her go?" In the next conversation the wife said, "I really think, husband, that our servant gets so much good where she goes, that we had better go and hear for ourselves;" and they were Soon members of the very same church which they had thought so lightly of at the first. Now, we can each of us in our station do that. We are not all called to preach in these boxes called pulpits, but we may preach more conveniently and much more powerfully behind the counter or in the drawing-room, or in the parlor, or in the field, or wherever else providence may have placed us. Let us endeavor to make men mark what kind of gospel we believe. Only a few weeks ago, a missionary in China took his gun to go up one of the rivers of the interior to shoot wild ducks; and, as he went along in the boat, he shot at some ducks, and down they fell; unfortunately they did not happen to be wild fowl, but tame ducks belonging to some of the neighbors. The owner was miles away, but the boat was drawn up to the side of the river, and the missionary went about carefully endeavoring to find out the owner of the ducks, for he could not rest until he had paid for the damage he had ignorantly done. The owner was much surprised, he had been so accustomed to have people shoot his ducks and never say a word about it, that he could not understand the honesty of the man of God, and he told others, until crowds of Chinese gathered round and stared at the missionary as if he had dropped from the moon; a man so extremely honest as not to be willing to take away ducks when he had killed them! They listened to the gospel with attention, and observed that the teaching must be good which made people so conscientious as the missionary had been. I should not wonder but what that little accident did more for the gospel than the preaching of twenty sermons might have done without it. So let it be with us; let us so act in every position that we shall adorn the gospel which is committed to our trust.

Lastly, it is committed to our trust if we have received it that we may spread it—spread it personally by telling it abroad. If more could preach the gospel it would be well. We have in all our congregations young men who are hard at work—at this very moment I do not doubt but what we have a hundred preaching in the street—perhaps more; but I have sometimes regretted that so few of the wealthier men enter into such labor. We could wish to see the men of ten talents preaching—the men of large abilities consecrating themselves to Christ. Many of our young members are more useful at literary institutions than in the church. Other useful occupations are all very well in their way, but I wish we could get the strength first of our men spent more in the preaching of the gospel. The first business of a Christian is his Christianity, all the rest, his patriotism even, must be kept subservient to that, for heaven is more his country than England is, and Jesus Christ is rather his King than any of the kings of earth. "Seek ye first the kingdom of God and his righteousness." I would ask young men now present who love the Lord, whether they really are doing for the cause of God what they ought to do? Whether they could not do something more by way of making manifest in every place the savor of Jesus Christ's name? My sisters, your voices are exceedingly sweet, but we like to hear them better anywhere than from a pulpit; but still you have your sphere—do you occupy in it for Christ? The Christian woman's first firsts call is to serve Jesus in the family; next to that to serve Christ in her neighborhood. Are we doing so? The "glorious gospel of the blessed God " is as much committed to your trust, Christian woman, as if there were not another Christian under heaven: how would it fare if it were so? If all other Christians died, would you have done by the gospel what it might demand of you? Ail the zeal and industry of ten thousand others cannot touch your personal responsibility as a Christian.

I have to ask you, this morning, to help me to spread the glorious gospel. Some years ago, having done my utmost to preach the word with my own mouth, finding that running up and down throughout the country, preaching ten or twelve times a week, I was still able to do but very little, I thought if I found other tongues and set them talking, found other brains and set them thinking, I might, perhaps, do more for the cause of my blessed Master. One young man was thrown in my way who was educated for me by an esteemed brother for the Christian ministry; and when he was greatly owned of God as preacher, the desire to assist students grew within my heart, and that one young man gave place to ten, then twenty, then thirty, then fifty, then ninety, as at present. The pastor's college, for which I ask your contributions this morning, has grown to be a power for good. We have had for some successive years between eighty and ninety brethren in training for the ministry. The whole of the support for them is found by the gifts of God's people, which they voluntarily send, without being waited upon by any collector, or asked for annual subscriptions. I have nothing to depend upon but the providence of God, which directs the generosity of his people. Sometimes my funds run rather short, but never so short that I am really in need, for when the treasury is scantily furnished, we call the young men together and pray about it, and many a time we have had as distinct answers to prayer as though God had stretched his hand out of heaven to give the needful money. Some five thousand pounds a-year are spent in this way, which God always sends when it is wanted. We have built several places of worship; we have formed and founded several fresh churches; we have evangelized the darkest districts of London and the country; and our men are now to be found in Australia, on the rock of St. Helena, in Southern Africa, in America, and all quarters of the earth. God has been pleased to bless them, and has given them souls for their hire, and we shall be glad if you feel moved to give towards their maintenance.

Before I dismiss you, I would like to press home to each one the question, "Dost thou believe in the Lord Jesus Christ? Has the gospel become a glorious gospel to thee ?" I do not know you as I know my own people, but when I look along my galleries I mourn over those who have been hearing the word ten years, and are the same as if they never heard it. I suppose there are some of you in the like case, and my esteemed brother, Mr. Tucker, must cast his eye around the gallery, and the area, and see many who have grown gospel-hardened. It is a horrible thing to think of! The same sun that melts wax hardens clay, and to some hearts the gospel becomes the savor of death unto death. If nothing comes of this morning's service but making every one inquire how it is with his own soul; if it shall only constrain you to go to your solitary chamber and shut the door and pray, "O Lord, let me know this glorious gospel; I have not understood it up till now, for it has not been glorious to me. Do make it so to me this day, that t may be saved!" My heart will be very glad if such shall be the case.

8

THE OLD, OLD STORY

Preached on March 30, 1862
Scripture: Romans 5:6
From: Metropolitan Tabernacle Pulpit Volume 8

"In due time Christ died for the ungodly."—Romans 5:6

THERE is a doctor of divinity here tonight who listened to me some years ago. He has been back to his own dwelling-place in America, and he has come here again. I could not help fancying, as I saw his face just now, that he would think I was doting on the old subject, and harping on the old strain; that I had not advanced a single inch upon any new domain of thought, but was preaching the same old gospel in the same old terms as ever. If he should think so he will be quite right. I suppose I am something like Mr. Cecil when he was a boy. His father once told him to wait in a gateway till he came back, and the father, being very busy, went about the city; and amidst his numerous cares and engagements, he forgot the boy. Night came on, and at last when the father reached home, there was great inquiry as to where Richard was. The father said, "Dear me, I left him early in the morning standing under such-and-such a gateway, and I told him to stay there until I came for him; I should not wonder but what he is there now." So they went, and there they found him. Such an example of childish simple faithfulness it is no disgrace to emulate. I received some years ago orders from my Master to stand at the foot of the cross until he came. He has not come yet, but I mean to stand there till he does. If I should disobey his orders and leave those simple truths which have been the means of the conversion of souls, I know not how I could expect his blessing, Here, then, I stand at the foot of the cross and tell out the old, old story, stale though it sound to itching ears, and worn threadbare as critics may deem it. It is of Christ I love to speak—of Christ who loved, and lived, and died, the substitute for sinners, the just for the unjust, that he might bring us to God.

It is somewhat singular, but just as they say fish go bad at the head first, so modern divines generally go bad first upon the head and main doctrine of the substitutionary work of Christ. Nearly all our modern errors, I might say all of them, begin with mistakes about Christ. Men do not like to be always preaching the same thing. There are Athenians in the pulpit as well as in the pew who spend their time in nothing but hearing some new thing. They are not content to tell over and over again the simple message, "He that believeth in the Lord Jesus Christ hath everlasting life." So they borrow novelties from literature, and garnish the Word of God with the words which man's wisdom teacheth. The doctrine of atonement they mystify. Reconciliation by the precious blood of Jesus ceases to be the corner-stone of their ministry. To shape the gospel to the diseased wishes and tastes of men enters far more deeply into their purpose, than to re-mold the mind and renew the heart of men that they receive the gospel as it is. There is no telling where they will go who once go back from following the Lord with a true and undivided heart, from deep to deep descending, the blackness of darkness will receive them unless grace prevent. Only this you may take for a certainty,

> *"They cannot be right in the rest,*
> *Unless they speak rightly of Him."*

If they are not sound about the purpose of the cross, they are rotten everywhere. "Other foundation can no man lay than that is laid, which is Jesus Christ." On this rock there is security. We may be mistaken on any other points with more impunity than this. They who are builded on the rock, though they build wood, and hay, and stubble, thereupon to their sore confusion, for what they build shall be burned, themselves shall be saved yet so as by fire. Now that grand doctrine which we take to be the keystone of the evangelical system, the very corner-stone of the gospel, that grand doctrine of the atonement of Christ we would tell to you again, and then, without attempting to prove it, for that we have done hundreds of times, we shall try to draw some lessons of instruction from that truth which is surely believed among us. Man having sinned, God's righteousness demanded that the penalty should be fulfilled. He had said, "The soul that sinneth shall die;" and unless God can be false, the sinner must die. Moreover, God's holiness demanded it, for the penalty was based on justice. It was just that the sinner should die. God had not appended a more heavy penalty than he should have done. Punishment is the just result of offending. God, then, must either cease to be holy, or the sinner must be punished. Truth and holiness imperiously demanded that God should lift his hand and smite the man who had broken his law and offended his majesty. Christ Jesus, the second Adam, the federal head of the chosen ones, interposed.

He offered himself to bear the penalty which they ought to bear; to fulfill and honor the law which they had broken and dishonored. He offered to be their day's-man, a surety, a substitute, standing in their room, place, and stead. Christ became the vicar of his people; vicariously suffering in their stead; vicariously doing in their stead that which they were not strong enough to do by reason of the weakness of the flesh through the fall. This which Christ proposed to do was accepted of God. In due time Christ actually died, and fulfilled what he promised to do. He took every sin of all his people, and suffered every stroke of the rod on account of those sins. He had compounded into one awful draft the punishment of the sins of all the elect. He took the cup; he put it to his lips; he sweat as it were great drops of blood while he tasted the first sip thereof, but he never desisted, but drank on, on, on, till he had exhausted the very dregs, and turning the vessel upside down he said, "It is finished!" and at one tremendous draft of love the Lord God of salvation had drained destruction dry. Not a dreg, not the slightest residue was left; he had suffered all that ought to have been suffered; had finished transgression, and made an end of sin. Moreover, he obeyed his Father's law to the utmost extent of it; he fulfilled that will of which he had said of old—"Lo, I come to do thy will, O God: thy law is my delight;" and having offered both an atonement for sin and a complete fulfilment of the law, he ascended up on high, took his seat on the right hand of the Majesty in heaven, from henceforth expecting till his enemies be made his footstool, and interceding for those whom he bought with blood that they may be with him where he is. The doctrine of the atonement is very simple. It just consists in the substitution of Christ in the place of the sinner; Christ being treated as if he were the sinner, and then the transgressor being treated as if he were the righteous one. It is a change of persons; Christ becomes the sinner; he stands in the sinner's place and stead; he was numbered with the transgressors; the sinner becomes righteous; he stands in Christ's place and stead, and is numbered with the righteous ones. Christ has no sin of his own, but he takes human guilt, and is punished for human folly. We have no righteousness of our own, but we take the divine righteousness; we are rewarded for it, and stand accepted before God as though that righteousness had been wrought out by ourselves. "In due time Christ died for the ungodly," that he might take away their sins.

It is not my present object to prove this doctrine. As I said before, there is no need to be always arguing what we know to be true. Rather let us say a few earnest words by way of commending this doctrine of the atonement; and afterwards I shall propound it by way of application to those who as yet have not received Christ.

I. First, then, BY WAY OF COMMENDATION.

There are some things to be said for the gospel which proclaims the atonement as its fundamental principle. And the first thing to be said of it is, that in comparison with all modern schemes how simple it is! Brethren, this is why our great gentlemen do not like it, it is too plain. If you will go and purchase certain books which teach you how sermons ought to be made, you will find that the English of it is this,—pick all the hard words you can out of all the books you read in the week, and then pour them out on your people on Sunday; and there is a certain set of people who always applaud the man they cannot understand. They are like the old woman who was asked when she came home from Church, "Did you understand the sermon?" "No;" she answered, "I would not have the presumption;" she thought it would be presumption to attempt to understand the minister. But the Word of God is understood with the heart, and makes no strange demands on the intellect.

Now, our first commendation on the doctrine of the atonement is, that it commends itself to the understanding. The way-faring man, though his intellect be but one grade beyond an idiot, may get a hold on the truth of substitution without any difficulty. Oh, these modern theologians, they will do anything to spirit away the cross! They hang over it the gaudy trappings of their elocution, or they introduce it with the dark mysterious incantations of their logic, and then the poor troubled heart looks up to see the cross and sees nothing there but human wisdom. Now I say it again, there is not one of you here but can understand this truth, that Christ died in the stead of his people. If you perish, it will not be because the gospel was beyond your comprehension. If you go down to hell, it will not be because you were not able to understand how God can be just, and yet the justifier of the ungodly. It is astonishing in this age how little is known of the simple truisms of the Bible; it seems to be always admonishing us how simple we ought to be in setting them forth. I have heard that when Mr. Kilpin was once preaching a very good and earnest sermon, he used the word "Deity," and a sailor sitting down below leaned forward and said, "Beg your pardon, sir, but who's he, pray? Do you mean God Almighty?" "Yes," said Mr. Kilpin, "I do mean God, and I ought not to have used a word which you could not understand." "I thank you, sir," said the Bailor, and looked as if he would devour the rest of the sermon in the interest which he felt in it even to the close. Now that one unvarnished fact is but an index of that which prevails in every land. There must be simple preaching. A doctrine of atonement that is not simple, a doctrine which comes from Germany, which needs a man to be a great scholar before he can comprehend it himself, and to be a still greater adept before he can tell it to others—such a doctrine is manifestly not of God, because it is not suited to God's creatures. It is fascinating to one in a thousand of them, but it is not suited to those poor of this world who are rich in faith; not suited to those babes to whom God has revealed the things of the kingdom while he has hidden them from the wise and prudent. Oh, you may always judge of a doctrine in this way. If it is not a simple doctrine, it does not come from God; if it puzzles you, if it is one which you cannot see through at once because of the mysterious language in which it is couched, you may begin to suspect that it is man's doctrine, and not the Word of God.

Nor is this doctrine of the atonement to be commended merely for its simplicity, but because while suiting the understanding it also suits the conscience. How it satisfies the conscience no tongue can tell! When a man is awakened and his conscience stings him, when the Spirit of God has shown him his sin and his guilt, there is nothing but the blood of Christ that can ever give him peace. Peter might have stood up at the prow of the boat and have said to the winds and to the waves, "Peace, be still," but they would have gone on roaring with unabated fury. The Pope of Rome, who pretends to be Peter's successor, may stand up with his ceremonies and say to the troubled conscience, "Peace, be still," but it will not cease it's terrible agitations. The unclean spirit that sets conscience in so much turmoil cries out, "Jesus I know, and his cross I know, but who are ye?" Yea, and it will not be cast out. There is no chance whatever of our finding a pillow for a head which the Holy Ghost has made to ache save in the atonement and the finished work of Christ. When Mr. Robert Hall first went to Cambridge to preach, the Cambridge folks were nearly Unitarians. So he preached upon the doctrine of the finished work of Christ, and some of them came to him in the vestry and said, "Mr. Hall, this will never do." "Why not?" said he, "Why, your sermon was only fit for old women." "And why only fit for old women?" said Mr. Hall. "Because," said they, "they are tottering on the borders of the grave, and they want comfort, and, therefore, it will suit them, but it will not do for us." "Very well," said Mr. Hall, "you have unconsciously paid me all the compliment that I can ask for; if this is good for old women on the borders of the grave, it must be good for you if you are in your right senses, for the borders on the grave is where we all stand." Here, indeed, is a choice feature of the atonement, it is comforting to us in the thought of death. When conscience is awakened to a sense of guilt, death is sure to cast his pale shadow on all our prospects, and encircle all our steps with dark omens of the grave. Conscience is accompanied generally in its alarms with the thoughts of the near-approaching judgment, but the peace which the blood gives is conscience-proof, sickness-proof, death-proof, devil-proof, judgment proof, and it will be eternity-proof. We may well be alarmed at all the uprisings of occupation and all the remembrance of past defilement, but only let our eyes rest on thy dear cross, O Jesus, and our conscience has peace with God, and we rest and are still. Now we ask whether any of these modern systems of divinity can quiet a troubled conscience? We would like to give them some cases that we meet with sometimes—some despairing ones—and say, "Now, here, cast this devil out if you can try your hand at it," and I think they would find, that this kind goeth not out save by the tears, and groans, and death of Jesus Christ the atoning sacrifice. A gospel without an atonement may do very well for young ladies and gentlemen who do not know that they ever did anything wrong. It will just suit your lackadaisical people who have not got a heart for anybody to see; who have always been quite moral, upright, and respectable; who would feel insulted if you told them they deserved to be sent to hell; who would not for a moment allow that they could be depraved or fallen creatures. The gospel, I say, of these modems will suit these gentlefolks very well I dare say, but let a man be really guilty and know it; let him be really awake to his lost state, and I aver that none but Jesus—none but Jesus, nothing but the precious blood can give him peace and rest. For these two things, then, commend us to the doctrine of the atonement, because it suits the understanding of the most lowly, and will quiet the conscience of the most troubled.

It has, moreover, this peculiar excellency, that it softens the heart. There is a mysterious softening and melting power in the story of the sacrifice of Christ. I know a dear Christian woman who loved her little ones and sought their salvation. When she prayed for them, she thought it right to use the best means she could to arrest their attention and awaken their minds. I hope you all do likewise. The means, however, which she thought best calculated for her object was the terrors of the Lord. She used to read to her children chapter after chapter of Alleine's Alarm to the Unconverted. Oh, that book! how many dreams it gave her boy at night about the devouring flames and the everlasting burnings. But the boy's heart grew hardened, as if it were annealed rather than melted by the furnace of fear. The hammer welded the heart to sin, but did not break it. But even then, when the lad's heart was hard, when he heard of Jesus' love to his people, though he feared he was not one of them, still it used to make him weep to think Jesus should love anybody after such a sort. Even now that he has come to manhood, law and terrors make him dead and stolid, but thy blood, Jesu, thine agonies in Gethsemane and on the tree, he cannot bear; they melt him; his soul flows through his eyes in tears; he weeps himself away from grateful love to thee for what thou hast done. Alas for those that deny the atonement! They take the very sting out of Christ's sufferings; and then, in taking out the sting, they take out the point with which the sufferings of Christ pierce, and probe, and penetrate the heart. It is because Christ suffered for my sin, because he was condemned that I might be acquitted and not be damned as the result of my guilt: it is this that makes his sufferings such a cordial to my heart.

> *"See on the bloody tree,*
> *The illustrious sufferer hangs,*
> *The torments due to thee,*
> *He bore the dreadful pangs;*
> *And canceled there, the mighty sum,*
> *Sins present, past, and sins to come."*

At this present hour there are congregations met in the theatres of London, and there are persons addressing them. I do not know what their subjects are, but I know what they ought to be. If they want to get at the intellects of those who live in the back-slums, if they want to get at the consciences of those who have been thieves and drunkards, if they want to melt the hearts of those who have grown stubborn and callous through years of lust and iniquity, I know there is nothing will do it but the death on Calvary, the five wounds, the bleeding side, the vinegar, the nails, and the spear. There is a melting power here which is not to be found in all the world besides.

I will detain you yet once more on this point. We commend the doctrine of the atonement because, besides suiting the understanding, quieting the conscience, and melting the heart, we know there is a power in it to affect the outward life. No man can believe that Christ suffered for his sins and yet live in sin. No man can believe that his iniquities were the murderers of Christ, and yet go and hug those murderers to his bosom. The sure and certain effect of a true faith in the atoning sacrifice of Christ is the purging out of the old leaven, the dedication of the soul to him who bought it with his blood, and the vowing to have revenge against those sins which nailed Jesus to the tree. The proof, after all, is in the trial. Go into any parish in England where there lives a philosophical divine who has cut the atonement out of his preaching, and if you do not find more harlots, and thieves, and drunkards there than is usual, write me down mistaken; but go, on the other hand, into a parish where the atonement is preached, and that with rigid integrity and with loving earnestness, and if you do not find the ale-houses getting empty, and the shops shut on the Sunday, and the people walking in honesty and uprightness, then I have looked about the world in vain. I knew a village once that was perhaps one of the worst villages in England for many things; where many an illicit still was yielding its noxious liquor to a manufacturer without payment of the duty to the Government, and where, in connection with that, all manner of riot and iniquity were rife. There went a lad into that village, and but a lad, and one who had no scholarship, but was rough, and sometimes vulgar. He began to preach there, and it pleased God to turn that village upside down, and in a short time the little thatched chapel was crammed, and the biggest vagabonds of the village were weeping floods of tears, and those who had been the curse of the parish became its blessing; and where there had been robberies and villainies of every kind all round the neighborhood, there were none, because the men who did the mischief were themselves in the house of God, rejoicing to hear of Jesus crucified. Mark me, I am not telling you an exaggerated story now, nor a thing that I do not know. Yet this one thing I remember to the praise of God's grace, it pleased the Lord to work signs and wonders in our midst. He showed the power of Jesus' name, and made us witnesses of that gospel which can win souls, draw reluctant hearts, and mold the life and conduct of men afresh. Why, there are some brethren here who go to the refuges and homes to talk to those poor fallen girls who have been reclaimed. I wonder what they would do if they had not the gospel tale to carry with them to the abodes of wretchedness and shame. If they should take a leaf out of some divinity essays, and should go and talk to them in high-flowing words, and philosophies, what good would it be to them? Well, what is not good to them is not good to us. We want something we can grasp, something we can rely upon, something we can feel; something that will mold our character and conversation, and make us to be like Christ.

II. Secondly, one or two points BY WAY OF EXHORTATION.

Christian man, you believe that your sins are forgiven, and that Christ has made a full atonement for them. What shall we say to you? To you first we say, what a joyful Christian you ought to be! How you should live above the common trials and troubles of the world! Since sin is forgiven, what matter what happens to you now? Luther said, "Smite, Lord, smite, for my sin is forgiven; if thou hast but forgiven me, smite as hard as thou wilt as if he felt like a child who had done wrong, and cared not how his father might whip him if he would but forgive him. So I think you can say, "Send sickness, poverty, losses, crosses, slander, persecution, what thou wilt, thou hast forgiven me, and my soul is glad, and my spirit is rejoiced."

And then, Christian, if thou art thus saved, and Christ really did take thy sin, whilst thou art glad, be grateful and be loving. Cling to that cross which took thy sin away; serve thou him who served thee. "I beseech you therefore, brethren, by the mercies of God, that ye present your bodies a living sacrifice, holy, acceptable unto God, which is your reasonable service." Let not your zeal bubble over with some little ebullition of song. You may say,

"I love my God with zeal so great, that I could give him all,"

but sing it not in words unless thou dost mean it. Oh, do mean it! Is there nothing in your life that you do because you belong to Christ? Are you never anxious to show your love in some expressive tokens? Love the brethren of him who loved thee. If there be a Mephibosheth anywhere who is lame or halt, help him for Jonathan's sake. If there be a poor tried believer, try and weep with him, and bear his cross for the sake of him who wept for thee and carried thy sins.

And yet, again, Christian, if this be true that there is an atonement made for sin, tell it, tell it, tell it. "We cannot all preach," say you; no, but tell it, tell it. "I could not prepare a sermon—tell it; tell out the story; tell out the mystry and wonder of Christ's love. "But I should never get a congregation—tell it in your house; tell it by the fireside. "But I have none but little 'children—tell it to your children, and let them know the sweet mystery of the cross, and the blessed history of him who lived and died for sinners. Tell it, for you know not into what ears you may speak. Tell it often, for thus you will have the better hope that you may turn sinners to Christ. Lacking talent, lacking the graces of oratory, be glad that you lack these, and glory in your infirmity that the power of Christ may rest upon you, but do tell it. Sometimes there are some of our young men get preaching who had better hold their tongues, but there are many others who have gifts and abilities which they might use for Christ, but who seem tongue-tied. I have often said that if you get a young man to join a rifle corps, he has got something to do, and he puts his heart in it; but if you get the same young man to join a church, well, his name is in the book, and he has been baptized, and so on, and he thinks he has nothing more to do with it. Why, brethren, I do not like to have members of the church who feel they can throw the responsibility on a few of us while they themselves sit still. That is not the way to win battles. If at Waterloo some nine out of ten of our soldiers had said, "Well, we need not fight ; we will leave the fighting to the few, there they are; let them go and do it all." Why, if they had said that, they would very soon have all been cut in pieces. They must every one of them take their turns, horse, and foot, and artillery; men who were light-armed, and men of all kinds; they must each march to the fray; yes, and even the guards, if they are held back as a reserve to the last, yet they must be called for,—"Up guards, and at 'em;" and if there are any of you here that are old men and women and think you are like the guards, and ought to be spared the heavy conflict, yet up and at them, for now the world needs you all, and since Christ has bought you with his blood, I beseech you be not content till you have fought for him, and have been victorious through his name. Tell it; tell it; tell it; with voice of thunder tell it; yea, with many voices mingling together as the sound of many waters; tell it till the dwellers in the remotest wilderness shall hear the sound thereof. Tell it till there shall be ne'er a cot upon the mountain where it is not known, ne'er a ship upon the sea where the story has not been told. Tell it till there is never a dark alley that has not been illuminated by its light, nor a loathsome den which has not been cleansed by its power. Tell out the story that Christ died for the ungodly.

With a few words of application to unbelievers I draw to a close. Unbeliever, if God cannot and will not forgive the sins of penitent men without Christ taking their punishment, rest assured he will surely bring you to judgment. If, when Christ, God's Son, had imputed sin laid on him, God smote him, how will he smite you who are his enemy, and who have your own sins upon your head? God seemed at Calvary, as it were, to take an oath—sinner, hear it!—he seemed, as it were, to take an oath and say, "'By the blood of my Son I swear that sin must be punished," and if it is not punished in Christ for you, it will be punished in you for yourselves. Is Christ yours, sinner? Did he die for you? Do you trust him? If you do, he died for you. Do you say, "No, I do not?" Then remember that if you live and die without faith in Christ, forevery idle word and forevery ill act that you have done, stroke for stroke, and blow for blow, vengeance must chastise you.

Again, to another class of you, this word. If God has in Christ made an atonement and opened a way of salvation, what must be your guilt who try to open another way; who say, "I will be good and virtuous; I will attend to ceremonies; I will save myself?" Fool that thou art, thou hast insulted God in his tenderest point, for thou hast insulted his Son. Thou hast said, "I can do it without that blood;" thou hast, in fact, trampled on the blood of Christ, and said, "I need it not." Oh, if the sinner who repents not be damned, with what accumulated terrors shall he be damned, who, in addition to his impenitence, heaps affronts upon the person of Christ by going about to establish his own righteousness. Leave it; leave your rags, you will never make a garment of them; leave that pilfered treasure of thine; it is a counterfeit; forsake it. I counsel thee to buy of Christ fine raiment, that thou mayest be clothed, and fine gold that thou mayest be rich.

And consider this, one and all of you, oh my hearers! If Christ hath made atonement for the ungodly, then let the question go round, let it go round the aisles and round the gallery, and let it echo in every heart, and let it be repeated by every lip,—"Why not for me?" and "Why not for me?" Hope, sinner, hope; he died for the ungodly. If it had said he died for the godly, there were no hope for thee. If it had been written that he died to save the good, the excellent, and the perfect, then thou hast no chance. He died for the ungodly; thou art such an one; what reason hast thou to conclude that he did not die for thee? Hark thee, man; this is what Christ saith to thee, "Believe, and thou shalt be saved;" that is, trust, and thou shalt be saved. Trust thy soul in the hands of him who carried thy load upon the cross; trust him now. He died for you; your faith is to us the evidence, and to you the proof that Christ bought you with his blood. Delay not; you need not even stay to go home to offer a prayer. Trust Christ with your soul now. You have nothing else to trust to; hang on him. You are going down; you are going down. The waves are gathering about you, and soon shall they swallow you up, and we shall hear your gurglings as you sink. See, he stretches out his hand. "Sinner," saith he, "I will bear thee up; though hell's fiery waves should dash against thee I will bear thee through them all, only trust me." What sayest thou, sinner? Wilt thou trust him? Oh, my soul, recollect the moment when first I trusted in him! There is joy in heaven over one sinner that repenteth, but I hardly think that is greater joy than the joy of the repenting sinner when he first finds Christ. So simple and so easy it seemed to me when I came to know it. I had only to look and live, only to trust and be saved. Year after year had I been running about hither and thither to try and do what was done beforehand, to try and get ready for that which did not want any readiness. Oh, happy was that day when I ventured to step in by the open door of his mercy, to sit at the table of grace ready spread, and to eat and drink, asking no questions! Oh, soul, do the same! Take courage. Trust Christ, and if he cast thee away when thou hast trusted him—my soul for thine as we meet at the bar of God, I will be pawn and pledge for thee at the last great day if such thou needest; but he cannot and he will not cast out any that come to him by faith. May God now accept and bless us all, for Jesus' sake! Amen.

9

THE TWO EFFECTS OF THE GOSPEL

Preached on May 27, 1855
Scripture: 2 Corinthians 2:15-16
From: New Park Street Pulpit Volume 1

"For we are unto God a sweet savor of Christ, in them that are saved, and in them that perish: To the one we are the savor of death unto death; and to the other the savor of life unto life. And who is sufficient for these things?" —2 Corinthians 2:15-16

These are the words of Paul, speaking on the behalf of himself and his brethren the Apostles, and they are true concerning all those who by the Spirit are chosen, qualified, and thrust into the vineyard to preach God's gospel. I have often admired the 14th verse of this chapter, especially when I have remembered from whose lips the words fell, "Now thanks be unto God, which always causeth us to triumph in Christ, and maketh manifest the savor of his knowledge by us in every place." Picture Paul, the aged, the man who had been beaten five times with forty stripes save one,' who had been dragged forth for dead, the man of great sufferings, who had passed through whole seas of persecution only think of him saying, at the close of his ministerial career, "Now thanks be unto God, which always causeth us to triumph in Christ!" to triumph when shipreckced, to triumph when scourged, to triumph in the stocks, to triumph under the stones, to triumph amidst the hiss of the world, to triumph when he was driven from the city and shook off the dust from his feet, to triumph at all times in Christ Jesus!

Now, if some ministers of modern times should talk thus, we would think little of it, for they enjoy the world's applause They can always go to their place in ease and peace; they have an admiring people, and no open foes; against them not a dog doth move his tongue; everything is safe and pleasant, For them to say, "Now thanks be unto God, which always causeth us to triumph" is a very little thing; but for one like Paul, so trampled on, so tried, so distressed, to say it-then, we say, outspoke a hero; here is a man who had true faith in God and in the divinity of his mission.

And, my brethren, how sweet is that consolation which Paul applied to his own heart amid all his troubles. "Notwithstanding all," he says, "God makes known the savor of his knowledge by us in every place." Ah! with this thought a minister may lay his head upon his pillow: "God makes manifest the savor of his knowledge." With this he may shut his eyes when his career is over, and with this he may open them in heaven: "God hath made known by me the savor of his knowledge in every place," Then follow the words of my text, of which I shall speak, dividing it into three particulars. Our first remark shall be, that although the gospel is "a sweet savor" in every place, yet it produces different effects in different persons; to one it is the savor of death unto death; and to the other the savor of life unto life." Our second observation shall be, that ministers of the gospel are not responsible for their success, for it is said. "We are unto God a sweet savor of Christ, in them that are saved, and in them that perish." And thirdly, yet the gospel ministers place is by no means a light one: his duty is very weighty; for the Apostle himself said, "Who is sufficient for these things?"

I. Our first remark is, that THE GOSPEL PRODUCES DIFFERENT EFFECTS. It must seem a strange thing, but it is strangely true, that there is scarcely ever a good thing in the world of which some little evil is not the consequence. Let the sun shine in brilliance—it shall moisten the wax, it shall harden clay; let it pour down floods of light on the tropics—it will cause vegetation to be extremely luxuriant, the richest and choicest fruits shall ripen, and the fairest of all flowers shall bloom, but who does not know, that there the worst of reptiles and the most venomous snakes are also brought forth? So it is with the gospel. Although it is the very sun of righteousness to the world, although it is God's best gift, although nothing can be in the least comparable to the vast amount of benefit which it bestows upon the human race, yet even of that we must confess, that sometimes it is the "savor of death unto death." But then we are not to blame the gospel for this; it is not the fault of God's truth; it is the fault of those who do not receive it. It is the "savor of life unto life" to every one that listens to its sound with a heart that is open to its reception. It is only "death unto death" to the man who hates the truth, despises it, scoffs at it, and tries to oppose its progress, It is of that character we must speak first.

    A. The gospel is to some men "a savor of death unto death." Now, this depends very much upon what the gospel is; because there are some things called gospel, that are "a savor of death unto death" to everybody that hears them. John Berridge says he preached morality till there was not a moral man left in the village; and there is no way of injuring morality like legal preaching. The preaching of good works, and the exhorting men to holiness, as the means of salvation, is very much admired in theory; but when brought into practice, it is found not only ineffectual, but more than that—it becomes even "a savor of death unto death." So it has been found; and I think even the great Chalmers himself confessed, that for years and years before he knew the Lord, he preached nothing but morality and precepts, but he never found a drunkard reclaimed by shewing him merely the evils of drunkenness; nor did he find a swearer stop his swearing because he told him the heinousness of the sin; it was not until he begin to preach the love of Jesus, in his great heart of mercy—it was not until he preached the gospel as it was in Christ, in some of its clearness, fullness, and power, and the doctrine, that "by grace ye are saved, through faith, and that not of yourselves, it is the gift of God" that he ever met with success. But when he did preach salvation by faith, by shoals the drunkards came from their cups, and swearers refrained their lips from evil speaking; thieves became honest men, and unrighteous and ungodly persons bowed to the scepter of Jesus. But ye must confess, as I said before, that though the gospel does in the main produce the best effect upon almost all who hear it either by restraining them from sin, or constraining them to Christ, yet it is a great fact, and a solemn one, upon which I hardly know bow to speak this morning, that to some men the preaching of Christ's gospel is "death unto death," and produces evil instead of good.

    1. And the first sense is this. Many men are hardened in their sins by hearing the gospel. Oh! 'tis terribly and solemnly true, that of all sinners some sanctuary sinners are the worst. Those who can dive deepest into sin, and have the most quiet consciences and hardest hearts, are some who are to be found in God's own house. I know that a faithful ministry will often prick them, and the stern denunciations of a Boanerges, will frequently make them shake. I am aware that the Word of God will sometimes make their blood curdle within them; but I know (for I have seen the men) that there are many who turn the grace of God into licentiousness, make even God's truth a stalking-horse for the devil, and abuse God's grace to pall ate their sin. Such men have I found amongst those who

hear the doctrines of grace in their fullness. They will say, "I am elect, therefore I may swear; I am one of those who were chosen of God before the foundation of the world, and therefore I may live as I list." I have seen the man who stood upon the table of a public house, and grasping the glass in his hand, said, "Mates! I can say more than any of you; I am one of those who are redeemed with Jesus' precious blood:" and then he drank his tumbler of ale and danced again before them, and sang vile and blasphemous songs. Now, that is a man to whom the gospel is "a savor of death unto death." He bears the truth, but he perverts it; he takes what is intended by God for his good, and what does he do, he commits suicide therewith. That knife which was given him to open the secrets of the gospel he drives into his own heart. That which is the purest of all truth and the highest of all morality, he turns into the panderer of his vice, and makes it a scaffold to aid in building up his wickedness and sin. Are there any of you here like that man—who love to hear the gospel, as ye call it, and yet live impurely? who can sit down and say you are the children of God, and still behave like liege servants of the devil? Be it known unto you, that ye are liars and hypocrites, for the truth is not in you at all. "If any man is born of God, he cannot sin." God's elect will not be suffered to fall into continual sin; they will never "turn the grace of God into licentiousness;" but it will be their endeavor, as much as in them lies, to keep near to Jesus. Rest assured of this: "By their fruits ye shall know them." A good tree cannot bring forth corrupt fruit; neither can an evil tree bring forth good fruit." Such men, however, are continually turning the gospel into evil, They sin with a high hand, from the very fact that they have heard what they consider excuses their vice. There is nothing under heaven, I conceive, more liable to lead men astray than a perverted gospel. A truth perverted is generally worse than a doctrine which all know to be false. As fire, one of the most useful of the elements, can also cause the fiercest of conflagrations, so the gospel, the best thing we have, can be turned to the vilest account. This is one sense in which it is "a savor of death unto death."

2. But another. It is a fact that the gospel of Jesus Christ will increase some mens damnation at the last great day. Again, I startle at myself when I have said it; for it seems too horrible a thought for us to venture to utter—that the gospel of Christ will make hell hotter to some men than it otherwise would have been. Men would all have sunk to hell had it not been for the gospel. The grace of God reclaims "a multitude that no man can number;" it secures a countless army who "shall be saved in the Lord with an everlasting salvation;" but, at the same time, it does to those who reject it, make their damnation even more dreadful. And let me tell you why.

First, because men sin against greater light; and the light we have is an excellent measure of our guilt. What a Hottentot might do without a crime, would be the greatest sin to me, because I am taught better; and what some even in London might do with impunity—set down, as it might be, as a sin by God, but not so exceeding sinful-would be to me the very height of transgression, because I have from my youth up been tutored to piety. The gospel comes upon men like the light from heaven. What a wanderer must he be who strays in the light! If he who is blind falls into the ditch we can pity him, but if a man, with the light on his eyeballs dashes himself from the precipice and loses his own soul, is not pity out of the question?

> *"How they deserve the deepest hell,*
> *That slight the joys above!*
> *What chains of vengeance must they feel,*
> *Who laugh at sov'reign love!"*

It will increase your condemnation, I tell you all, unless you find Jesus Christ to he your Savior; for to have had the light and not to walk by it, shall be the condemnation, the very essence of it, This shall be the virus of the guilt—that the, "light came into the world, and the darkness comprehended it not;" for "men love darkness rather than light, because their deeds are evil."

Again: it must increase your condemnation if you oppose the gospel. If God devises a scheme of mercy, and man rises up against it, how great must be his sin? Who shall tell the great guilt incurred by such men as Pilate, Herod, and the Jews? Oh! who shall picture out, or even faintly sketch, the doom of those who cried, "Crucify him! Crucify him!" And who shall tell what place in hell shall be hot enough for the man who slanders God's minister, who speaks against his people, who hates his truth, who would, if he could, utterly cut off the godly from the land? Ah! God help the infidel! God help the blasphemer! God save his soul: for of all men least would I choose to be that man. Think you, sirs, that God will not take account of what men have said? One man has cursed Christ; he has called him a charlatan. Another has declared, (know that he spoke a lie) that the gospel was false. A third has proclaimed his licentious maxims, and then has pointed to God's Word and still, "There are worse things there!" A fourth has abused God's ministers and held up their imperfections to radicals. Think you God shall forget all this: it the last day? When his enemies come before him, shall he take then by the hand and say, "The other day thou didst call my servant a dog, and spit on him, and for this I will give thee heaven!" Rather, if the sin has not been canceled by the blood of Christ, he will not say, "Depart, cursed one, into the hell which thou didst scoff at; leave that heaven which thou didst despise; and learn that though thou saidst there was no God, this right arm shall teach thee eternally the lesson that there is one; for he who discovers it not by my works of benevolence shall learn it by my deeds of vengeance: therefore depart, again, I say!" It shall increase men's hell that they have opposed God's truth. Now, is not this a very solemn view of the gospel, that it is indeed to many "a savor of death unto death?"

3. Yet, once more. I believe the gospel make some men in this world more miserable than they would be. The drunkard could drink, and could revel in his intoxication with greater joy, if he did not hear it said, "All drunkards shall have their portion in the lake that burneth with fire and brimstone." How jovially the Sabbath-breaker would riot through his Sabbaths, if the Bible did not say, "Remember the Sabbath day to keep it holy!" And how happily could the libertine and licentious man drive on his mad career, if he were not told, "The wages of sin is death, and after death the judgment!" But the truth puts the bitter in his cup; the warnings of God freeze the current of his soul. The gospel is like the skeleton at the Egyptian feast. Though by day he laughed at it, by night he will quiver as the aspen leaf, and when the shades of evening gather around him, he will shake at a whisper. At the thought of a future state his joy is spoiled, and immortality instead of being a boon to him, is in its very contemplation the misery of his existence. The sweet wooings of mercy are to him no more harmonious than peals of thunder, because he knows he despises them. Yea, I have known some who have, been in such misery under the gospel, because they would not give up their sins, that they have been ready to take their own lives. Oh! terrible thought! The, gospel is "a savor of death unto death!" Unto how many here is it so? Who are now hearing God's Word to be damned by it? Who shall retire hence to be hardened by the sound of the truth? Why, every man who does not believe it; for unto those that receive it, it is "a savor of life unto life," but to unbelievers it is a curse, and a savor of death unto death."

B. But, blessed be God, the gospel has a second power. Besides being "death unto death," it is "a savor of life unto life." Ah! my brethren, some of us could speak, if we were allowed this meaning, of the gospel as being "a savor of life" to us. We can look back to that hour when we were "dead in trespasses and sin." In vain all Sinai's thunders; in vain the rousing of the watchmen; we slept on in the death-sleep of our transgressions; nor could, an angel have aroused us. But we look back with joy to that hour when first we stepped within the walls of a sanctuary, and savingly heard the voice of mercy. With some of you it is but a few weeks. I know where ye are and who ye are. But a few weeks or months ago ye too were far from God, but now ye are brought to love him. Canst thou look back my brother Christian, to that very moment when the gospel was to thee—when thou didst cast away thy sins, renounce thy lusts, and turning to God's Word, received it with full purpose of heart? Ah! that hour—of all hours the sweetest! Nothing can be compared, therewith. I knew a person who for forty or fifty years had been completely deaf. Sitting one morning at her cottage door as some vehicle was passing, she thought she heard melodious music. It was not music; it was but the sound of the vehicle. Her ear had suddenly opened, and that rough sound seemed to her like the music of heaven, because it was the first she had heard for so many years. Even so, the first time our ears were opened to hear the words of love—the assurance of our pardon—we never heard the word so well as we did then; it never seemed so sweet; and perhaps, even now, we look back and say,

"What peaceful hours I then enjoyed!
How sweet their memory still!"
When first it was "a savor of life" unto our souls.

Then, beloved, if it ever has been "a savor of life," it will always be "of life;" because it says it is not of savor of life unto death, but a savor of life unto life. "Now I must aim another blow at my antagonists the Arminians; I cannot help it. They will have it that sometimes the gospel is a savor of life unto death. They tell us that a man may receive spiritual life, and yet may die eternally. That is to say, a man may be forgiven, and yet be punished afterwards; he may be justified from all sin, and yet after that, his transgressions can be laid on his shoulders again. A man may be born of God, and yet die; a man may be loved of God, and yet God may hate him tomorrow. Oh! I cannot bear to speak of such doctrines of lies; let those believe them that like. As for me, I so deeply believe in the immutable love of Jesus that I suppose that if one believer were, to be in hell, Christ himself' would not long stay in heaven, but would cry, "To the rescue!" Oh! if Jesus Christ were in glory with one the gems wanting in his crown, and Satan had that gem, he would say, "Aha! prince of light and glory, I have one of thy jewels!" and he would hold it up, and then he would say, "Aha! thou didst die for this man, but thou hadst not strength enough to save him; thou didst love him once—where is thy love? It is not worth having, for thou didst hate him afterwards!" And how would he chuckle over that heir of heaven, and hold him up, and say, "This man was redeemed; Jesus Christ purchased him with his blood:" and plunging him in the waves of hell, he would say, "There purchased one see how I can rob the Son of God!" And then again he would say, This man was forgiven, behold the justice of God! He is to be punished after he is forgiven. Christ suffered for this mans sins, and yet," says Satan with a malignant joy, "I have him afterwards; for God exacted the punishment twice!" Shall that e'er be said? Ah! no. It is "a savor of life unto life," and not of life unto death. Go, with your vile gospel; preach it where you please; but my Master said, "I give unto my sheep ETERNAL life." You give to your sheep temporary life, and they lose it; but, says Jesus, "I give unto my sheep ETERNAL life, and they shall never perish, neither shall man pluck them out of my hands." I generally wax warm when I got to this subject, because I think few doctrines more vital than that of the perseverance of the saints; for if ever one child of God did perish, or if I knew it were possible that one could, I should conclude at once that I must, and suppose each of you would do the same; and then where is the joy and happiness of the gospel? Again I tell you the Arminian gospel is the shell without the kernel; it is the husk without the fruit; and those who love it may take it to themselves. We will not quarrel with them. Let them go and preach it. Let them go and tell poor sinners, that if they believe in Jesus they will be damned after all, that Jesus Christ will forgive them and yet the Father send them to hell. Go and preach your gospel, and who will listen to it? And if they do listen, is it worth their hearing? I say no; for if I am to stand after conversion on the same footing as I did before conversion then it is of no use for me to have been converted at all. But whom he loves he loves to the end.

> *"Once in Christ, in Christ forever;*
> *Nothing from his love can sever."*

It is "a savor of life unto life." And not only, "life unto life" in this world, but of "life unto life" eternal. Every one who has this life shall receive the next life; for "the Lord will give grace and glory, and no good thing will he withhold from them that walk uprightly."

I am obliged to leave this point; but if my Master will but take it up, and make his word a savor of "life unto life" this morning, I shall rejoice in what I have said.

II. But our second remark was, that THE MINISTER IS NOT RESPONSIBLE FOR HIS SUCCESS. He is responsible for what he preaches; he is accountable for his life and actions; but he is not responsible for other people. If I do but preach God's word, if there never were a soul saved, the King would say, "Well done, good and faithful Servant!" If I do but tell my message, if none should listen to it, he would say, "Thou hast fought the good fight: receive thy crown." You hear the words of the text: "We are unto God a sweet savor of Christ, as well in them that perish, as in them that are saved." This will appear, if I just tell you what a gospel minister is called in the Bible. Sometimes he is called an ambassador. Now, for what is an ambassador responsible? He goes to a country as a plenipotentiary; he carries terms of peace to the conference; he uses all his talents for his master; he tries to show that the war is inimical to the prosperity of the different countries; he endeavors to bring about peace; but the other kings haughtily refuse it. When he comes home does his master say, "Why did not you make peace?" "Why, my Lord," he would say, "I told them the terms; but they said nothing." "Well, then," he will say, "thou hast done thy duty; I am not to condemn thee if the war continues." Again the minister of the gospel is called a fisherman. Now a fisherman is not responsible for the quantity of fish he catches, but for the way he fishes. That is a mercy for some ministers, I am sure, for they have neither caught fish, for neither caught fish nor even attracted any round their nets. They have been spending all their life fishing with most elegant silk lines, and gold and silver hooks; they always use nicely polished phrases; but the fish will not bite for all that, whereas we of a rougher order have put the hook into the jaws of hundreds. However, if we cast the gospel net in the right place, even if we catch none, the Master will find no fault with us He will say, "Fisherman! didst thou labor? Didst thou throw the net into the sea in the time of storms?" "Yes, my Lord, I did." "What hast thou caught?" "Only one or two." "Well, I could have sent thee a shoal, if it so pleased me; it is not thy fault; I give in my sovereignty where I please; or withhold when I choose; but as for thee, thou hast well labored, therefore there is thy reward." Sometimes the minister is called a sower. Now, no farmer expects a sower to be responsible for the harvest; all he is responsible for is, does be sow the seed? and does he sow the right seed? If he scatters it on good soil, then he is happy; but if it falls by the way-side, and the fowls of the air devour it, who shall blame the sower? Could he help it? Nay, he did his duty; he scattered the seed broad-cast, and there he left it. Who is to blame? Certainly not the sower. So, beloved, if a minister comes to heaven with but one sheaf on his shoulder, his Master will say, "O reaper! once a sower! where didst thou gather thy sheaf?" "My Lord, I sowed upon the rock, and it would not grow; only one seed on a chance Sabbath morning was blown a little awry by the wind, and it fell on a prepared heart; and this is my one sheaf." "Hallelujah!" the angelic choirs resound, "one sheaf from a rock is more honor to God than a thousand sheaves from a good soil; therefore, let him take his seat as near the throne as yon man, who, stooping beneath his many sheaves, comes from some fertile land, bringing his sheaves with him." I believe that if there are degrees in glory, they will not be in proportion to success, but in proportion to the earnestness of our endeavors. If we mean right, and if with all our heart we strive to do the right thing as ministers if we never see any effect, still shall we receive the crown. But how much more happy is the man who shall have it in heaven said to him, "He shines forever, because he was wise, and won many souls unto righteousness." It is always my greatest joy to believe, that if I should enter heaven, I shall in future days see heaven's gates open, and in shall fly a cherub, who, looking me in the face, will smilingly pass along to God's throne, and there bow down before him and when has paid his homage and his adoration, he may fly to me, and though unknown, shall clasp my hand. and if there were tears in heaven, surely I should weep, and he would say, "Brother, from thy lips I heard the word; thy voice first admonished me of my sin; here I am, and thou the instrument of my salvation." And as the gates open one after another, still will they come in; souls ransomed, souls ransomed; and for each one of these a star—for each one of these another gem in the diadem of glory—for each one of them another honor, and another note in the song of praise. Blessed be that man that shall die in the Lord, and his works shall follow him; for thus saith the Spirit.

What will become of some good Christians now in Exeter Hall, if crowns in heaven are measured in value by the souls that are saved? Some of you will have a crown in heaven without a single star in it. I read a little while ago, a piece upon the starless crown in heaven—a man in heaven with a crown without a star! Not one saved by him! He will sit in heaven as happy as he can be, for sovereign mercy saved him; but oh! to be in heaven without a single star! Mother! what sayest thou to be in heaven without one of thy children to deck thy brow with a star? Minister! what wouldst thou say to be a polished preacher and yet have no star? Writer! will it well become thee to have written even as gloriously as Milton, if thou shouldst be found in heaven without a star? I am afraid we pay too little regard to this. Men will sit down and write huge folios and tomes, that they may have them put in libraries forever, and have their names handed down by fame! but how few are looking to win stars forever in heaven! Toil on, child of God, toil on; for if thou wishest to serve God, thy bread cast upon the waters shall be found after many days. If thou sendest in the feet of the ox or the ass, thou shalt reap a glorious harvest in that day when he comes to gather in his elect. The minister is not responsible for his success.

III. But yet, in the last place, TO PREACH THE GOSPEL IS HIGH AND SOLEMN WORK. The ministry has been very often degraded into a trade. In these days men are taken and made into ministers who would have made good captains at sea, who could have waited well at the counter, but who were never intended for the pulpit. They are selected by man, they are crammed with literature; they are educated up to a certain point; they are turned out ready dressed; and persons call them ministers. I wish them all God-speed, every one of them; for as good Joseph Irons used to say, "God be with many of them, if it be only to make them hold their tongues." Man-made ministers are of no use in this world, and the sooner we get rid of them the better. Their way is this: they prepare their manuscripts very carefully, then read it on the Sunday most sweetly in *sotto voce*, and so the people go away pleased. But that is not God's way of preaching. If so, I am sufficient to preach forever. I can buy manuscript sermons for a shilling; that is to say, provided they have been preached fifty times before, but if I use them for the first time the price is a guinea, or more. But that is not the way. Preaching God's word is not what some seem to think, mere child's play—a mere business or trade to be taken up by any one. A man ought to feel first that he has a solemn call to it; next, he ought to know that he really possesses the Spirit of God, and that when he speaks there is an influence upon him that enables him to speak as God would have him, otherwise out of the pulpit he should go directly; he has no right to be there, even if the living is his own property. He has not been called to preach God's truth, and unto him God says, "What hast thou to do, to declare my statutes?"

But you say, "What is there difficult about preaching God's gospel?" Well it must be somewhat hard; for Paul said, "Who is sufficient for these things?" And first I will tell you, it is difficult because it is so hard as not to be warped by your own prejudices in preaching the word. You want to say a stern thing; and your heart says, "Master! in so doing thou wilt condemn thyself;" then the temptation is not to say it. Another trial is, you are afraid of displeasing the rich in your congregations. Your think, "If I say such-and-such a thing, so-and-so will be offended; such an one does not approve of that doctrine; I had better leave it out." Or perhaps you will happen to win the applause of the multitude, and you must not say anything that will displease them, for if they cry, "Hosanna" to day, they will cry, "Crucify, crucify," tomorrow. All these things work on a minister heart. He is a man like yourselves; and he feels it. Then comes again the sharp knife of criticism, and the arrows of those who hate him and hate his Lord; and he cannot help feeling it sometimes. He may put on his armor, and cry, "I care not for your malice;" but there were seasons when the archers sorely grieved even Joseph. Then he stands in another danger, lest he should come out and defend himself; for he is a great fool whoever tries to do it. He who lets his detractors alone, and like the eagle cares not for the chattering of the sparrows, or like the lion will not turn aside to rend the snarling jackal—he is the man, and he shall be honored. But the danger is, we want to set ourselves right. And oh! who is sufficient to steer clear from these rocks of danger? "Who is sufficient," my brethren, "for these things?" To stand up, and to proclaim, Sabbath after Sabbath, and weekday after weekday, "the unsearchable riches of Christ."

Having said thus much, I may draw the inference—to close up—which is: if the gospel is "a savor of life unto life," and if the minister's work be solemn work, how well it becomes all lovers of the truth to plead for all those who preach it, that they may be "sufficient for these things." To lose my Prayer-book, as I have often told you, is the worst thing that can happen to me. To have no one to pray for me would place me in a dreadful condition. "Perhaps," says a good poet, "the day when the world shall perish, will be the day unwhitened by a prayer;" and, perhaps, the day when a minister turned aside from truth, was the day when his people left off to pray for him, and when there was not a single voice supplicating grace on his behalf. I am sure, it must be so with me. Give me the numerous hosts of men whom it has been my pride and glory to see in my place before I came to this hall: give me those praying people, who on the Monday evening met in such a multitude to pray to God for a blessing, and we will overcome hell itself, in spite of all that may oppose us. All our perils are nothing, so long as we have prayer. But increase my congregation; give me the polite and the noble,—give me influence and understanding; and I should fail to do anything without a praying church. My people! shall I ever lose your prayers? Will ye ever cease your supplications? Our toils are nearly ended in this great place, and happy shall we be to return to our much-loved sanctuary. Will ye then ever cease to pray? I fear ye have not uttered so many prayers this morning as ye should have done; I fear there has not been so much earnest devotion as might have been poured forth. For my own part, I have not felt the wondrous power I sometimes experience. I will not lay it at your doors; but never let it be said, "Those people, once so fervent, have become cold!" Let not Laodiceanism get into Southwark; let us leave it here in the West end, if it is to be anywhere; let us not carry it with us. Let us "strive together for the faith once delivered unto the saints:" and knowing in what a sad position the standard. bearer stands, I beseech you rally round him; for it will be ill with the army,

> "If the standard bearer fall, as fall full well he may.
> For never saw I promise yet, of such a deadly fray."

Stand up my friends; grasp the banner yourselves, and maintain it erect until the day shall come, when standing on the last conquered castle of hell's domains, we shall raise the shout, "Hallelujah! Hallelujah! Hallelujah! The Lord God Omnipotent reigneth!" Till that time, fight on.

10

THE GOSPEL'S HEALING POWER

Preached on November 11, 1866
Scripture: Luke 5:17
From: Metropolitan Tabernacle Pulpit Volume 12

"And it came to pass on a certain day, as he was teaching, that there were Pharisees and doctors of the law sitting by, which were come out of every town of Galilee, and Judaea, and Jerusalem: and the power of the Lord was present to heal them." —Luke 5:17.

LUKE, the writer of this gospel, was a physician, and therefore had a quick eye for cases of disease and instances of cure; you can trace throughout the whole of his gospel the hand of one who was skilled in surgery and medicine. From which I gather that whatever may be our calling, or in whatever art or science we may have attained proficiency, we should take care to use our knowledge for Christ; and that if we be called being physicians we may understand the work of the Lord Jesus all the better by what we see in our own work, and we may also do much for our Lord in real substantial usefulness among our patients. Let no man despise his calling; whatever instrument of usefulness God hath put into thine hand, consider that the Great Captain knew what weapon it were best for thee to wield. Covet not thy neighbor's sword or spear, but use that which thy Lord hath given thee, and go forth to the battle of life to serve according to thy capacity. If thou be placed in this corner of the vineyard or that, consider that thou art in the best place for thyself, and the best place for thy Master; and do not always be judging what thy fellow servants ought to do in their place, nor what thou couldst do if thou wert in another place; but see what it is that thou canst do where thou art, and use such things as thou hast in glorifying thy Lord and Master. One is pleased to observe in the language of a true man how the man's self shows itself. David frequently sings like one who had been a shepherd boy, and though a king he is not ashamed to own that he once grasped the crook. There is a manifest difference between the prophecies of Amos the herdsman and of Isaiah the royal seer. True men do not imitate one another, but each one, moved of God, speaketh according to his native bias, and according to the circumstances in which Providence has cast him. It was destructive to Egyptian art when the great men of the land framed articles of taste, and laws of statuary and of painting by which every sculptor must be bound, for then everything like freshness and originality was driven away; the proportions of every colossal statue and of every figure upon the wall were rigidly fixed, and then the glory and excellence of art vanished from the land. To do the same in religion is even more unwise; to say, "Ye shall all speak after one fashion, and ye all shall conform to this manner of talk and life," is folly at its height. Let each man speak after his own manner, every man in his own order, each quickened soul bringing out its own individuality, and seeking in that individuality to magnify God and to show forth the riches of his grace. These remarks were suggested by the abundant record of cures in this chapter and elsewhere in Luke's gospel. Luke does not write like John, nor copy the style of Matthew; he writes not as a fisherman or a publican, but as a physician. Luke did not cease to be Luke when he was called by grace, but he was the same man elevated and refined, and taught to consecrate to noblest ends the gifts which he had acquired in his earthly calling; he was a physician before, and he became "the beloved physician" after his conversion.

I. The text, as we read it, suggests in the first place, that THE POWER OF CHRIST IN THE GOSPEL IS MAINLY A POWER TO HEAL. "The power of the Lord was present to heal them." The power of the gospel, of which Christ is the sum and substance, is a healing power. My brethren, when Christ came on earth he might have come with destroying power. Justly enough might God have sent his only Son with the armies of vengeance to destroy this rebellious world. But—

"Thy hands, dear Jesus, were not arm'd
With an avenging rod;
No hard commission to perform,
The vengeance of a God.

> *"But all was mercy, all was mild,*
> *And wrath forsook the throne,*
> *When Christ on the kind errand came,*
> *And brought salvation down."*

"I have not come," said he, "to destroy men's lives, but to save them." Elias calls fire from heaven upon the captains of fifties, and their fifties, so that they are utterly consumed; but Christ brings fire from heaven for quite another purpose, namely, that by its power men might be saved from the wrath to come. The gospel is not intended to be a power to destroy. "God sent not his Son into the world to condemn the world, but that the world through him might be saved." And if that gospel be made a savor of death unto death unto any, it is not on account of its own intrinsic qualities or design, but because of the perversity and wickedness of the human heart. If men perish by the gospel of life, it is because they make that to be a stumbling-stone which was meant to be a foundation.

The gospel does not even come into the world merely to reveal disease. It is true it does discover, detect, and describe the maladies of fallen man. One of the clearest exposures of man's fallen estate is the gospel of the grace of God; but it is rather the design of the law than of the gospel to discover to man his ruin. It is by the glare of Sinai's lightnings that men tremblingly read the sentence of condemnation upon those who have broken God's law: by the gentler light of Calvary they may read the same truth, and must read it; but this is not the main design of Calvary. Calvary is the place for the healing balm rather than for the lancet and the knife. The work of Jesus, our heavenly Physician, is not so much to point out disease as to indicate and to apply the remedy. Certain philosophers have made it their business and delight, with grim sardonic smile upon their faces, to put forth the finger and mark out human wickedness and weakness as a theme for ridicule and sarcasm. The philosophy of the Stoics, the wisdom of such men as Diogenes, was but a heartless unpitying showing up of human folly and sin; it knew no remedy, and cared not to search for one. They showed poor manhood to be besotted, befooled, debased, and depraved, and there they left it, passing by on the other side as the priest and Levite did with the wounded man in the parable. But Jesus came upon no such fruitless errand; he does convince the world of sin by his Spirit, but it is not to leave the world hopelessly despairing of its restoration, but to recover it by his power. Jesus bears with him power to heal; this is his honor and renown. He has the eagle's eye to see our sicknesses, the lion's heart bravely to encounter them, and the lady's hand gently to apply the heavenly ointment; in him the three necessaries of a good surgeon meet in perfection.

Beloved, I trust you and I have known this power to heal in our own cases, and if it be so we know of a certainty that it is a divine power which comes from our Lord Jesus because he is most surely God. It is the sole prerogative of God to heal spiritual disease. Natural disease may be instrumentally healed by men, but even then the honor is to be given to God who giveth virtue unto medicine, and bestoweth power unto the human frame to cast off disease. But as for spiritual sicknesses, these remain with the great Physician alone; he claims it as his prerogative, "I kill and I make alive, I wound and I heal;" and one of the Lord's choice titles is Jehovah Rophi, the Lord that healeth thee. "I will heal thee of thy wounds," is a promise which could not come from the lip of man, but only from the mouth of the eternal God. On this account the psalmist cried unto the Lord, "O Lord, heal me, for my bones are sore vexed," and again, "Heal my scul, for I have sinned against thee." For this also, the godly praise the name of the Lord, saying, "He healeth all our diseases." He who made man can heal man; he who was at first the creator of our nature can new create it. What a transcendent comfort it is that in the person of Jesus Christ of Nazareth we have Deity Incarnate! "In him dwelleth all the fullness of the Godhead bodily." My soul, whatever thy disease may be, this great Physician can heal thee. If he be God, there can be no limit to his infinite power; if he be truly divine, there can be no boundary to the majesty of his might. Come then with the blind eye of thine understanding, come with the limping foot of thine energy, come with the maimed hand of thy faith, come just as thou art, for he who is God can certainly heal thee. None shall say unto the healing flood of his love, "Hitherto canst thou go and no further." The utmost length of human sickness can be reached by this great Physician. Have thou confidence, O poor doubting heart! have thou unstaggering confidence in the Divine Healer.

Although our Lord Jesus healed as Divine, remember that he also possessed power to heal because of his being human. Is it not written, "The chastisement of our peace was upon him, and with his stripes we are healed"? He used no other remedy in healing our sin-sickness but that of taking our sicknesses and infirmities upon himself. This is the one great cure-all. Blessed be the Son of God that the medicine, bitter as it is, is not for us to drink, but was all drained by himself. He took the terrible cup in Gethsemane, and drank it dry on our account. The sharp but healing cuts of the lancet are not made in our bodies, but he bore them in his own flesh. When the plowers made deep furrows, those furrows were not upon the sinner's shoulders, but upon the shoulders of the sinner's Substitute. Didst ever hear, O Earth, of such a Physician as this? who heals by suffering himself, whose pains, and sorrows, and griefs, and pangs, and torments, and anguish, and death are the only medicine by which he removes the woes of men! Blessed Son of God, if I trust thee, seeing that thou art Divine, how will I love thee! how will I cling to thee, seeing thou art human! With what gratitude will I look up to thy cross and view thee, while those blessed founts of health are streaming crimson floods, and while thy heart, the source of all spiritual sanity, is pouring forth a heavenly torrent, efficacious to wash the sinner from all his sicknesses! Come hither, all ye sin-sick ones, and behold the glorious Son of God, made in the likeness of human flesh, breathing out his life upon the cross! Come hither, ye that mourn for sin, ye who are palsied and diseased with iniquity! here is power, power still present in the dying Savior to heal you, whatsoever your diseases may be. He healed all that had need of healing while he sojourned here, and the costly balm of his atonement has lost none of its power.

The power which dwelt in Christ to heal, coming from him as divine and human, was applicable, most eminently, to the removal of the guilt of sin. Reading this chapter through, one pauses with joy over that twentyfourth verse, "The Son of Man hath power upon earth to forgive sin." Here, then, is one of the great Physician's mightiest arts: he has power to forgive sin. While here he lived below, before the ransom had been paid, before the blood had been literally sprinkled on the mercy-seat, he had power to forgives in. Hath he not power to do it now that he hath died? Brethren, what power must dwell in him who to the utmost farthing has faithfully discharged the debts of his people! He has indeed power, seeing that he has finished transgression and made an end of sin. If ye doubt it, see him rising from the dead! behold him in ascending splendor raised to the right hand of God! hear him pleading before the Eternal Father, pointing to his wounds, urging the merit of his sacred passion! What power to forgive is here! "He hath ascended on high, and received gifts for men." "He is exalted on high to give repentance and remission of sins." At this moment, sinner, Christ has power to pardon, power to pardon thee, and millions such as thou art. He has nothing more to do to win thy pardon; all the atoning work is done. He can, in answer to thy tears, forgive thy sins today, and make thee know it. He can breathe into thy soul at this very moment a peace with God which passeth all understanding, which shall spring from perfect remission of thy manifold iniquities. Dost thou believe that? I trust thou believest it. Mayest thou experience now that the healing power of the gospel is power to forgive sin! Waste no time in applying to the Physician of souls, but hasten to him with words like these—

> "Jesus! Master! hear my cry;
> Save me, heal me with a word;
> Fainting at thy feet I lie,
> Thou my whisper'd plaint hast heard."

This is not the only form of the healing power which dwells without measure in our glorious Lord. He heals the sorrow of sin. It is written, "He healeth the broken in heart and bindeth up their wounds." When sin is really manifest to the conscience it is a most painful thing, and for the conscience to be effectually pacified is an unspeakable blessing. Sharper than a dagger in the heart, or an arrow piercing through the loins is conviction of sin. He that has ever smarted under the prickings of an awakened conscience well knows that there is no pain of body that can be compared to it. When crushed under the hand of God a man may form some idea of what the miseries of hell must be. Correspondingly joyous is the relief which Immanuel brings to us when he brings better balm than that of Gilead, and ministers Heaven's infallible specific to a soul disease. When Jesus is received by faith, he lifts all our sorrow from us in a moment. One promise applied by his Spirit, one drop of his blood brought home to the conscience, and at once there is such a peace, so deep and profound that nothing can rival it. What the poet wrote concerning recovery from bodily sickness is doubly true of spiritual restoration.

> *"See the Man that long has tost*
> *On the thorny bed of pain,*
> *At length repair his vigour lost,*
> *And breathe and walk again:*
> *The meanest floweret of the vale,*
> *The simplest note that swells the gale,*
> *The common sun, the air, the skies,*
> *To him are opening Paradise."*

God grant, that to you who fear his name the Sun of righteousness may arise with healing beneath his wings!

Jesus also heals the power of sin. Sin may be in your case, dear friend, so mighty, that like a whirlwind it hurries you away at its pleasure. You feel like the sere leaves which are driven by the tempest; you have scarce power to resist your passions; you have perhaps, yielded so long to certain forms of evil that now you are positively powerless in strife against them. Do not however despair; Christ can surely deliver you. The demoniac had such an energy of evil within him that he brake the chains and bands with which he had been bound, he cut himself with stones, and howled all night amidst the tombs; but when Jesus came near to him he was soon seen clothed and in his right mind, sitting meekly at the great Physician's feet. And so wilt thou, poor captive of evil. Do not think that thou needst to be a drunkard, or that thy angry temper need always be thy master. Do not conceive that thou must always be a slave to lust, or led captive at the devil's will. There is hope for thee, man, where Christ is, and though thy disease be of as long standing as thy very life, yet a word from the powerful lips of the Son of God can make even thee whole. The power of the gospel is a power to heal the guilt, the sorrow, and the influence of sin; Jesus Christ came into the world to destroy the works of the devil in all their forms.

It should not be forgotten that the Lord Jesus is able to heal us of our relapses. I have heard men say that a relapse is what the physician frequently fears more than the primary disease, and that there is frequently a period in the healing process when the virus of disease gathers renewed energy, and the physician feels that now and not at the first the true battle has to be fought. We have met with men who have professed conversion, and we trust were changed, who have gone back like the dog to his vomit, and the sow that was washed to her wallowing in the mire. We have had to mourn over those in whom the change appeared to be great, but it was superficial, and soon the power of evil returned upon them. But, my backsliding hearer, Jesus is able to heal your backslidings. What a mercy that is! "I will heal their backslidings, I will love them freely, for mine anger is turned away from him." What if thou be sevenfold more a child of hell than thou wast before, yet even now eternal mercy that drove out a legion of devils from one of old can drive them out of thee. The healing power of my Master is such, that if thou hast backslidden ever so far yet he saith unto thee, "Return! return! return." There shall be more joy over thee, thou poor lost sheep, than over ninety and nine that went not astray. He shall be more glad to receive thee, thou wandering prodigal child, than he hath joy even over that righteous son who remained always in the father's house.

To sum up much in little, my Master, as a physician, works cures very suddenly; he touches, and the deed is done at once. He works cures of all kinds. Such as have been the stumbling-stones of other physicians have been readily overcome by him. He never fails. He has not in his diary one single case that has over-matched his mighty power. He heals effectually, the disease never again reigns when he has once dethroned it. When he casteth the devil out of the man he shall not return. He healeth with his word even those who think that they cannot be healed. There is no hospital for incurables now as to souls, for incurables there are none. The Friend of sinners is "able to save unto the uttermost those that come unto God by him." Cases of disease so putrid that men say, "Put them out of sight;" vice so detestable that the very mention of it makes the cheek of modesty to blush; such as these the master-hand of Immanuel can heal. With God nothing is impossible, and with the Son of God nothing is difficult. He can save the chief of sinners, and the vilest of the vile. In the highest conceivable degree the power of the gospel is power to heal, Come, poor sinner, and behold him who is able to heal thee of thy deadly wounds; come look upon him now and live.

> *"Raise to the cross thy tearful eyes,*
> *Behold, the Prince of Glory dies;*
> *He dies extended on the tree,*
> *And sheds a sovereign balm for thee."*

II. A second remark arises from the text; THERE ARE SPECIAL PERIODS WHEN THE POWER TO HEAL IS MOST MANIFESTLY DISPLAYED. The verse before us says that on a certain day the power of the Lord was present to heal, by which I understand, not that Christ is not always God, not that he was ever unable to heal, but this,—that there were certain periods when he pleased to put forth his divine energy in the way of healing to an unusual degree. The sea is never empty; it is indeed always as full at one time as at another, but yet it is not always at flood. The sun is never dim, he shines with equal force at all hours, and yet it is not always day with us, nor do we always bask in the warmth of summer. Christ is fullness itself, but that fullness does not always overflow; he is able to heal, but he is not always engaged in healing. There are times when the power to save is more than usually manifest—times of refreshing, seasons of revival, days of visitation, acceptable days, days of salvation. Any student of the world's history who has read it in the light of true religion will have observed that there have been favored periods when the power of God has been peculiarly present to heal men. My solemn conviction is that we are living in such an era, that this present moment is one of the set times when God's power is peculiarly manifest; I gather this from many signs, but even the text assists me in my belief. Observe that on the occasion mentioned in the text there was a great desire among the multitude to hear the word. In the opening of the chapter we read that they pressed upon our Lord by the sea. Further on we find them coming from all parts of the country in multitudes. Especial mention is made of doctors of the law and Pharisees, the last people to be impressed, who nevertheless, overcome by the common enthusiasm, were found mingling with the throng: we are told that the people thronged the house at such a rate that the palsied man could not be brought into the congregation except by the expedient of breaking through the roof. When God's power is moving, there will be a corresponding motion among the people; they will long to hear when God's power is with the speaker. Take it as a sign of grace when the houses dedicated to worship are full. Consider that the Lord is about to fill the net, when the fishes crowd around the boat. We cannot expect the gospel to be blessed to those who do not hear it, we may lawfully and properly expect it will be a blessing to those who have an intense anxiety to listen to it. At the present hour I see a religious awakening amongst the masses of London, not so great a one as we could desire, but still there it is, and we must be grateful for it. We shall not long have to put up with the pernicious nonsense of Puseyism, public opinion will aid us in putting it down. It has taken a long time to wake up our nation, but it will awaken after all. I think I see the tide of popular feeling turning in the right direction. Men are just now occupied about religious thought, and whether they think rightly or wrongly, there is more attention just now paid to religious truth than has been for many a day; and where ministers do but preach simply and lovingly the gospel of Christ at this moment they find no lack of hearers. This is a sure sign that the power of the Lord is present to heal.

Observe next that the healing power was conspicuously present when Christ was teaching. Note carefully the favored hour, "when he was teaching in a certain place." Jesus linked the healing with the teaching. It was so with the material healing, much more with the spiritual healing, for "faith cometh by hearing, and hearing by the Word of God." Brethren, is there not among our own brethren, of whom we can speak with the most certainty, more teaching of Christ now than there was. I am persuaded that the most of my brethren preach more faithfully and fully the simple truth of Christ Jesus than they once did. Teaching is returning to the pulpits. Now mark, dear hearer, whether thou be saved or not, if thou art present where Christ is fully preached, where he is lifted up, exalted, proclaimed, and commended to thee, thou art in a place where he also is present to heal; for is it not written, "I, if I be lifted up, will draw all men unto me"?

A further sign of present power is found most clearly in the sick folk who were healed by Jesus. Now we know that in this very house not a Sunday passes without souls being converted. We have before our church meetings the cases of hundreds whom God has blessed by the simple telling of the story of the cross. This then is proof positive, that Christ being taught, and souls being blessed, he is in a remarkable manner present to heal.

One other thing must be noted, namely, that this particular time mentioned in the text was prefaced by a special season of prayer on the part of the principal actor in it. Did you notice it? He withdrew himself and prayed, and then the power of the Lord was present to heal them. Is it so that even with regard to Christ himself, the Lord and Giver of Life, in whom dwelleth the fullness of the Godhead, and who has the Spirit without measure, yet before that Spirit is publicly manifested in any high degree there must be a special retirement for fervent prayer? How plainly does this say to us that the church must pray if she would have the healing power! But, my brethren, we have prayed. There has been such prayer put up by this congregation as I believe was never excelled, even in apostolic times; and last Monday was a day of wrestling of such a kind that the blessing could not be withheld. I have almost ceased to ask further, I wait in joyful anticipation of the heavenly visitation. I come not forth today so much as a sower as a reaper. I believe that the fish are taken in the net, and that we have only to pull it to land. God grant the net may not break by reason of the multitude of fishes! For God is with us, and that of a truth in this house this day. Wonders of grace are being wrought; while we are yet speaking men are being inclined to look to Christ, while we are lifting him up tearful eyes are looking to him; and in many a heart there may be heard the cry, "I will arise and go to my Father." Now all these signs meeting together, a desire to hear, a set time of private prayer, the teaching of the word, and the manifest blessing of souls under that word, I gather that we have arrived at this present moment at that state which is described in the text.

III. Passing on to a third thought, we observe, that WHEN THE POWER OF THE LORD IS PRESENT TO HEAL, IT MAY NOT BE SEEN IN ALL, BUT MAY BE SHOWN IN SPECIAL CASES AND NOT IN OTHERS. It is a melancholy reflection that men may be in the region of divine power, and yet not feel its operations. I have read this verse through a great many times with one object, I have tried, if I could, to make the text mean that the Pharisees and doctors of the law were present, and that the power of the Lord was present to heal them. But the text does not so teach us; the power of the Lord was not present to heal the doctors and Pharisees, for they were not healed. The word "them" agrees with the noun further back, according to the frequent usage of the New Testament by which the pronouns are not made to refer to the nearer noun, but to another more remote. The power of God was present to heal the sick, not to heal the doctors, nor the Pharisees; and yet how nearly they seem to have gained it, for had they but known their sickness, and been willing to confess their infirmity, there was power enough to have healed even them; but as it was, we do not find that one of them was healed—not so much as a single doctor of the law, or a Pharisee felt the power which was passing so near to them that they were amazed and staggered and fell to cavilling at it. Dear hearers, this very melancholy observation must be applied to some that are present now. You may be in the midst of this congregation, which is under remarkable visitations of God's grace, and yet there may be no power present operating in your heart to heal you. You will observe that those who missed this grace were not the harlots; infamous as they were by character, they felt the power of the love of Jesus and entered into his kingdom. We do not find that this power was wanting among the publicans; we have an instance here of one of them who made a great feast in his house for Christ. Where then was the power lacking? Where was it unsought and unfelt? It was in the first place among the knowing people, the doctors of the law. These teachers knew too much to submit to be taught by the Great Rabbi. There is such a thing as knowing too much to know anything, and being too wise to be anything but a fool. The knowledge of the doctors was that which puffeth up, and not the knowledge which cometh from God. Ah, dear hearer, beware of head knowledge without heart knowledge; beware of being so orthodox as to set yourself up as a judge of the preacher, and to refuse to be obedient to the truth. Beware of saying, "Oh yes, yes, yes, yes, that is very applicable to So-and-so, and very well put." Do not criticise but feel. It were better for you that you had been a common plow-boy, whistling at the plow, who never heard these things until today, and have now listened to them, and have received them in all their novelty, and power, and beauty for the first time; this were better for you than to have heard them till they ring in your ears like the bell which you have heard every Sabbath day, of whose monotony you are weary. Beware of going down to hell with a millstone of sound doctrine about your necks, for if ye will be damned you may as well perish knowing the truth as not knowing it. Nay, if you catch the formula and lay hold upon the creed, and imagine yourself to be teachers of others, it is even easier to perish in that state than it is if you came in to hear the Word untaught heretofore in its glad message. These were the knowing ones who had no power to be healed.

Those, moreover, who had a good opinion of themselves were left unblest. The Pharisees! no better people anywhere, from Dan to Beersheba, than the Pharisees, if you would take them upon their own reckoning. Observe with due respect their public character. Were they not most eminent? See the breadth of the borders of their garments! How visible were their phylacteries! How diligently did they wash their hands before they ate! How scrupulous about straining out gnats from their wine! How careful to tithe the anise, and mint, and cummin! Yet these were the people who obtained no blessing from Jesus. They were too good to be saved. How many people there are of this kind! "Well," says one, "I know I never robbed anybody; I have brought up my family respectably, and conducted myself with such decorum that nobody could possibly find fault with me." Just so, and you will not have Christ because you are whole, and have no need of a physician. "Ah!" says another, "surely if we do our duty to the best of our ability it will be all right with us." If you think thus you will find that when you have done your duty to the best you can, you will have no part nor lot in a Savior, because manifestly, on your own showing, you do not require one. The Lord Jesus will take your own showing, and will say, "I never knew you. How should I know you? You were never sick; you never needed me; you declared that you were whole, and you would not stoop to accept the salvation which I, the Savior, came to bring." Thus will Jesus speak to you who now proudly despise his grace.

Once again, the people who did not get the blessing were not only the knowing ones and the very good ones, but they were also the people who stood by. As one observes, they did not come to be preached at, they came for Christ to preach before them. That used to be the old style of sermon prefaces—"A sermon preached before the honorable or worshipful company of So-and-so." Now that is the worst kind of preaching anywhere, preaching before people; preaching right at people is the only preaching worth hearing and worth uttering. But they did not come for Christ to operate upon them; they were not patients, they were visitors in the hospitals. Like visitors they went round to the beds and looked at the prescriptions put over the sick, and observed upon each case, and when the physician came in and began to exercise his art upon the sick, they stood by and criticized his treatment, imagining all the while that they were not sick themselves. If they had been lying on the bed sick they could have been healed, but they took only a superficial interest in the healing, for they came not to partake in it. Beware, my dear hearers, of going to places of worship merely to be lookers on. There will be no lookers on in heaven, and there will be no lookers on in hell. Take care that you do not play the looker on in the worship of God here. Every truth as spoken by God's servants has a bearing upon you. If it be threatening, and you are in the gall of bitterness, it is yours, tremble under it! If it be the promise of divine love, then if you have no part in it, be afraid, be ashamed, be alarmed, and fly to Christ that you may partake in it. Those who get no blessing are those who suppose they do not particularly need it and stand by, having merely come to see and to be seen, but not to receive a cure.

Those who felt not the healing power sneered and cavilled. They said further down in the chapter, "Who can forgive sins but God only?" When a man gets no good out of the ministry, he is pretty sure to think there is no good in the ministry; and when he himself for want of stooping down to drink finds no water in the river, he concludes it is dry; whereas it is his own stubborn knee that will not bend, and his own willful mouth that will not open to receive the gospel. But if they quarrel, if they raise questions, if they dispute, we know their breed, we understand the race to which they belong, and we know how Jesus said to them of old, "Ye generation of vipers, how shall ye escape the damnation of hell?" If any shall not escape, surely they shall not whose only hearing of the gospel is to make it the butt of their sarcasm and the object of their ridicule, who look derisively even at the cross itself with a dying Savior upon it, and thrust their tongue into their cheek, and make jests and merriment of the agonies of the world's Redeemer. Beware, lest you have those jests in your mouth on earth which you will have to digest in hell! Beware, lest your mockery return upon you at the last great day, when the words of Solomon shall be fulfilled, "Because I called and ye refused, I stretched out my hands and no man regarded, I also will mock at your calamity, I will laugh when your fear cometh." There were persons then to whom the present power of Christ to heal was of no service whatever, there may be such now. Friend, art thou such an one?

IV. In the last place, I want Christian people here to observe that WHEN THE POWER OF CHRIST WAS PRESENT, IT CALLED FORTH THE ENERGY OF THOSE WHO WERE HIS FRIENDS TO WORK WHILE THAT POWER WAS MANIFEST.

My dear brethren, the members of this church especially, what I have to say is earnestly addressed to you. You will perceive that as soon as ever it was discovered that the power of healing was present, loving hearts desired to bring in others that they might experience it. Four persons took each a corner of the bed and brought in a palsied man who could not come of himself, and they let him down with much inconvenience through the roof. God is blessing the church now. Christian men and women, join together to pray for your friends who cannot or will not pray for themselves; and if you meet with any in deep distress, palsied with despair, who cannot lift the finger of faith, strive to bring them to hear the gospel, bring them where Christ is working miracles. If one of you cannot prevail to lay the case before the Lord, let two of you unite; if two should not be enough, let four blend their petitions; if four should not suffice, tell it to the church, and ask the whole to pray; but do strive to bring dying sinners where Christ is working spiritual miracles.

If you read further on in the chapter you will learn how to bring some persons to the Savior who would never hear of him else. Levi made a great feast, for he thought to himself, "I should like Jesus to come and preach to the publicans.

They are such great sinners, just such as I am; if I could but get them to hear him they might be converted. But," he thought, "if I ask them they would say they could not afford to give up a day's work, they will not care to listen to a sermon; so (said he) I will get them this way, I will invite them to my house to a feast; they will be sure to come then, and then I will ask Jesus to come and eat with them, and I know he will not let them go without saying a good word." So you see he used arts as fowlers do when they are anxious to catch their prey. Now cannot you be as watchful and thoughtful in your generation as Levi was? Cannot you get the outcasts and the neglecters of the Sabbath to your own house or to anybody else's house, and use means to bring them under the sound of God's word? Why, if you have a few flowers in your back room, if it rains in the summer time, do not you always put them out in it? All the pots you put out in the garden to let them catch the shower. Do so with your friends, your neighbors, your children, your kinsfolk, while the rain of grace is dropping try to get them under the influence of it, and if they will not come by one means try another, only do get them where the power of the Lord is present, for perhaps Jesus may look upon them and they may look to him and may be healed.

And oh! let me say in closing, if they should not be saved the responsibility will not then rest with you, even as the responsibility this morning does not rest with me. We have proclaimed to you in this house many times that Christ Jesus came into the world to save sinners. We have told you that the heavenly Father is willing to receive returning sinners, that he delights in mercy, that he is free to blot out sin. We have told you that the blood of Christ can make the blackest clean, that all manner of sin and blasphemy shall be forgiven unto men. We have urged you to flee away like doves to Jesus' wounds. The power of the Spirit of God has led many of you to come to him, and you are saved; but alas! there still remains a multitude who are unsaved still. Well, if you perish, it is not because Christ has not been taught in your streets. You will go down to hell, some of you, with the light shining on your eyelids, but with your eyes willfully closed against it; you will perish with the voice of mercy ringing in your ears; and in hell you will be awful monuments to the justice of God, who will then say to you, "You sinned against light and knowledge, and against love and mercy." If they perish who despised Moses' law, how shall ye escape if ye neglect so great salvation? May the Holy Spirit now with mighty energy apply the precious blood of Jesus to every hearer, and unto God shall be glory world without end. Amen.

"Blest Savior, at thy feet I lie,
Here to receive a cure or die;
But grace forbids that painful fear,
Almighty grace, which triumphs here.
"Thou wilt withdraw the poison'd dart,
Bind up and heal the wounded heart;
With blooming health my face adorn,
And change the gloomy night to morn."

11

PREACH THE GOSPEL

Preached on August 5, 1855
Scripture: 1 Corinthians 9:16
From: New Park Street Pulpit Volume 1

"For though I preach the gospel, I have nothing to glory of; for necessity is laid upon me; yea woe is unto me, if I preach not the gospel."—1 Corinthians 9:16

The greatest man of Apostolic times was the apostle Paul. He was always great in everything. If you consider him as a sinner, he was exceeding sinful; if you regard him as a persecutor, he was exceeding mad against the Christians, and persecuted them even unto strange cities, if you take him as a convert, his conversion was the most notable one of which we read, worked by miraculous power, and by the direct voice of Jesus speaking from heaven—"Saul, Saul, why persecutest thou me?"—If we take him simply as a Christian, he was an extraordinary one, loving his Master more than others, and seeking more than others to exemplify the grace of God in his life. But if you take him as an apostle, and as a preacher of the Word, he stands out preeminent as the prince of preachers, and a preacher to kings—for he preached before Agrippa, he preached before Nero Caesar—he stood before emperors and kings for Christ's name's sake. It was the characteristic of Paul, that whatever he did, he did with all his heart. He was one of the men who could not allow one half of his frame to be exercised, while the other half was indolent but, when he set to work, the whole of his energies—every nerve, every sinew—were strained in the work to be done, be it bad work or be it good. Paul, therefore, could speak from experience concerning his ministry; because he was the chief of ministers. There is no nonsense in what he speaks; it is all from the depth of his soul. And we may be sure that when he wrote this, he wrote it with a strong, unpalsied hand— "Though I preach the gospel, I have nothing to glory of, for necessity is laid upon me, yea, woe is me if I preach not the gospel."

Now, these words of Paul, I trust, are applicable to many ministers in the present day; to all those who are especially called, who are directed by the inward impulse of the Holy Spirit to occupy the position of gospel ministers. In trying to consider this verse, we shall have three inquiries this morning:—First, What is it to preach the gospel? Secondly, Why is it that a minister has nothing to glorify of? And thirdly, What is that necessity and that woe, of which it is written, "Necessity is laid upon me, yea, woe is unto me, if I preach not the gospel?"

I. The first inquiry is, WHAT IS IT TO PREACH THE GOSPEL? There are a variety of opinions concerning this question, and possibly amongst my own audience—though I believe we are very uniform in our doctrinal sentiments—there might be found two or three very ready answers to this question: What is it to preach the gospel? I shall therefore attempt to answer it myself according to my own judgment, if God will help me; and if it does not happen to be the correct answer, you are at liberty to supply a better to yourselves at home.

1. The first answer I shall give to the question is this: To preach the gospel is to state every doctrine contained in God's Word, and to give every truth its proper prominence. Men may preach a part of the gospel; they may only preach one single doctrine of it; and I would not say that a man did not preach the gospel at all if he did but maintain the doctrine of justification by faith—"By grace are ye saved through faith." I should put him down for a gospel minister, but not for one who preached the whole gospel. No man can be said to preach the whole gospel of God if he leaves it out, knowingly and intentionally, one single truth of the blessed God. This remark of mine must be a very cutting one, and ought to strike into the consciences of many who make it almost a matter of principle to keep back certain truths from the people, because they are afraid of them. In conversation, a week or two ago, with an eminent professor, he said to me, "Sir, we know that we ought not to preach the doctrine of election, because it is not calculated to convert sinners." "But," said I to him, "who is the men that dares to find fault with the truth of God? You admit, with me, that it is a truth, and yet you say it must not be preached. I dare not have said that thing. I should

reckon it supreme arrogance to have ventured to say that a doctrine ought not to be preached when the all-wise God has seen fit to reveal it. Besides, is the whole gospel intended to convert sinners? There are some truths which God blesses to the conversion of sinners; but are there not other portions which were intended for the comfort of the saint? and ought not these to be a subject of gospel ministry as well as the others? And shall I look at one and disregard the other? No: if God says, 'Comfort ye, comfort ye, my people' if election comforts God's people, then must I preach it." But I am not quite so sure, that after all, that doctrine is not calculated to convert sinners. For the great Jonathan Edwardes tells us, that in the greatest excitement of one of his revivals, he preached the sovereignty of God in the salvation or condemnation of man, and showed that God was infinitely just if he sent men to hell! that he was infinitely merciful if he saved any; and that it was all of his own free grace, and he said, "I found no doctrine caused more thought nothing entered more deeply into the heart than the proclamation of that truth." The same might be said of other doctrines. There are certain truths in God's word which are condemned to silence; they, forsooth, are not to be uttered, because, according to the theories of certain persons, looking at these doctrines, they are not calculated to promote certain ends. But is it for me to judge God's truth? Am I to put his words in the scale, and say, "This is good, and that is evil?' Am I to take God's Bible, and sever it and say, "this is husk, and this is wheat?" Am I to cast away any one truth, and say, "I dare not preach it?" No: God forbid. Whatsoever is written in God's Word is written for our instruction: and the whole of it is profitable, either for reproof, or for consolation, or for edification in righteousness. No truth of God's Word ought to be withheld, but every portion of it preached in its own proper order.

Some men purposely confine themselves to four or five topics continually. Should you step into their chapel, you would naturally expect to hear them preaching, either from this, "Not of the will of the flesh, but of the will of God," or else, "Elect according to the foreknowledge of God the Father." You know that the moment you step in you are sure to hear nothing but election and high doctrine that day. Such men err also, quite as much as others, if they give too great prominence to one truth to the neglect of the others. Whatsoever is here to be preached, "all it whatever name you please, write it high, write it low—the Bible, the whole Bible, and nothing but the Bible, is the standard of the true Christian. Alas! alas! many make an iron ring of their doctrines, and he who dares to step beyond that narrow circle, is not reckoned orthodox. God bless heretics, then! God send us more of them! Many make theology into a kind of wheel, consisting of five doctrines, which are everlastingly rotated; for they never go on to anything else. There ought to be every truth preached. And if God has written in his word that "he that believeth not is condemned already," that is as much to be preached as the truth that "there is no condemnation to them that are in Jesus Christ." If I find it written, "O Israel, thou hast destroyed thyself," that man's condemnation is his own fault, I am to preach that as well as the next clause, "In me is thy help found." We ought, each of us who are entrusted with the ministry, to seek to preach all truth. I know it may be impossible to tell you all of it. That high hill of truth hath mists upon its summit. No mortal eye can see its pinnacle; nor hath the foot of man ever trodden it. But yet let us paint the mist, if we cannot paint the summit. Let us depict the difficulty itself if we cannot unravel it. Let us not hide anything, but if the mountain of truth be cloudy at the top, let us say, "Clouds and darkness are around him," Let us not deny it; and let us not think of cutting down the mountain to our own standard, because we cannot see its summit or cannot reach its pinnacle. He who would preach the gospel must preach all the gospel. He who would have it said he is a faithful minister, must not keep back any part of revelation.

2. Again, am I asked what it is to preach the gospel? I answer to preach the gospel is to exalt Jesus Christ. Perhaps this is the best answer that I could give. I am very sorry to see very often how little the gospel is understood even by some of the best Christians. Some time ago there was a young woman under great distress of soul; she came to a very pious Christian man, who said "My dear girl, you must go home and pray." Well I thought within myself, that is not the Bible way at all. It never says, "Go home and pray." The poor girl went home; she did pray, and she still continued in distress. Said he, "You must wait, you must read the Scriptures and study them." That is not the Bible way; that is not exalting Christ; find a great many preachers are preaching that kind of doctrine. They tell a poor convinced sinner, "You must go home and pray, and read the Scriptures; you must attend the ministry;" and so on. Works, works, works—instead of "By grace are ye saved through faith," If a penitent should come and ask me, "What must I do to be saved?" I would say, "Christ must save you—believe on the name of the Lord Jesus Christ." I would neither direct to prayer, nor reading of the Scriptures nor attending God's house; but simply direct to faith, naked faith on God's gospel. Not that I despise prayer—that must come after faith. Not that I speak a word against the searching of the Scriptures—that is an infallible mark of God's children. Not that I find fault with attendance on God's word—God forbid! I love to see people there. But none of those things are the way of salvation. It is nowhere written—"He that attendeth chapel shall be saved," or, "He that readeth the Bible shall be saved." Nor do I read—"He that prayeth and is baptized shall be

saved;" but, "He that believeth,"—he that has a naked faith on the "Man Christ Jesus,"—on his Godhead, on his manhood, is delivered from sin. To preach that faith alone saves, is to preach God's truth. Nor will I for one moment concede to any man the name of a gospel minister, if he preaches anything as the plan of salvation except faith in Jesus Christ, faith, faith, nothing but faith in his name. But we are, most of us, very much muddled in our ideas. We get so much work stored into our brain, such an idea of merit and of doing, wrought into our hearts, that it is almost impossible for us to preach justification by faith clearly and fully; and when we do, our people won't receive it. We tell them, "Believe on the name of the Lord Jesus Christ and thou shalt be saved." But they have a notion that faith is something so wonderful, so mysterious, that it is quite impossible that without doing something else they can ever get it. Now, that faith which unites to the Lamb is an instantaneous gift of God, and he who believes on the Lord Jesus is that moment saved, without anything else whatsoever. Ah! my friends, do we not want more exalting Christ in our preaching, and more exalting Christ in our living? Poor Mary said, "They have taken away my Lord and I know not where they have laid him," And she might say so now-a-days if she could rise from the grave. Oh! to have a Christ-exalting ministry! Oh! to have preaching that magnifies Christ in his person, that extols his divinity, that loves his humanity; to have preaching that shows him as prophet, priest, and king to his people! to have preaching whereby the spirit manifests the Son of God unto his children: to have preaching that says, "Look unto him and be ye saved all the ends of the earth,"—Calvary preaching, Calvary theology, Calvary books, Calvary sermons! These are the things we want, and in proportion as we have Calvary exalted and Christ magnified, the gospel is preached in our midst.

3. The third answer to the question is: to preach the gospel is to give every class of character his due. "You are only to preach to God's dear people, if you go into that pulpit," said a deacon once to a minister. Said the minister, "Have you marked them all on the back, that I may know them?" What is the good of this large chapel if I am only to preach to God's dear people? They are few enough. God's dear people might be held in the vestry. We have many more here besides God's dear people, and how am I to be sure, if I am told to preach only to God's dear people, that somebody else wont take it to himself? At another time some one might say, "Now, be sure you preach to sinners. If you do not preach to sinners this morning, you won't preach the gospel. We shall only hear you once; and we shall be sure you are not right if you do not happen to preach to sinner this particular morning, in this particular sermon." What nonsense, my friends! There are times when the children must be fed, and there are times when the

sinner must be warned. There are different times for different objects. If a man is preaching to God's saints if it so happen that little is said to sinners, is he to be blamed for it, provided that at another time when he is not comforting the saints, he directs his attention specially to the ungodly? I heard a good remark from an intelligent friend of mine the other day. A person was finding fault with "Dr. Hawker's Morning and Evening Portions" because they were not calculated to convert sinners. He said to the gentleman, "Did you ever read; 'Grote's History of Greece?'" "Yes." Well, that is a shocking book, is it not? for it is not calculated to convert sinners. "Yes, but," said the other, "*Grote's History of Greece* was never meant to convert sinners." "No," said my friend, "and if you had read the preface to *Dr. Hawker's Morning and Evening Portion*, you would see that it was never meant to convert sinners, but to feed God's people, and if it answers its end the man has been wise, though he has not aimed at some other end." Every class of person is to have his due. He who preaches solely to saints at all times does not preach the gospel; he who preaches solely and only to the sinner; and never to the saint, does not preach the whole of the gospel. We have amalgamation here. We have the saint who is full of assurance and strong; we have the saint who is weak and low in faith; we have the young convert; we have the man halting between two opinions; we have the moral man; we have the sinner; we have the reprobate; we have the outcast. Let each have a word. Let each have a portion of meat in due season; not at every season, but in due season. He who omits one class of character does not know how to preach the entire gospel. What! Am I to be put into the pulpit and to be told that I am to confine myself to certain truths only, to comfort God's saints? I will not have it so. God gives men hearts to love their fellow-creatures, and are they to have no development for that heart? If I love the ungodly am I to have no means of speaking to them? May I not tell them of judgment to come, of righteousness, and of their sin? God forbid I should so stultify my nature and so brutalize myself, as to have a tearless eye when I consider the loss of my fellow creatures, and to stand and say "Ye are dead, I have nothing to say to you!" and to preach in effect if not in words that most damnable heresy, that if men are to be saved they will be saved—that if they are not to be saved they will not be saved; that necessarily, they must sit still and do nothing whatever; and that it matters not whether they live in sin or in righteousness—some strong fate has bound them down with adamantine chains; and their destiny is so certain that they may live on in sin. I believe their destiny is certain—that as elect, they will be saved, and if not elect they are damned forever. But I do not believe the heresy that follows as an inference that therefore men are irresponsible and may sit still. That is a heresy against which I have ever protested, as being a doctrine of the devil and not of God at all. We believe in destiny; we believe in predestination; we believe in election and non-election: but, notwithstanding that, we believe that we must preach to men, "Believe on the Lord Jesus Christ and ye shall be saved," but believe not on him and ye are damned.

4. I had thought of giving one more answer to this question, but time fails me. The answer would have been somewhat like this—that to preach the gospel is not to preach certain truths about the gospel, not to preach about the people, but to preach to the people. To preach the gospel is not to talk about what the gospel is, but to preach it into the heart, not by your own might, but by the influence of the Holy Ghost—not to stand and talk as if we were speaking to the angel Gabriel, and telling him certain things, but to speak as man to man and pour our heart in to our fellow's heart. This I take it, is to preach the gospel, and not to mumble some dry manuscript over on Sunday morning or Sunday evening. To preach the gospel is not to send a curate to do your duty for you; it is not to put on your fine gown and then stand and give out some lofty speculation. To preach the gospel is not, with the hands of a bishop, to turn over some beautiful specimen of prayer, and then to go down again and leave it to some humbler person to speak. Nay; to preach the gospel is to proclaim with trumpet tongue and flaming zeal the unsearchable riches of Christ Jesus, so that men may hear, and understanding, may turn to God with full purpose of heart. This is to preach the gospel.

II. The second question is—How IS IT THAT MINISTERS ARE NOT ALLOWED TO GLORY? "For though I preach the gospel I have nothing to glorify it." There are some weeds that will grow anywhere; and one of them is Pride. Pride will grow on a rock as well as in a garden. Pride will grow in the heart of a shoe-black as well as in the heart of an alderman. Pride will grow in the heart of a servant girl and equally as well in the heart of her mistress. And pride will grow in the pulpit. It is a weed that is dreadfully rampant. It wants cutting down every week, or else we should stand up to our knees in it. This pulpit is a shocking bad soil for pride. It grows terribly; and I scarcely know whether you ever find a preacher of the gospel who will not confess that he has the greatest temptation to pride. I suppose that even those ministers of whom nothing is said, but that they are very good people, and who have a City church, with some six people attending it, have a temptation to pride. But whether that is so or not, I am quite sure wherever there is a large assembly, and wherever a great deal of noise and stir is made concerning any man there is a great danger of pride. And, mark you, the more proud a man is the greater will be his fall at last. If people will hold a minister up in their hands and do not keep hold of him, but let him go, what a fall he will have, poor fellow, when it is all over. It has been so with many. Many men have been held up by the arms of men, they have been held up by the arms of praise, and not of prayer; these arms have become weak, and down they have fallen. I say there is temptation to pride in the pulpit; but there is no ground for it in the pulpit; there is no soil for pride to grow on; but it will grow without any. "I have nothing to glorify of." But, notwithstanding, there often comes in some reason why we should glory, not real, but apparent to our ownselves.

1. Now, how is it that a true minister feels he has "nothing to glorify of." First, because he is very conscious of his own imperfections. I think no man will ever form a more just opinion of himself than he who is called constantly and incessantly to preach. Some man once thought he could preach, and on being allowed to enter the pulpit, he found his words did not come quite so freely as he expected, and in the utmost trepidation and fear, he leaned over the front of the pulpit and said "My friends, if you would come up here, it would take the conceit out of you all, I verily believe it would out of a great many, could they once try themselves whether they could preach. It would take their critical conceit out of them, and make them think that after all it was not such easy work. He who preaches best feels that he preaches worst. He who has set up some lofty model in his own mind of what eloquence should be, and what earnest appeal ought to be, will know how much he falls below it. He, best of all, can reprove himself when he knows his own deficiency. I do not believe when a man does a thing well, that therefore he will glory in it. On the other hand, I think that he will be the best judge of his own imperfections, and will see them most clearly. He knows what he ought to be: other men do not. They stare, and gaze, and think it is wonderful, when he thinks it is wonderfully absurd and retires wondering that he has not done better. Every true minister will feel that he is deficient. He will compare himself with such men as Whitfield, with such preachers as those of puritanical times, and he will say, "What am I? Like a dwarf beside a giant, an ant-hill by the side of the mountain." When he retires to rest on Sabbath-night, he will toss from side to side on his bed, because he feels that he has missed the mark, that he has not had that earnestness, that solemnity, that death-like intenseness of purpose which became his position. He will accuse himself of not having dwelt enough on this point, or for having shunned the other, or not having been explicit enough on some certain subject, or expanded another too much. He will see his own faults, for God always chastises his own children at night-time when they have done something wrong. We need not others to reprove us; God himself

takes us in hand, The most highly honored before God will often feel himself dishonored in his own esteem.

2. Again, another means of causing us to cease from all glory is the fact that God reminds us that all our gifts are borrowed. And strikingly have I this morning been reminded of that great truth—that all our gifts are borrowed, by reading in a newspaper to the following effect:—

"Last week, the quiet neighborhood of New Town was much disturbed by an occurrence which has thrown a gloom over the entire neighborhood. A gentleman of considerable attainment, who has won an honorable degree at the university has for some months been deranged. He had kept an academy for young gentlemen, but his insanity had obliged him to desist from his occupation, and he has for some time lived alone in a house in the neighborhood. The landlord obtained a warrant of eviction; and it being found necessary to handcuff him, he was, by sad mismanagement, compelled to remain on the steps, exposed to the gaze of a great crowd, until at last a vehicle arrived, which conveyed him to the asylum. One of his pupils (says the paper) is Mr. Spurgeon."

The man from whom I learned whatever of human learning I have, has now become a raving lunatic in the Asylum! When I saw that, I felt I could bend my knee with humble gratitude and thank my God that not yet had my reason reeled, not yet had those powers departed. Oh! how thankful we ought to be that our talents are preserved to us, and that our mind is not gone! Nothing came nearer and closer to me than that. There was one who had taken all pains with me—a man of genius and of ability; and yet there he is! how fallen! how fallen! How speedily does human nature come from its high estate and sink below the level of the brutes? Bless God my friends, for your talents! thank him for your reason! thank him for your intellect! Simple as it may be, it is enough for you, and if you lost it you would soon mark the difference. Take heed to yourself lest in aught you say. "This is Babylon that I have builded;" for, remember, both trowel and mortar must come from him. The life, the voice, the talent, the imagination, the eloquence—all are the gift of God; and he who has the greatest gifts must feel that unto God belong the shield of the mighty, for he has given might to his people, and strength unto his servants.

3. One more answer to this question. Another means whereby God preserves his ministers from glorying is this: He makes them feel their constant dependence upon the Holy Ghost. Some do not feel it, I confess. Some will venture to preach without the Spirit of God, or without entreating it. But I think that no man, who is really commissioned from on high, will ever venture to do so, but he will feel that he needs the Spirit. Once, while preaching in Scotland, the Spirit

of God was pleased to desert me, I could not speak as usually I have done. I was obliged to tell the people that the chariot wheels were taken off; and that the chariot dragged very heavily along. I have felt the benefit of that ever since. It humbled me bitterly, for I could have crept into a nut-shell, and I would have hidden myself in any obscure corner of the earth. I felt as if I should speak no more in the name of the Lord, and then the thought came "Oh! thou art an ungrateful creature: hath not God spoken by thee hundreds of times? And this once, when he would not do so wilt thou upbraid him for it? Nay, rather thank him, that a hundred times he hath stood by thee; and, if once he hath forsaken thee, admire his goodness, that thus he would keep thee humble." Some may imagine that want of study brought me into that condition, but I can honestly affirm, that it was not so. I think that I am bound to give myself unto reading, and not tempt the Spirit by unthought-of effusions. Usually, I deem it a duty to seek a sermon of my Master and implore him to impress it on my mind, but on that occasion, I think I had even prepared more carefully then than I ordinarily do, so that unpreparedness was not the reason. The simple fact was this—"The wind bloweth where it listeth;" and winds do not always blow hurricanes. Sometimes the winds themselves are still. And, therefore, if I rest on the Spirit, I cannot expect I should always feel its power alike. What could I do without the celestial influence, for to that I owe everything. By this thought God humbles his servants. God will teach us how much we want it. He will not let us think we are doing anything ourselves. "Nay, says he, "thou shalt have none of the glory. I will take thee down. Art thou thinking 'I am doing this?' I will show thee what thou art without me "Out goes Samson. He attacks the Philistines. He fancies he can slay them; but they are on him. His eyes are out. His glory is gone, because he trusted not in his God, but rested in himself. Every minister will be made to feel his dependence upon the Spirit; and then will he, with emphasis, say, as Paul did, "If I preach the gospel, I have nothing to glorify of."

III. Now comes the third question, with which we are to finish WHAT IS THAT NECESSITY WHICH IS LAID UPON US TO PREACH THY GOSPEL?

1. First, a very great part of that necessity springs from the call itself: If a man be truly called of God to the ministry, I will defy him to withhold himself from it. A man who has really within him the inspiration of the Holy Ghost calling him to preach cannot help it. He must preach. As fire within the bones, so will that influence be until it blazes forth Friends may check him, foes criticize him, despisers sneer at him, the man is indomitable; he must preach if he has the call of heaven. All earth might forsake him; but he would preach to the barren

mountain-tops. If he has the call of heaven, if he has no congregation, he would preach to the rippling waterfalls, and let the brooks hear his voice. He could not be silent. He would become a voice crying in the wilderness, "Prepare ye the way of the Lord." I no more believe it possible to stop ministers, than to stop the stars of heaven. I think it no more possible to make a man cease from preaching, if he is really called, than to stop some mighty cataract, by seeking, with an infant's cup, to drink its waters. The man has been moved of heaven, who shall stop him? He has been touched of God, who shall impede him? With an eagle's wing he must fly; who shall chain him to the earth? With seraph's voice he must speak, who shall stop his lips? Is not his word like a fire within me? Must I not speak if God has placed it there? And when a man does speak as the Spirit gives him utterance, he will feel a holy joy akin to heaven; and when it is over he wishes to be at his work again, and longs to be once more preaching. I do not think young men are called of God to any great work who preach once a week, and think they have done their duty. I think if God has called a man, he will impel him to be more or less constantly at it, and he will feel that he must preach among the nations the unsearchable riches of Christ.

2. But another thing will make us preach: we shall feel that woe is unto us if we preach not the gospel; and that is the sad destitution of this poor fallen world. Oh, minister of the gospel! stand for one moment and bethink thyself of thy poor fellow creatures! See them like a stream, rushing to eternity—ten thousand to their endless home each solemn moment fly! See the termination of that stream, that tremendous cataract which dashes streams of souls into the pit! Oh, minister, bethink thyself that men are being damned each hour by thousands, and that each time thy pulse beats another soul lifts up its eyes in hell, being in torments; bethink thyself how men are speeding on their way to destruction, how "the love of many waxeth cold" and "iniquity doth abound." I say, is there not a necessity laid upon thee? Is it not woe unto thee if thou preachest not the gospel? Take thy walk one evening through the streets of London when the dusk has gathered, and darkness veils the people. Mark you not yon profligate hurrying on to her accursed work? See you not thousands and tens of thousands annually ruined? Up from the hospital and the asylum there comes a voice, "Woe is unto you if ye preach not the gospel." Go to that huge place built around with massive walls, enter the dungeons, and see the thieves who have for years spent their lives in sin. Wend your way sometimes to that sad square of Newgate, and see the murderer hanged. A voice shall come from each house of correction, from each prison, from each gallows, saying, "Woe is unto thee if thou preachest not the gospel." Go thou to the thousand death-beds, and mark how men are perishing

in ignorance, not knowing the ways of God. See their terror as they approach their Judge, never having known what it was to be saved, not even knowing the way; and as you see them quivering before their Maker, hear a voice, "Minister, woe is unto thee if thou preachest not the gospel." Or take another course. Travel round this great metropolis, and stop at the door of some place where there is heard the tinkling of bells, chanting and music, but where the whore of Babylon hath her sway, and lies are preached for truth; and when thou comest home and thinkest of Popery and Puseyism, let a voice come to thee, "Minister woe is unto thee if thou preachest not the gospel." Or step into the hall of the infidel where he blasphemes thy Maker's name; or sit in the theater where plays, libidinous and loose are acted, and from all these haunts of vice there comes the voice, "Minister, woe is unto thee if thou preachest not the gospel." And take thy last solemn walk down to the chambers of the lost; let the abyss of hell be visited, and stand thou and hear:

> "The sullen groans, the hollow moans,
> And shrieks of tortured ghosts."

Put thine ear at hell's gate, and for a little while list to the commingled screams and shrieks of agony and fell despair that shall lend thine ear; and as thou comest from that sad place with that doleful music still affrighting thee, thou wilt hear the voice, "Minister! minister! woe is unto thee if thou preaches not the gospel." Only let us have these things before our eyes, and we must preach. Stop preaching! Stop preaching! Let the sun stop shining, and we will preach in darkness. Let the waves stop their ebb and flow, and still our voice shall preach the gospel, let the world stop its revolutions, let the planets stay their motion; we will still preach the gospel. Until the fiery center of this earth shall burst through the thick ribs of her brazen mountains, we shall still preach the gospel; till the universal conflagration shall dissolve the earth, and matter shall be swept away, these lips, or the lips of some others called of God, shall still thunder forth the voice of Jehovah. We cannot help it. "Necessity is laid upon us, yea woe is unto us if we preach not the gospel.

Now, my dear hearers, one word with you. There are some persons in this audience who are verily guilty in the sight of God because they do not preach the gospel. I cannot think out of the fifteen hundred or two thousand persons now present, within the reach of my voice, there are none who are qualified to preach the gospel besides myself. I have not so bad an opinion of you as to conceive myself to be superior in intellect to one half of you, or even in the power of preaching God's Word: and even supposing I should be, I cannot believe that

I have such a congregation that there are not among you many who have gifts and talents that qualify you to preach the Word. Among the Scotch Baptists it is the custom to call upon all the brethren to exhort on the Sabbath morning; they have no regular minister to preach on that occasion, but every man preaches who likes to get up and speak. That is all very well, only, I fear, many unqualified brethren would be the greatest speakers, since it is a known fact, that men who have little to say will often keep on the longest; and if I were chairman, I should say, "Brother, it is written, 'Speak to edification.' I am sure you would not edify yourself and your wife, you had better go and try that first, and if you cannot succeed, don't waste our precious time."

But still I say, I cannot conceive but what there are some here this morning who are flowers "wasting their sweetness in the desert air, "gems of purest ray serene," lying in the dark caverns of ocean's oblivion. This is a very serious question. If there be any talent in the Church at Park Street, let it be developed. If there be any preachers in my congregation let them preach. Many ministers make it a point to check young men in this respect. There is my hand, such as it is, to help any one of you if you think you can tell to sinners round what a dear Savior you have found. I would like to find scores of preachers among you; would to God that all the Lord's servants were prophets. There are some here who ought to be prophets, only they are half afraid—well, we must devise some scheme of getting rid of their bashfullness. I cannot bear to think that while the devil sets all his servants to work there should be one servant of Jesus Christ asleep. Young man, go home and examine thyself, see what thy abilities are, and if thou findest that thou hast ability, then try in some poor humble room to tell to a dozen poor people what they must do to be saved. You need not aspire to become absolutely and solely dependent upon the ministry, but if it should please God, even desire it. He that desireth a bishopric desireth a good thing. At any rate seek in some way to be preaching the gospel of God. I have preached this sermon especially, because I want to commence a movement from this place which shall reach others. I want to find some in my church, if it be possible, who will preach the gospel. And mark you, if you have talent and power, woe is unto you if you preach not the gospel.

But oh! my friends, if it is woe unto us if we preach not the gospel, what is the woe unto you if ye hear and receive not the gospel? May God give us both to escape from that woe! May the gospel of God be unto us the savor of life unto life, and not of death unto death.

12

GOSPEL MISSIONS

Preached on April 27, 1856
Scripture: Acts 13:49
From: New Park Street Pulpit Volume 2

"And the word of the Lord was published throughout all the region."
—Acts 13:49

I shall not confine myself to the text. It being an old custom to take texts when we preach, I have taken one, but I shall address you, at large, upon a subject which I am sure will occupy your attention, and has done for many days and years past—the subject of gospel missions. We feel persuaded that all of you are of one mind in this matter, that it is the absolute duty as well as the eminent privilege of the Church to proclaim the gospel to the world. We do not conceive that God will do his own work without instruments, but that, as he has always employed means in the work of the regeneration of this world, he will still continue to do the same, and that it becomes the Church to do its utmost to spread the truth wherever it can reach the ear of man. We have not two opinions on that point. Some churches may have, but we have not. Our doctrines, although they are supposed to lead to apathy and sloth, have always proved themselves to be eminently practical; the fathers of the mission were all zealous lovers of the doctrines of the grace of God; and we believe, the great supporters of missionary enterprise, if it is to be successful, must always come from those who hold God's truth firmly and boldly, and yet have fire and zeal with it, and desire to spread it everywhere. But there is a point on which we have great division of opinion, and that is as to the reason why we have had so little success in our missionary labors. There may be some who say the success has been proportionate to the agency, and that we could not have been more successful. I am far from being of their opinion, and I do not think they themselves would express it on their knees before Almighty God. We have not been successful to the extent we might have expected, certainly not to an apostolic extent, certainly with nothing like the success of Paul or Peter, or even of those imminent men who have preceded us in modern times, and who were able to evangelize whole countries, turning thousands to God. Now, what is the reason of this? Perhaps we may turn our eyes on high, and think we find that reason in the sovereignty of God, which hath withholden his Spirit, and hath not poured out his grace as aforetime. I shall be prepared to grant all men may say on that point, for I believe in the ordination of everything by Almighty God. I believe in a present God in our defeats as well as in our successes; a God as well in the motionless air as in the careering tempest; a God of ebbs as well as a God of floods. But still we must look at home for the cause. When Zion travails, she brings forth children; when Zion is in earnest, God is in earnest about his work; when Zion is prayerful, God blesses her. We must not, therefore, arbitrarily look for the cause of our failure in the will of God, but we must also see what is the difference between ourselves and the men of Apostolic times, and what it is that renders our success so trifling in comparison with the tremendous results of Apostolic preaching. I think I shall be able to show one or two reasons why our holy faith is not so prosperous as it was then. In the first place, we have not Apostolic men; in the second place, they do not set about their work in an Apostolic style; in the third place, we have not Apostolic churches to back them up; and in the fourth place, we have not the Apostolic influence of the Holy Ghost. in the measure which they had it in ancient times.

I. First, WE HAVE FEW APOSTOLIC MEN IN THESE TIMES. I will not say we have none; here and there we may have one or two, but unhappily their names are never heard; they do not start out before the world, and are not noted as preachers of God's truth. We had a Williams once, a true apostle, who went from island to island, not counting his life dear unto him; but Williams is called to his reward. We had a Knibb, who toiled for his Master with seraphic earnestness, and was not ashamed to call an oppressed slave his brother; but Knibb, too, has entered into his rest. We have one or two still remaining, precious and treasured names; we love them fervently, and our prayers shall ever rise to heaven on their behalf. We always say, in our prayers, "God bless such men as Moffat! God bless those who are earnestly toiling and successfully laboring!" But cast your eyes around, and where can we find many such men? They are all good men; we find no fault with them; they are better than we; we, ourselves, shrink into nothingness compared with them; but we must still say of them that they are less than their fathers, they differ from the mighty Apostles in many respects, which we think even they would not be slow to own. I am not speaking of missionaries only, but of ministers too; for I take it we have as much to mourn over in regard to the spread of the gospel in England as in foreign lands, and much to regret the lack of men filled with the Holy Ghost and with fire.

In the first place, we have not men with Apostolic zeal. Converted in a most singular way, by a direct interposition from heaven, Paul, from that time forward became an earnest man. He had always been earnest, in his sin and in his persecutions; but after he heard that voice from heaven, "Saul, Saul, why persecutest thou me?" and had received the mighty office of an apostle, and had been sent forth a chosen vessel to the Gentiles, you can scarce conceive the deep, the awful earnestness which he manifested. Whether he did eat, or drink, or whatsoever he did, he did all for the glory of his God; he never wasted an hour; he was employing his time either in ministering with his own hands unto his necessities, or else lifting those hands in the Synagogue, on Mars-hill, or anywhere where he could command the attention of the multitude. His zeal was so earnest, and so burning, that he could not (as we unfortunately do) restrain himself within a little sphere; but he preached the Word everywhere. It was not enough for him to have it handed down that he was the Apostle of Pisidia, but he must go also to Pamphylia; it was not enough that he should be the great preacher of Pamphylia and Pisidia, but he must go also to Attalia; and when he had preached throughout all Asia, he must needs take ship to Greece, and preach there also. I believe not once only did Paul hear in his dream the men of Macedonia saying, "Come over and help us," but every day and hour he heard the cry in his ears from multitudes of souls, "Paul, Paul, come over and help us." He could not restrain himself from preaching. "Woe is unto me" he said "if I preach not the gospel. God forbid that I should glory save in the cross of Christ." Oh! if you could have seen Paul preach, you would not have gone away as you do from some of us, with half a conviction, that we do not mean what we say. His eyes preached a sermon without his lips, and his lips preached it, not in a cold and frigid manner, but every word fell with an overwhelming power upon the hearts of his hearers. He preached with power, because he was in downright earnest. You had a conviction, when you saw him, that he was a man who felt he had a work to do and must do it, and could not contain himself unless he did do it. He was the kind of preacher whom you would expect to see walk down the pulpit stairs straight into his coffin, and then stand before his God, ready for his last account. Where are the men like that man? I confess I cannot claim that privilege, and I seldom hear a solitary sermon which comes up to the mark in earnest, deep, passionate longing for the souls of men.

We have no eyes now like the eyes of the Savior, which could weep over Jerusalem; we have few voices like that earnest impassioned voice which seemed perpetually to cry, "Come unto me, and I will give you rest." "O Jerusalem, Jerusalem, how often would I have gathered thee as a hen gathereth her chickens under her wings, but ye would not." If ministers of the gospel were more hearty in their work of preaching; if, instead of giving lectures and devoting a large part of their time to literary and political pursuits, they would preach the Word of God, and preach it as if they were pleading for their own lives, ah! then, my brethren, we might expect great success; but we cannot expect it while we go about our work in a half-hearted way, and have not that zeal, that earnestness, that deep purpose which characterized those men of old.

Then, again, I take it we have not men in our days who can preach like Paul—as to their faith. What did Paul do? He went to Philippi; did he know a soul there? Not one. He had his Master's truth, and he believed in the power of it. He was unattended and devoid of pomp, or show, or parade; he did not go to a pulpit with a soft cushion in it to address a respectable congregation, but he walked through the streets and began to preach to the people. He went to Corinth, to Athens, alone, single-handed, to tell the people the gospel of the blessed God. Why? Because he had faith in the gospel and believed it would save souls, and hurl down idols from their thrones. He had no doubt about the power of the gospel; but now-a-days, my brethren, we have not faith in the gospel we preach. How many there are who preach gospel, which they are afraid will not save souls; and, therefore, they add little bits of their own to it in order, as they think, to win men to Christ! We have known men who believed Calvinistic doctrines, but who preached Calvinism in the morning and Arminianism in the evening, because they were afraid God's gospel would not convert sinners, so they would manufacture one of their own. I hold that a man who does not believe his gospel to be able to save men's souls, does not believe it all. If God's truth will not save men's souls, man's lies cannot; if God's truth will not turn men to repentance, I am sure there is nothing in this world that can. When we believe the gospel to be powerful, then we shall see it is powerful. If I walk into this pulpit, and say, "I know what I preach is true," the world says I am an egotist. "The young man is dogmatical." Ay, and the young man means to be; he glories in it, he keeps it to himself as one of his peculiar titles, for he does most firmly believe what he preaches. God forbid that I should ever come tottering up the pulpit stairs to teach anything I was not quite sure of, something which I hoped might save sinners, but of which I was not exactly certain. When I have faith in my doctrines, those doctrines will prevail, for confidence is the winner of the palm. He who hath courage enough to grasp the standard, and hold it up, will be sure enough to find followers. He who says, "I know," and asserts it boldly in his Master's name, without disputing, will not be long before he will find men who will listen to what he says, and who will say, "This man speaks with authority, and not as the Scribes and Pharisees." That is one reason why we do not succeed: we have not faith in the gospel. We send educated men to India in order to confound the learned Brahmins. Nonsense! Let the Brahmins say what they like, have we any business to dispute with them? "Oh, but they are so intellectual and so clever." What have we to do with that? We are not to seek to be clever in order to meet them. Leave the men of the world to combat their metaphysical errors; we have merely to say, "This is truth: he that believeth it shall be saved, and he that denieth it shall be damned." We have no right to come down from the high ground of divine authoritative testimony; and until we maintain that ground, and come out as we ought to do, girded with the belt of divinity—preaching not what may be true, but asserting that which God has most certainly revealed— we shall not see success. We want a deeper faith in our gospel; we want to be quite sure of what we preach. Brethren, I take it we have not the faith of our fathers. I feel myself a poor drivelling thing in point of faith. Why, methought sometimes I could believe anything; but now a little difficulty comes before me, I am timid, and I fear. It is when I preach with unbelief in my heart that I preach unsuccessfully; but when I preach with faith and can say, "I know my God has said, that in the self-same hour he will give me what I shall preach, and careless of man's esteem, I preach what I believe to be true," then it is that God owns faith and crowns it with his own crown.

Again: we have not enough self-denial, and that is one reason why we do not prosper. Far be it from me to say aught against the self-denial of those worthy brethren who have left their country to cross the stormy deep and preach the Word. We hold them to be men who are to be had in honor; but still I ask, where is the self-denial of the Apostles now-a-days? I think one of the greatest disgraces that ever was cast upon the church in these days was that last mission to Ireland. Men went over to Ireland, but like men who have valor's better part, brave bold men, they came back again, which is about all we can say of the matter. Why do they not go there again? Why, they say the Irish "hooted" at them. Now, don't you think you see Paul taking a microscope out of his pocket, and looking at the little man who should say to him, "I shall not go there to preach because the Irish hooted me?" "What!" he says, "is this a preacher? —what a small edition of a minister he must be, to be sure!" "Oh! but they threw stones at us; you have no idea how badly they treated us!" Just tell that to the Apostle Paul. I am sure you would be ashamed to do so. "Oh! but in some places the police interfered, and said that we should only create a riot." What would Paul have said to that? The police interfering! I did not know that we had any right to care about governments. Our business is to preach the Word, and if we must be put in the stocks there let us lie; there would come no hurt of it at last. "Oh! but they might have killed some of us." That is just it. Where is that zeal which counted not its life dear so that it might win Christ? I believe that the killing of a few of our ministers would have prospered Christianity. However we might mourn over it, and none more than myself, I say the murder of a dozen of them would have been no greater ground for grief than the slaughter of our men by hundreds in a successful fight for hearths and homes. I would count my own blood most profitably shed in so holy a struggle. How did the gospel prosper aforetime? Were there not some who laid down their lives for it; and did not others walk to victory over their slain bodies; and must it not be so now? If we are to start back because we are afraid of being killed, heaven knows when the gospel is to spread over the world—we do not. What have other missionaries done? Have they not braved death in its direst forms, and preached the Word amid countless dangers? My brethren, we say again, we find no fault, for we, ourselves, might err in the same manner; but we are sure we are therein not like Paul. He went to a place where they stoned him with stones, and dragged him out as dead. Did he say, "Now for the future I will not go where they will ill-treat me?" No, for he says, "Of the Jews five times received I forty stripes save one. Thrice was I beaten with rods, thrice I suffered shipwreck." I am sure we have not the self-denial of the Apostles. We are mere carpet-knights and Hyde-park-warriors. When I go to my own house and think how comfortable and happy I am, I say to myself, "How little I do for my Master! I am ashamed that I cannot deny myself for his truth, and go everywhere preaching his Word." I look with pity upon people who say "Do not preach so often; you will kill yourself." O my God! what would Paul have said to such a thing as that? "Take care of your constitution; you are rash; you are enthusiastic." When I compare myself with one of those men of old, I say, "Oh that men should be found calling themselves Christians, who seek to stop our work of faith and labor of love, for the sake of a little consideration about the 'constitution,' which gets all the stronger for the preaching of God's Word."

But I hear some one whispering, "You ought to make a little allowance." My dear friend, I make all allowance. I am not finding fault with those brethren; they are a good sort of people; we are "all honorable men;" but I will only say, that in comparison with Paul, we are less than nothing, and vanity; little insignificant Lilliputian creatures, who can hardly be seen in comparison with those gigantic men of old.

Ones of my hearers may perhaps hint that this is not the sole cause, and he observes, "I think you ought to make excuse, for ministers now cannot work miracles." Well, I have considered that too, and certainly it is a drawback, but, I take it, not a very great one; for if it had been, God would not have allowed it to exist. He gave that gift to the Church in its infancy, but now it needs it no longer. We mistake in attributing too much to miracles. What was one of them? Wherever the Apostles went they could speak the language of the people. Well, in the time it would have taken Paul to walk from here to Hindostan, we could learn Hindostani, and we can go over in a very little time by the means of travelling that are now provided: so that is no great gain there. Then, again, in order to make the gospel known amongst the people, it was necessary that miracles should be worked, so that every one might talk about it; but now there is a printing press to aid us. What I say today, within six months will be read across the Alleghanies; and so with other ministers, what they say and what they do can soon be printed off and distributed everywhere; so they have facilities for making themselves known which are not much behind the power of miracles. Again, we have a great advantage over the Apostles. Wherever they went they were persecuted, and sometimes put to death; but now, although occasionally we hear of the massacre of a missionary, the occurrence is rare enough. The slaughter of an Englishman anywhere would provoke a fleet of men-of-war to visit the offence with chastisement. The world respects an Englishman wherever he goes; he has the stamp of the great Caesar upon him; he is the true cosmopolite—the citizen of the world. That could not be said of the poor despised Jews. There might be some respect paid to Paul, for he was a Roman citizen, but there would be none paid to the rest. We cannot be put to death now without a noise being made. The murder of two or three ministers in Ireland would provoke a tumult through the country; the government would have to interpose, the orderly of the land would be up in arms, and then we might preach with an armed constabulary around us, and so go through the land, provoking the priests, startling antichrist, and driving superstition to its dens forever.

II. In the second place, WE DO NOT GO ABOUT OUR WORK IN AN APOSTOLIC STYLE. How is that? Why, in the first place, there is a general complaint that there is not enough preaching by ministers and missionaries. They sit down interpreting, establishing schools, and doing this, that, and the other. We have nothing to find fault with in this; but that is not the labor to which they should devote themselves; their office is preaching, and if they preached more, they might hope for more success. The missionary Chamberlain preached once at a certain place, and years afterwards disciples were found there from that one sermon. Williams preached wherever he went, and God blessed him; Moffat preached wherever he went, and his labors were owned. Now we have our churches, our printing-presses, about which a great deal of money is spent. This is doing good, but it is not doing the good. We are not using the means which God has ordained, and we cannot therefore expect to prosper. Some say there is too much preaching now-a-days, in England. Well, it is the tendency of the times to decry preaching, but it is "the foolishness of preaching" which is to change the world. It is not for men to say, "If you preached less, you might study more." Study is required well enough if you have a settled church; but the Apostles needed no study, I apprehend, but they stood up and delivered out the simple cardinal truths of religion, not taking one text, but going through the whole catalogue of truth. So I think, in itinerant evangelical labors, we are not bound to dwell on one subject, for then we need to study, but we shall find it profitable to deal out the whole truth wherever we go. Thus we should always find words to hand, and truths ever ready to teach the people.

In the next place I conceive that a great mistake has been made in not affirming the divinity of our mission, and standing fast by the truth, as being a revelation not to be proved by men, but to be believed; always holding out this, "He that believeth and is baptized shall be saved; he that believeth not shall be damned." I am often grieved when I read of our missionaries holding disputes with the Brahmins, and it is sometimes said that the missionary has beaten the Brahmin because he kept his temper, and so the gospel had gained great honor by the dispute. I take it that the gospel was lowered by the controversy. I think the missionary should say, "I am come to tell you something which the One God of heaven and earth hath said, and I tell you before I announce it, that if you believe it you shall be saved, and if not, you shall be damned. I am come to tell you that Jesus Christ, the Son of God, became flesh, to die for poor unworthy man, that through his mediation, and death, and suffering, the people of God might be delivered. Now, if you will listen to me you shall hear the word of God: if you do not, I shake the dust of my feet against you, and go somewhere else."

Look at the history of every imposture; it shows us that the claim of authority insures a degree of progress. How did Mahommed come to have so strong a religion in his time? He was all alone, and he went into the market-place and said, "I have received a revelation from heaven." It was a lie, but he persuaded men to believe it. People looked at his face; they saw that he looked upon them earnestly as believing what he said, and some five or six of them joined him. Did he prove what he said? Not he. "You must," he said, "believe what I say, or there is no Paradise for you." There is power in that kind of thing, and wherever he went his statement was believed, not on the ground of reasoning, but on his authority, which he declared to be from Allah; and in a century after he first proclaimed his imposture, a thousand sabres had flashed from a thousand sheaths, and his word had been proclaimed through Africa, Turkey, Asia, and even in Spain. The man claimed authority—he claimed divinity; therefore he had power. Take again the increase of Mormonism. What has been its strength? Simply this—the assertion of power from heaven. That claim is made, and the people believe it, and now they have missionaries in almost every country of the habitable globe, and the book of Mormon is translated into many languages. Though there never could be a delusion more transparent, or a counterfeit less skilful, and more lying upon the very surface, yet this simple pretension to power has been the means of carrying power with it. Now, my brethren, we have power; we are God's ministers; we preach God's truth; the great Judge of heaven and earth has told us the truth, and what have we to do to dispute with worms of the dust? Why should we tremble and fear them? Let us stand out and say, "We are the servants of the living God; we tell unto you what God has told us, and we warn you, if you reject our testimony, it shall be better for Tyre and Sidon in the day of judgment than for you." If the people cast that away we have done our work. We have nothing to do with making men believe; ours is to testify of Christ everywhere, to preach and to proclaim the gospel to all men.

But there is one passage in the Bible which seems to militate against what I have said, if the common translation be true—the passage which says that Paul "disputed in the school of one Tyrannus." But this is better rendered in English, he "dialogued in the school of one Tyrannous." Albert Barnes says, that "disputed is not a happy translation," for there is no such idea conveyed by the word. Jesus, when he preached, "dialogued." When the man came and said to him, "Master, what shall I do to inherit eternal life?" he "dialogued" with him. When another said unto him, "Speak, Lord, unto my brother, that he divide with me the inheritance," Christ did not dispute with him, but he "dialogued." His usual style was to address the people, and but rarely to dispute with men.

We might give up all the books that have been written in defense of Christianity if we would but preach Christ, if, instead of defending the outposts, we were to say, "God will take care of them," and were at once to make a sortie on the enemy; then by God's Holy Spirit we should carry everything before us. O, Church of God! believe thyself invincible, and thou art invincible; but stay to tremble, and fear, and thou art undone. Lift up thy head and say, "I am God's daughter; I am Christ's bride." Do not stop to prove it, but affirm it; march through the land, and kings and princes shall bow down before thee, because thou hast taken thine ancient prowess and assumed thine ancient glory.

I have one more remark to make here with regard to the style in which we go to work. I fear that we have not enough of the divine method of itinerancy. Paul was a great itinerant: he preached in one place, and there were twelve converted there; he made a church at once; he did not stop till he had five hundred; but when he had twelve, he went off to another place. A holy woman takes him in; she has a son and daughter; they are saved and baptized—there is another church. Then he goes on; wherever he goes the people believe and are baptized, wherever he meets a family who believe, he or his companion baptizes all the house, and goes about his way still forming churches and appointing elders over them. We, now-a-days, go and settle in a place, make a station of it, and work around it by little and little, and think that is the way to succeed. No, no! ravage a continent; attempt great things and great things shall be done. But they say if you just pass over a place it will be forgotten like the summer shower, which moistens all, but satisfies none. Yes, but you do not know how many of God's elect may be there; you have no business to stop in one place; go straight on; God's elect are everywhere. I protest if I could not itinerate this country of England, I could not bear to preach. If I preached here always, many of you would become gospel hardened. I love to go ranging here, there, and everywhere. My highest ambition is this, that I may be found going through the entire land, as well as holding my head quarters in one position. I do hold that itinerancy is God's great plan. There should be fixed ministers and pastors, but those who are like apostles should itinerate far more than they do.

III. But I have a third thing to say which will strike home to some of us: that is, that WE HAVE NOT APOSTOLIC CHURCHES. Oh! had you seen an Apostolic church, what a different thing it would appear to one of our churches! as different, I had almost said, as light from darkness, as different as the shallow bed of the brook that is dried by summer is from the mighty rolling river, ever full, ever deep and clear, and ever rushing into the sea. Now, where is our prayerfulness compared with theirs? I trust that we know something of the power of prayer here, but I do not think we pray like they did. "They broke bread from house to house, and did eat their meat with singleness of heart, giving glory to God." There was not a member of the Church, as a rule, who was half-hearted; they gave their souls wholly to God; and when Ananias and Sapphira divided the price, they were smitten with death for their sin. Oh! if we prayed as deeply and as earnestly as they did, we should have as much success. Any measure of success we may have had here has been entirely owing under God to your prayers; and wherever I have gone, I have boasted that I have a praying people. Let other ministers have as prayerful a people; let missionaries have as many prayers from the Church, and, all things being equal, God will bless them, and there will be greater prosperity than ever.

We have not the Apostolic mode of liberality. In the Apostles' days they gave all their substance. It was not demanded of them then, and it is not now, no one thinks of asking such a thing; still we have run to the other extreme, and many give nothing at all. Men who have thousands and tens of thousands are so eternally considerate for their families, albeit they are provided for, that they give nothing more than the servant girl who sits next to them. It is a common saying, that members of Christian Churches do not give in proportion to their wealth. We give because it is genteel and respectable. A great many of us give I hope, because we love the cause of God; but many of us say, "There is a poor bricklayer, working hard all the week and only earning just enough to keep his wife and family: he will give a shilling; now, I have so many pounds a week—I am a rich man—what shall I give? why, I will give half-a-crown." Another says, "I will give ten shillings this morning." Now, if they measured their wealth in comparison with his, they would see that he gives all he has left above his maintenance, while they give comparatively nothing. My brethren, we are not half Christians; that is the reason why we have not half success. We are Christianized, but I question whether we are thoroughly so. The Spirit of God hath not entered into us to give us that life, and fire, and soul, which they had in these ancient times.

IV. But lastly, as the result of the other things which have gone before, and perhaps partly as the cause of them too, WE HAVE NOT THE HOLY SPIRIT IN THAT MEASURE WHICH ATTENDED THE APOSTLES. I see no reason whatever, why, this morning, if God willed it, I should not stand up and preach a sermon which should be the means of converting every soul in the place. I see no reason why I should not, tomorrow, preach a sermon which should be the means of the salvation of all who heard it, if God the Spirit were poured out. The word is able to convert, just as extensively as God the Spirit pleases to apply it; and I can see no reason why, if converts come in by ones and twos now, there should not be a time when hundreds and thousands shall come to God. The same sermon which God blesses to ten if he pleased he could bless to a hundred. I know not but that in the latter days when Christ shall come and shall begin to take the kingdom to himself, every minister of God shall be as successful as Peter on the day of Pentecost. I am sure the Holy Spirit is able to make the word successful, and the reason why we do not prosper is that we have not the Holy Spirit attending us with might and energy as they had then. My brethren, if we had the Holy Spirit upon our ministry, it would signify very little about our talent. Men might be poor and uneducated; their words might be broken and ungrammatical; there might be no polished periods of Hall, or glorious thunders of Chalmers; but if there were the might of the Spirit attending them, the humblest evangelists would be more successful than the most pompous of divines, or the most eloquent of preachers. It is extraordinary grace, not talent, that wins the day; extraordinary spiritual power, not extraordinary mental power. Mental power may fill a chapel; but spiritual power fills the Church. Mental power may gather a congregation; spiritual power will save souls. We want spiritual power. Oh! we know some before whom we shrink into nothing as to talent, but who have no spiritual power, and when they speak they have not the Holy Spirit with them; but we know others, simple hearted worthy men who speak their country dialect, and who stand up to preach in their country place, and the Spirit of God clothes every word with power; hearts are broken, souls are saved, and sinners are born again. Spirit of the living God! we want thee. Thou art the life, the soul; thou art the source of thy people's success; without thee they can do nothing, with thee they can do everything.

Thus I have tried to show you what I conceive to be the causes of our partial non-success. And now permit me, with all earnestness, to plead with you on behalf of Christ and Christ's Holy Gospel, that you would stir yourselves up to renewed efforts for the spread of his truth, and to more earnest prayers, that his kingdom may come, and his will be done on earth even as it is in heaven. Ah! my friends, could I show you the tens of thousands of spirits who are now walking in outer darkness; could I take you to the gloomy chamber of hell, and show you myriads upon myriads of heathen souls in unutterable torture, not having heard the word, but being justly condemned for their sins; methinks you could ask yourselves, "Did I do anything to save these unhappy myriads? They have been damned, and can I say I am clear of their blood?" Oh! God of mercy, if these skirts be clear of my fellow creatures' blood, I shall have eternal reason to bless thee in heaven. Oh! Church of Christ! thou hast great reason to ask thyself whether thou art quite clean in this matter. Ye say too often, ye sons of God, "Am I my brother's keeper?" Ye are too much like Cain; ye do not ask yourselves whether God will require your fellow-creatures blood at your hands. Oh! there is a truth which says, "If the watchman warn them not, they shall perish, but their blood will he require at the watchman's hands." Ah! there ought to be more of us who are preaching to the heathen, and yet, perhaps, we are indolent and doing little or nothing. There are many of you, yea all of you, who ought to be doing far more than you are for evangelical purposes and the spread of Christ's gospel. Oh! put this question to your hearts; shall I be able to say to the damned spirit if he meets me in hell, "Sinner, I did all I could for thee?" I am afraid some will have to say, "No, I did not; it is true I might have done more; I might have labored more, even though I might have been unsuccessful, but I did not do it." AH, my dear friends, I believe there is a great reason for some of us to suspect whether we believe our religion at all. An infidel once met a Christian. "Because," said the other, "for years you have passed me on my way to my house of business. You believe, do you not, there is a hell, into which men's spirit are cast?" "Yes, I do," said the Christian. "And you believe that unless I believe in Christ I must be sent there?" "Yes." "You do not, I am sure, because if you did you must be a most inhuman wretch to pass me, day by day, and never tell me about it or warn me of it." I do hold that there are some Christians who are verily guilty in this matter; God will forgive them, the blood of Christ can even wash that out, but they are guilty. Did you ever think of the tremendous value of a single soul. My hearers, if there were but one man in Siberia unsaved, and all the world were saved besides, if God should move our minds, it would be worth while for all the people in England to go after that one soul. Did you ever think of the value of a soul? Ah! ye have not heart the howls and yells of hell; ye have not heard the mighty songs and hosannas of the glorified; ye have no notion of what eternity is, or else ye would know the value of a soul. Ye who have been broken by conviction, humbled by the Spirit, and led to cry for mercy through the covenant Jesus; ye know something of what a soul's value is, but many of my hearers do not. Could we preach carelessly, could we pray coldly, if we knew what a precious thing it is about which we are concerned? No, surely we should be doubly in earnest that God will please to save sinners. I am sure the present state of affairs cannot go on long; we are doing next to nothing; Christianity is at a low ebb. People think it will never be much better; that it is clear impossible to do wonders in these days. Are we in a worse condition than the Roman Catholic nations were when one man, a Luther, preached? Then God can find a Luther now. We are not in a much worse state than when Whitfield began to preach, and yet God can find his Whitfields now. It is a delusion to suppose that we cannot succeed as they did. God helping us we will; God helping us by his Spirit we will see greater things than this, at any rate, we will never let God's Church rest if we do not see it prosper, but we will enter our earnest hearty protest against the coldness and lethargy of the times, and as long as this our tongue shall move in our mouth, we will protest against the laxity and false doctrine so rampant throughout the Churches, and then that happy double reformation—a reformation in doctrine and Spirit, will be brought about together. Then God knoweth but what we shall say, "Who are these that fly as a cloud, and as the doves to their windows," and ere long the shout of Christ shall be heard. He, himself, shall descend from heaven; and we shall hear it said and sung, "Alleluia! Alleluia! Alleluia! the Lord God Omnipotent reigneth."

13

THE DOCTRINES OF A GRACIOUS GOSPEL

The following messages, encompass five key doctrines that undergird God's gracious Gospel—also known as the Doctrines of Grace. These are basic tenets of Calvinism and were considered synonymous with The Gospel *by Spurgeon; so much so that The Prince of Gospel Preachers chose to judiciously invite several fellow ministers to expound upon these doctrines on the auspicious occasion of the ceremony at the Metropolitan Tabernacle officially inaugurating its opening after all the construction was completed. Preached on April 11, 1861, they form a timeless exposition of the principles that define and inform The Gospel.*

(Note: The Acronym T.U.L.I.P. is commonly used to delineate these five doctrines but they are each also known by various other monikers. You'll find next to each in the following chapter the name that corresponds to the TULIP acronym is included in paranthesis.)

From: Metropolitan Tabernacle Pulpit Volume 7

The proceedings were commenced by singing the 21st Hymn,

Saved from the damning power of sin,
The law's tremendous curse,
We'll now the sacred song begin
Where God began with us.

We'll sing the vast unmeasured grace
Which, from the days of old,
Did all his chosen sons embrace,
As sheep within the fold.

> *The basis of eternal love*
> *Shall mercy's frame sustain;*
> *Earth, hell, or sin, the same to move*
> *Shall all conspire in vain.*
>
> *Sing, O ye sinners bought with blood,*
> *Hail the Great Three in One;*
> *Tell how secure the cov'nant stood*
> *Ere time its race begun.*
>
> *Ne'er had ye felt the guilt of sin,*
> *Nor sweets of pard'ning love,*
> *Unless your worthless names had been*
> *Enroll'd to life above.*
>
> *O what a sweet exalted son*
> *Shall rend the vaulted skies,*
> *When, shouting, grace, the blood-wash'd throng*
> *Shall see the Top Stone rise.*

The Rev. George Wyard, of Deptford, began by leading in a commencement prayer. The Rev. C. H. Spurgeon in opening the proceedings said, we have met together beneath this roof already to set forth most of those truths in which consists the peculiarity of this Church. Last evening we endeavored to show to the world, that we heartily recognized the essential union of the Church of the Lord Jesus Christ. And now, this afternoon and evening, it is our intention, through the lips of our brethren, to set forth those things which are verily received among us, and especially those great points which have been so often attacked, but which are still upheld and maintained,—truths which we have proved in our experience to be full of grace and truth. My only business upon this occasion is to introduce the brethren who shall address you, and I shall do so as briefly as possible, making what I shall say a preface to their remarks.

The controversy which has been carried on between the Calvinist and the Arminian is exceedingly important, but it does not so involve the vital point of personal godliness as to make eternal life depend upon our holding either system of theology. Between the Protestant and the Papist there is a controversy of such a character, that he who is saved on the one side by faith in Jesus, dare not allow that his opponent on the opposite side can be saved while depending on his own works. There the controversy is for life or death, because it hinges mainly upon the doctrine of justification by faith, which Luther so properly called the *test doctrine*, by which a Church either stands or falls. The controversy again between the believer in Christ and the Socinian, is one which affects a vital point. If the Socinian be right, we are most frightfully in error; we are, in fact, idolaters, and how dwelleth eternal life in us? and if we be right, our largest charity will not permit us to imagine that a man can enter heaven who does not believe the real divinity of the Lord Jesus Christ. There are other controversies which thus cut at the very core, and touch the very essence of the whole subject. But, I think we are free to admit, that while John Wesley, for instance, in modern times zealously defended Arminianism, and on the other hand, George Whitfield with equal fervor fought for Calvinism, we should not be prepared either of us, on either side of the question, to deny the vital godliness of either the one or the other. We cannot shut our eyes to what we believe to be the gross mistakes of our opponents, and should think ourselves unworthy of the name of honest men, if we could admit that they are right in all things and ourselves right too. An honest man has an intellect which does not permit him to believe that "yes" and "no" can both subsist at the same hour and both be true. I cannot say, "It is," and my brother point blank say, "It is not," and yet both of us be right on that point. We are willing to admit, in fact, we dare not do otherwise, that opinion upon this controversy does not determine the future of even the present state of any man; but still, we think it to be so important, that in maintaining our views, we advance with all courage and fervency if spirit, believing that we are doing God's work and upholding most important truth. It may not be misunderstood, we only use the term for shortness. That doctrine which is called "Calvinism" did not spring from Calvin; we believe that it sprang from the great founder of all truth. Perhaps Calvin himself derived it mainly from the writings of Augustine. Augustine obtained his views, without doubt, through the Spirit of God, from the diligent study of the writings of Paul, and Paul received them of the Holy Ghost, from Jesus Christ the great founder of the Christian dispensation. We use the term then, not because we impute any extraordinary importance to Calvin's having taught these doctrines. We would be just as willing to call them by any other name, if we could find one which would be better understood, and which on the whole would be as consistent with fact. And then again, this afternoon, we shall have very likely to speak of Arminians, and by that, we would not for a moment insinuate that all who are in membership with the Arminian body, hold those particular views. There are Calvinists in connection with Calvinistic Churches, who are not Calvinistic, bearing the name but discarding the system. There are, on the other hand, not a few in the Methodist Churches, who, in most points perfectly agree with us, and I believe that if the matter came to be thoroughly sifted, it would be found that we are more agreed in our private opinions than in our public confessions, and our devotional religion is more uniform than our theology. For instance, Mr. Wesley's hymn-book, which may be looked upon as being the standard of his divinity, has in it upon some topics higher Calvinism than many books used by ourselves. I have been exceedingly struck with the very forcible expressions there used, some of which I might have hesitated to employ myself. I shall ask your attention while I quote verses from the hymns of Mr. Wesley, which we can all endorse as fully and plainly in harmony with the doctrines of grace, far more so than the preaching of some modern Calvinists. I do this because our low-doctrine Baptists and Morisonians ought to be aware of the vast difference between themselves and the Evangelical Arminians.

[HYMN 131, verses 1, 2, 3]

"Lord, I despair myself to heal:
I see my sin, but cannot feel;
I cannot, till thy Spirit blow,
And bid the obedient waters flow.

'Tis thine a heart of flesh to give;
Thy gifts I only can receive:
Here, then, to thee I all resign;
To draw, redeem, and seal,—is thine.

With simple faith on thee I call,
My Light, my Life, my Lord, my all:
I wait the moving of the pool;
I wait the word that speaks me whole."

[HYMN 133, verse 4]

"Thy golden sceptre from above
Reach forth; lo! my whole heart I bow;
Say to my soul, Thou art my love;
My chosen midst ten thousand, thou."

This is very like election.

[HYMN 136, verses 8, 9, 10]

"I cannot rest, till in thy blood
I full redemption have:
But thou, through whom I come to God,
Canst to the utmost save.

From sin, the guilt, the power, the pain,
Thou wilt redeem my soul:
Lord, I believe, and not in vain;
My faith shall make me whole.

I too, with thee, shall walk in white;
With all thy saints shall prove,
What is the length, and breadth, and height,
And depth of perfect love."

Brethren, is not this somewhat like final perseverance? and what is meant by the next quotation, if people of God can perish at all?

[HYMN 138, verses 6, 7]

"Who, who shall in thy presence stand,
And match Omnipotence?
Ungrasp the hold of thy right hand,
Or pluck the sinner thence?

Sworn to destroy, let earth assail;
Nearer to save thou art:
Stronger than all the powers of hell,
And greater than my heart."

The following is remarkably strong, especially in the expression "force." I give it in full:—

[HYMN 158]

"O my God, what must I do?
Thou alone the way canst show;
Thou canst save me in this hour;
I have neither will nor power:
God, if over all thou art,
Greater than my sinful heart,
All thy power on me be shown,
Take away the heart of stone.

Take away my darling sin,
Make me willing to be clean;
Make me willing to receive
All thy goodness waits to give.
Force me, Lord, with all to part;
Tear these idols from my heart;
Now thy love almighty show,
Make even me a creature new.

Jesus, mighty to renew,
Work in me to will and do;
Turn my nature's rapid tide,
Stem the torrent of my pride;
Stop the whirlwind of my will;
Speak, and bid the sun stand still;
Now thy love almighty show,
Make even me a creature new.

Arm of God, thy strength put on;
Bow the heavens, and come down;
All my unbelief o'erthrow;
Lay th' aspiring mountain low:
Conquer thy worst foe in me,
Get thyself the victory;
Save the vilest of the race;
Force me to be saved by grace."

[HYMN 206, verses 1, 2]

"What am I, O thou glorious God!
And what my father's house to thee,
That thou such mercies hast bestow'd
On me, the vilest reptile, me!
I take the blessing from above,
And wonder at the boundless love.

Me in my blood the love pass'd by,
And stopp'd, my ruin to retrieve;
Wept o'er my soul thy pitying eye;
Thy bowels yearn'd, and sounded, "Live!"
Dying, I heard the welcome sound,
And pardon in thy mercy found."

Nor are these all, for such good things as these abound, and they constrain me to say, that in attacking Arminianism we have no hostility towards the men who bear the name rather than the nature of that error, and we are opposed not to any body of men, but to the notions which they have espoused.

And now, having made these remarks upon terms used, we must observe that there is nothing upon which men need to be more instructed than upon the question of what Calvinism really is. The most infamous allegations have been brought against us, and sometime, I must fear, by men who knew them to be utterly untrue; and, to this day, there are many of our opponents, who, when they run short of matter, invent and make for themselves a man of straw, call that John Calvin, and then shoot all their arrows at it. We are not come here to defend your man of straw—shoot at it or burn it as you will, and, if it suit your convenience, still oppose doctrines which were never taught, and rail at fictions which, save in your own brain, were never in existence. We come here to state what our views really are, and we trust that any who do not agree with us will do us the justice of not misrepresenting us. If they can disprove our doctrines, let them state them fairly and then overthrow them, but why should they first caricature our opinions and then afterwards attempt to put them down? Among the gross falsehoods which have been uttered against the Calvinists proper, is the wicked calumny that we hold the damnation of little infants. A baser lie was never uttered. There may have existed somewhere, in some corner of the earth, a miscreant who would dare to say that there were infants in hell, but I have never met with him, nor have I met with a man who ever saw such a person. We say, with regard to infants, Scripture saith but little, and, therefore, where Scripture is confessedly scant, it is for no man to determine dogmatically. But I think I speak for the entire body, or certainly with exceedingly few exceptions, and those unknown to me, when I say, we hold that all infants are elect of God and are therefore saved, and we look to this as being the means by which Christ shall see of the travail of his soul to a great degree, and we do sometimes hope that thus the multitude of the saved shall be made to exceed the multitude of the lost. Whatever views our friends may hold upon the point, they are not necessarily connected with Calvinistic doctrine. I believe that the Lord Jesus, who said, "Of such is the kingdom of heaven," doth daily and constantly receive into his loving arms those tender ones who are only shown, and then snatched away to heaven. Our hymns are no ill witness to our faith on this point, and one of them runs thus:

> *"Millions of infant souls compose*
> *The family above."*

"Toplady, one of the keenest of Calvinists, was of this number. "In my remarks," says he, "on Dr. Nowell, I testified my firm belief that the souls of all departed infants are with God in glory; that in the decree of predestination to life, God hath included all whom he decreed to take away in infancy, and that the decree of reprobation hath nothing to do with them." Nay, he proceeds farther, and asks, with reason, how the anti-Calvinistic system of conditional salvation and election, or good works foreseen, will suit with the salvation of infants? It is plain that Arminians and Pelagians must introduce a new principle of election; and in so far as the salvation of infants is concerned, become Calvinists. Is it not an argument in behalf of Calvinism, that its principle is uniform throughout, and that no change is needed on the ground on which man is saved, whether young or old? John Newton, of London, the friend of Cowper, noted for his Calvinism, holds that the children in heaven exceed its adult inhabitants in all their multitudinous array. Gill, a very champion of Calvinism, held the doctrine, that all dying in infancy are saved. An intelligent modern writer, (Dr. Russell, of Dundee,) also a Calvinist, maintains the same views; and when it is considered that nearly one-half of the human race die in early years, it is easy to see what a vast accession must be daily and hourly making to the blessed population of heaven."

A more common charge, brought by more decent people,—for I must say that the last charge is never brought, except by disreputable persons,—a more common charge is, that we hold clear fatalism. Now, there may be Calvinists who are fatalists, but Calvinism and fatalism are two distinct things. Do not most Christians hold the doctrine of the providence of God? Do not all Christians, do not all believers in a God hold the doctrine of his foreknowledge? All the difficulties which are laid against the doctrine of predestination might, with equal force, be laid against that of Divine foreknowledge. We believe that God hath predestinated all things from the beginning, but there is a difference between the predestination of an intelligent, all-wise, all-bounteous God, and that blind fatalism which simple says, "It is because it is to be." Between the predestination of Scripture and the fate of the Koran, every sensible man must perceive a difference of the most essential character. We do not deny that the thing is so ordained that it must be, but why is it to be, but that the Father, God, whose name is love, ordained it; not because of any necessity in circumstances that such and such a thing should take place. Though the wheels of providence revolve with rigid exactness, yet not without purpose and wisdom. The wheels are full of eyes, and everything ordained is so ordained that it shall conduce to the grandest of all ends, the glory of God, and the next to that the good of his creatures. But we are next met by some who tell us that we preach the wicked and horrible doctrine of sovereign and unmerited reprobation. "Oh," say they, "you teach that men are damned because God made them to be damned, and that they go to hell, not because of sin, not because of unbelief, but because of some dark decree with which God has stamped their destiny." Brethren, this is an unfair charge again. Election does not involve reprobation. There may be some who hold unconditional reprobation. I stand not here as their defender, let them defend themselves as best they can; I hold God's election, but I testify just as clearly that if any man be lost he is lost for sin; and this has been the uniform statement of Calvinistic ministers. I might refer you to our standards, such as "The Westminster Assembly's Catechism," and to all our Confession, for they all distinctly state that man is lost for sin, and that there is no punishment put on any man except that which he richly and righteously deserves. If any of you have ever uttered that libel against us, do it not again, for we are as guiltless of that as you are yourselves. I am speaking personally—and I think in this I would command the suffrages of my brethren—I do know that the appointment of God extendeth to all things; but I stand not in this pulpit, nor in any other, to lay the damnation of any man anywhere but upon himself. If he be lost, damnation is all of man; but, if he be saved, still salvation is all of God. To state this important point yet more clearly and explicitly, I shall quote at large from an able Presbyterian divine:

"The pious Methodist is taught that the Calvinist represents God as creating men in order to destroy them. He is taught that Calvinists hold that men are lost, not because they sin, but because they are non-elected. Believing this to be a true statement, it is not wonderful that the Methodist stops short, and declares himself, if not an Arminian, at least an Anti-Predestinarian. But no statement can be more scandalously untrue. It is the uniform doctrine of Calvinism, that God creates all for his own glory; that he is infinitely righteous and benignant, and that where men perish it is only for their sins.

In speaking of suffering, whether in this world or in the world to come; whether it respects angels or men, the Westminster standards (which may be considered as the most authoritative modern statement of the system) invariably connect the punishment with previous sin, and sin only. "As for those wicked and ungodly men whom God as a righteous judge FOR FORMER SINS doth blind and harden, from them he not only withholdeth his grace, whereby they might have been enlightened in their understandings and wrought upon in their hearts, but sometimes also with draweth the gifts which they had, and exposeth them to such objects as their corruption makes occasion of sin; and withal gives them over to their own lusts, the temptations of the world, and the power of Satan, whereby it comes to pass that they harden themselves even under those means which God useth for the softening of others." The Larger Catechism, speaking of the unsaved among angels and men, says, "God according to his Sovereign power and the unsearchable counsel of his own will (whereby he extendeth or withholdeth favor as he pleaseth) hath passed by and fore-ordained the rest to dishonor and wrath, to be for their sin inflicted, to the praise of the glory of his justice." Again, "the end of God appointing this day (of the last judgment) is for the manifestation of the glory of his mercy, in the eternal salvation of the elect, and of his justice in the damnation of the reprobate who are wicked and disobedient." This is no more than what the Methodist and all other Evangelical bodies acknowledge—that where men perish it is in consequence of their sin. If it be asked, why sin which destroys, is permitted to enter the world, that is a question which bears not only on the Calvinist, but equally on all other parties. They are as much concerned and bound to answer it as he; nay, the question in not confined to Christians. All who believe in the existence of God—in his righteous character and perfect providence, are equally under obligation to answer it. Whatever may be the reply of others, that of the Calvinist may be regarded as given in the statement of the Confession of Faith, which declares that God's providence extendeth itself even to the first fall, and other sins of angels and men, &c.; "yet so as the sinfulness thereof proceedeth only from the creature, and not from God, who, being most holy and righteous, neither is nor can be the author or approver of sin." It is difficult to see what more could be said upon the subject; and if such be the undoubted sentiments of Calvinists, then what misrepresentation can be more gross than that which describes them as holding that sinners perish irrespective of their sin, or that God is the author of their sin? What is the declaration of Calvin? "Every soul departs (at death) to that place which it has prepared for itself while in this world."

It is hard to be charged with holding as sacred truth what one abhors as horrid blasphemy, and yet this is the treatment which has been perseveringly meted out to Calvinists in spite of the most solemn and indignant disclaimers. Against nothing have they more stoutly protested than the thought that the infinitely holy, and righteous, and amiable Jehovah is the author of sin; and yet how often do the supporters of rival systems charge them with this as an article of faith?

A yet further charge against us is, that we dare not preach the gospel to the unregenerate, that, in fact, our theology is so narrow and cramped that we cannot preach to sinners. Gentlemen, if you dare to say this, I would take you to any library in the world where the old Puritan fathers are stored up, and I would let you take down any one volume and tell me if you ever read more telling exhortations and addresses to sinners in any of your own books. Did not Bunyan plead with sinners, and whoever classed him with any but the Calvinist? Did not Charnock, Goodwin, and Howe agonize for souls, and what were they but Calvinist? Did not Jonathan Edwards preach to sinners, and who more clear and explicit on these doctrinal matters. The works of our innumerable divines teem with passionate appeals to the unconverted. Oh, sirs, if I should begin the list, time should fail me. It is an indisputable fact that we have labored more than they all for the winning of souls. Was George Whitfield any the less seraphic? Did his eyes weep the fewer tears or his bowels move with the less compassion because he believed in God's electing love and preached the sovereignty of the Most High? It is an unfounded calumny. Our souls are not stony; our bowels are not withdrawn the compassion which we ought to feel for our fellowmen; we can hold all our views firmly, and yet can weep as Christ did over a Jerusalem which was certainly to be destroyed. Again, I must say, I am not defending certain brethren who have exaggerated Calvinism. I speak of Calvinism proper, not that which has run to seed, and outgrown its beauty and verdure. I speak of it as I find it in Calvin's Institutes, and especially in his Expositions. I have read them carefully. I take not my views of Calvinism from common repute but from his books. Nor do I, in this speaking, even vindicate Calvinism as if I cared for the name, but I mean that glorious system which teaches that salvation is of grace from first to last. And again, then, I say it is an utterly unfounded charge that we dare not preach to sinners.

And then further, that I may clear up these points and leave the less rubbish for my brethren to wheel away, we have sometimes heard it said, but those who say it ought to go to school to read the first book of history, that we who hold Calvinistic views are the enemies of revivals. Why, sirs, in the history of the Church, with but few exceptions, you could not find a revival at all that was not produced by the orthodox faith. What was the great work which was done by Augustine, when the Church suddenly woke up from the pestiferous and deadly sleep into which Pelagian doctrine had cast it? What was the Reformation itself but the waking up of men's minds to those old truths? However far modern Lutherans may have turned aside from their ancient doctrines, and I must confess some of them would not agree with what I now say, yet, at any rate, Luther and Calvin had no dispute about Predestination. Their views were identical, and Luther, *On the Bondage of the Will*, is as strong a book upon the free grace of God as Calvin himself could have written. Hear that great thunderer while he cries in that book, "Let the Christian reader know then, that God foresees nothing in a contingent manner; but that he foresees, proposes, and acts, from his eternal and unchangeable will. This is the thunder stroke which breaks and overturns Free Will." Need I mention to you better names than Huss, Jerome of Prague, Farrel, John Knox, Wickliffe, Wishart, and Bradford? Need I do more than say that these held the same views, and that in their day anything like an Arminian revival was utterly unheard of and undreamed of. And then, to come to more modern times, there is the great exception, that wondrous revival under Mr. Wesley, in which the Wesleyan Methodists had so large a share; but permit me to say, that the strength of the doctrine of Wesleyan Methodism lay in its Calvinism. The great body of the Methodists disclaimed Palagianism, in whole and in part. They contended for man's entire depravity, the necessity of the direct agency of the Holy Spirit, and that the first step in the change proceeds not from the sinner, but from God. They denied at the time that they were Pelagians. Does not the Methodist hold as firmly as ever we do, that man is saved by the operation of the holy Ghost, and the Holy Ghost alone? And are not many of Mr. Wesley's sermons full of that great truth, that the Holy Ghost is necessary to regeneration? Whatever mistakes he may have made, he continually preached the absolute necessity of the new birth by the Holy Ghost, and there are some other points of exceedingly close agreement; for instance, even that of human inability. It matters not how some may abuse us, when we say man could not of himself repent or believe; yet, the old Arminian standards said the same. True, they affirm that God has given grace to every man, but they do not dispute the fact, that apart from that grace there was no ability in man to do that which was good in his own salvation. And then, let me say, if you turn to the continent of America, how gross the falsehood, that Calvinistic doctrine is unfavorable to revivals. Look at that wondrous shaking under Jonathan Edwards, and others which we might quote. Or turn to Scotland—what shall we say of M'Cheyne? What shall we say of those renowned Calvinists, Dr. Chalmers, Dr. Wardlow, and before them Livingstone, Haldane, Erskine, and the like? What shall we say of the men of their school, but that, while they held and preached unflinchingly the great truths which we would propound today, yet God owned their word, and multitudes were saved. And if it were not perhaps too much like boasting of one's own work under God, I might say, personally I have never found the preaching of these doctrines lull this Church to sleep, but ever while they have loved to maintain these truths, they have agonized for the souls of men, and the 1600 or more of whom I have myself baptized, upon profession of their faith, are living testimonies that these old truths in modern times have not lost their power to promote a revival of religion.

I have thus cleared away these allegations at the outset; I shall now need a few minutes more to say, with regard to the Calvinistic system, that there are some things to be said in its favor, to which of course I attach but little comparative importance, but they ought not to be ignored. It is a fact that the system of doctrines called the Calvinistic, is so exceedingly simple and so readily learned, that as a system of Divinity it is more easily taught and more easily grasped by unlettered minds than any other. The poor have the Gospel preached to them in a style which assists their memories and commends itself to their judgments. It is a system which was practically acknowledged an high philosophic grounds by such men as Bacon, Leibnitz, and Newton, and yet it can charm the soul of a child and expand the intellect of a peasant. And then it has another virtue. I take it that the last is no mean one, but it has another—that when it is preached there is a something in it which excites thought. A man may hear sermons upon the other theory which shall glance over him as the swallow's wing gently sweeps the brook, but these old doctrines either make a man so angry that he goes home and cannot sleep for very hatred, or else they bring him down into lowliness of thought, feeling the immensity of the things which he has heard. Either way it excites and stirs him up not temporarily, but in a most lasting manner. These doctrines haunt him, he kicks against the pricks, and full often the word forces a way into his soul. And I think this is no small thing for any doctrine to do, in an age given to slumber, and with human hearts so indifferent to the truth of God. I know that many men have gained more good by being made angry under a sermon than by being pleased by it, for being angry they have turned the truth over and over again, and at last the truth has burned its way right into their hearts. They have played with edge-tools, but they have cut themselves at last.

It has this singular virtue also—it is so coherent in all its parts. You cannot vanquish a Calvinist. You may think you can, but you cannot. The stones of the great doctrines so fit into each other, that the more pressure there is applied to remove them the more strenuously do they adhere. And you may mark, that you cannot receive one of these doctrines without believing all. Hold for instance that man is utterly depraved, and you draw the inference then that certainly if God has such a creature to deal with salvation must come from God alone, and if from him, the offended one, to an offending creature, then he has a right to give or withhold his mercy as he wills; you are this forced upon election, and when you have gotten that you have all: the others must follow. Some by putting the strain upon their judgments may manage to hold two or three points and not the rest, but sound logic I take it requires a man to hold the whole or reject the whole; the doctrines stand like soldiers in a square, presenting on every side a line of defense which it is hazardous to attack, but easy to maintain. And mark you, in these times when error is so rife and neology strives to be so rampant, it is no little thing to put into the hands of a young man a weapon which can slay his foe, which he can easily learn to handle, which he may grasp tenaciously, wield readily, and carry without fatigue; a weapon, I may add, which no rust can corrode and no blows can break, trenchant, and well annealed, a true Jerusalem blade of a temper fit for deeds of renown. The coherency of the parts, though it be of course but a trifle in comparison with other things, is not unimportant. And then, I add,—but this is the point my brethren will take up—it has this excellency, that it is scriptural, and that it is consistent with the experience of believers. Men generally grow more Calvinistic as they advance in years. Is not that a sign that the doctrine is right. As they are growing riper for heaven, as they are getting nearer to the rest that remaineth for the people of God, the soul longs to feed on the finest of the wheat, and abhors chaff and husks. And then, I add—and, in so doing, I would refute a calumny that has sometimes been urged,—this glorious truth has this excellency, that it produces the holiest of men. We can look back through all our annals, and say, to those who oppose us, you can mention no names of men more holy, more devoted, more loving, more generous than those which we can mention. The saints of our calendar, though uncanonized by Rome, rank first in the book of life. The names of Puritan needs only to be heard to constrain our reverence. Holiness had reached a height among them which is rare indeed, and well it might for they loved and lived the truth. And if you say that our doctrine is inimical to human liberty, we point you to Oliver Cromwell and to his brave Ironsides, Calvinists to a man. If you say, it leads to inaction, we point you to the Pilgrim Fathers and the wildernesses they subdued. We can put our finger upon every spot of land, the wide world o'er, and say, "Here was something done by a man who believed in God's decrees; and, inasmuch as he did this, it is proof it did not make him inactive, it did not lull him to sloth."

The better way, however of proving this point is for each of us who hold these truths, to be more prayerful, more watchful, more holy, more active than we have ever been before, and by so doing, we shall put to silence the gainsaying of foolish men. A living argument, is an argument which tells upon every man; we cannot deny what we see and feel. Be it ours, if aspersed and calumniated, to disprove it by a blameless life, and it shall yet come to pass, that our Church and its sentiments too shall come forth "Fair as the moon, clear as the sun, and terrible as an army with banners."

1. HUMAN DEPRAVITY ("T" TOTAL DEPRAVITY)

(Delivered by the Rev. Evan Probert, of Bristol)

My Christian friends, you are quite aware that the subject which is to engage our further attention this afternoon, is HUMAN DEPRAVITY—a subject about which there are different opinions, which I shall not attempt to examine at the present time, but I shall confine myself to the teachings of God's word, which is the only infallible rule of faith and practice, and from which we learn what man was when he came from the hands of his Maker, and what he is now as a fallen creature. It is explicitly declared by the sacred writers, that God made man upright, and therefore his condition was one of perfect innocence and high moral excellence. There was no tendency to evil in any part of his nature, nothing that deviated in the least from the rule of moral rectitude. Whatever his duty was, it was to him his invariable and delightful employment. But, alas! man in honor did not long continue. Through the insinuating wiles of the devil, our first parents were induced to violate the positive command of their Maker, the observance of which was the condition of their happiness, and, as punishment for their transgression, they were driven out of Paradise, and became liable to be cut off by the sentence of death, and consigned to everlasting misery; and, in consequence of our connection with Adam, as our federal head and representative, we became subject to the dreadful consequences of his fall. This is evident from the testimony of the Apostle Paul, in the fifth Chapter of his Epistle to the Romans. There we read, "By one man sin entered into the world, and death by sin, so that death passed upon all men, for that all have sinned." And, again, "By the offence of one, judgment came upon all men to condemnation, and by the disobedience of one, many were made sinners." It is evident from these passages that God viewed Adam in the covenant of works as the head and representative of his natural posterity, and consequently, when he fell we fell in him, and became subject to the tremendous consequences of his fall. Here it may be asked, what are the consequences of his fall? what were they to him, and what are they to us? To answer this question, we must ascertain what the Apostle means when he uses the words death, judgment, and condemnation. I think that he uses these words in opposition to the grace of God, to justification of life, and to the reign of the redeemed in life by Jesus Christ. These are the benefits which result from the grace of God through Christ, and which stand opposed to the evils which sin has introduced into our world; and, as it cannot be supposed that these benefits relate to temporal life, or solely to the resurrection of the body, it cannot be that the evils involved in the words, death, judgment, and condemnation, relate simply to temporal death, but they must be considered as including temporal, legal, and spiritual death.

From the very hour that Adam transgressed, he became mortal,—the sentence of death was pronounced upon him, and the seeds of depravity were sown in his system; thus the fair and beautiful and glorious creature began to fade, wither, and die, and all his posterity became mortal in him, and have from that day to this come into the world dying. Whatever the case of man might have been if he had not sinned we cannot say. This however we know, that he would not have died; for death is the result of the federal failure of the father of our race. "Dust thou are," God said to him, "and unto dust shalt thou return." "By one man sin entered into the world, and death by sin." "In Adam all died." So that it may be said to every one of Adam's sons and daughters, "Dust thou art, and unto dust shalt thou return."

But Adam by his transgression not only brought temporal death upon himself and his posterity, he also brought legal death. Having violated the law that was given him to observe, he became under the curse of that law, which involved not only temporal death and expulsion from Paradise, but an exposure to suffer the just demerits of his transgression; and, in consequence of our connection with him as our federal head, we are under the curse of the same law—"By one man's disobedience judgment came upon all men to condemnation;" and further, "By the offence of one many were made sinners." The very moment our progenitor transgressed, all his descendants became subject to the curse. The holy nature of God abhorred the apostate race; the curse of his holy and righteous law has ever rested upon that race; judgment has been given and recorded against us as a fallen world, in the court of Heaven, and unless it is reversed it must fall upon us with all its tremendous consequences.

We are also, in consequence of Adam's transgression, become the subjects of spiritual death, which consists not merely in the deprivation of the principle of life; but in having become depraved creatures, all the faculties of our souls and members of our bodies are depraved, so that it may be said of us, as the prophet says of the Jewish nation, "The head is sick, the whole heart is faint; from the sole of the foot unto the head there is no soundness." What! no soundness in any part? nothing good in any part? nothing spiritually good? nothing if cherished and fostered that will not lead to God, to Heaven, and to happiness? Nothing whatever. Let no one mistake me. I do not mean to say for a single moment, that sin has destroyed any of the faculties of man's soul, for they are all there. They all exist as they did when they were produced; but I mean to say, that sin has deprived man of the principle of spiritual life, and made him a depraved and debased creature; and we believe that we can prove this from the word of God, as well as from observation.

First,—From the conduct of little children. Children begin to sin very early in life. If there were any good in us, it would show itself in infancy, before good habits became corrupted, and evil principles were produced by our connection with the world. But do little children prefer good? Are they inclined to the good and the excellent? Do you see from the earliest period of their existence that they are desirous of good? On the contrary, I say, as soon as they begin to act, they prove by their action, that in them there is a depraved nature, from which they act. "Madness," says a wise man, "is bound up in the heart of a child," they go astray from the womb telling lies. But it may be said, in the way of objection, that this may arise from the unfavorable circumstance in which some children are placed. No doubt, unfavorable circumstances have a bad influence upon the minds of children; but it is not so with the whole race. Point out to me, one child who is disposed from infancy to seek that which is good, that which is holy. And surely, if the tendency of infants from their earliest history is to evil, it is a proof that it must arise from the evil propensities within them, which grow with their growth, and strengthen with their strength.

Secondly,—We have further proof of human depravity from the aversion of sinners to come to Christ. They are invited to come, persuaded to come, and are assured that they shall find pardon, acceptance, and salvation. But they cannot be induced to come to him; and why will they not come? Is it because he is not willing to receive them, or because there is anything in him to prevent them? No, but it is because of the deep-rooted depravity in their hearts. The heart is averse to all that is good, and therefore rejects the Savior and turns away from him. Hence he complained when in our world, "How often would I have gathered you, even as a hen gathereth her chickens under her wings, and ye would not." "Ye will not come to me, that ye might have life." What more needed to be added? Man turns away in proud disdain from all the blessings of the gospel, and the glories of heaven brought before him, and rushes on with steady purpose to damnation. "Light is come into the world, and men loved darkness rather than light, because their deeds are evil." Oh, to how many in this land may it be said, "They hate knowledge and did not choose the fear of the Lord; they would none of his counsel, they despised all his reproof."

Thirdly,—We have further evidence of native depravity from the testimony of Scripture. In the first place, let me refer you to the fifth chapter of the Book of Genesis, and the third verse. There we read, that Adam, after he had lived one hundred and thirty years, begat a son in his own likeness after his image. Mind, the image in which Adam was created was the image of God, but that image he had lost before he begat Seth; therefore, the image in which Seth was born must have been the image of his progenitor, as a fallen and depraved creature. Let me refer you, in the second place, to the third chapter of the Gospel of John. "He that is born of the flesh," said the Savior to Nicodemus, "is flesh, and he that is born of the Spirit is spirit." To be born of the flesh, according to the wisest interpretation of that passage, is to be born of a depraved nature; to be born of the Spirit is to be born of the Holy Spirit of God—which birth, the Savior told Nicodemus he must experience before he could see the kingdom of God. And again, we have several passages in proof of this point. In the seventh chapter of the Epistle to the Romans, at the fifth verse of that chapter, the Apostle says, "When we were in the flesh, the motions of sin by the law which worked in us to bring forth fruit unto death." "When we were in the flesh," means this—when we were in an unrenewed depraved state. In the same chapter he says, at the 14th verse, "We know that the law is spiritual, but I am carnal, sold under sin;" as if he had said, "I am as a sinner, a depraved creature." In accordance with this the Apostle says, at the 18th verse of the same chapter, "In me—that is, in my flesh—there dwelleth no good thing." No love to God, no holy aspirations! No, none whatever. At the beginning of the eighth chapter the same Epistle, we find the terms "flesh" and "Spirit" placed in opposition to each other, "Who walk not after the flesh," says the Apostle, describing Christians, "but after the Spirit." To be in the flesh is to be in a depraved state, to be in the Spirit is to be a partaker of his grace; to walk after the flesh is to walk after the dictates of corrupt principles and propensities, to walk after the Spirit is to be governed by spiritual principles and by the Holy Spirit of God; and the Apostle, in writing to the Galatians, says to them, "Walk in the Spirit, and ye shall not fulfill the lusts of the flesh." These passages, I think, prove beyond all contradiction, that man as a fallen creature, is a depraved creature, destitute of any good. There are many other passages of Scripture that confirm this doctrine, such as the following, "Who can bring a clean thing out of a unclean." Not one. What is man that he should be clean, or the son of man that he should be just. "Behold," says a Psalmist, "I was shapen in iniquity, and in sin did my mother conceive me." Read the account of man before the deluge, and there we find that every imagination and the thought of his heart were only evil, and that continually. The same account is given of him after the flood. The deluge could not wipe away the stains of moral pollution, could not destroy in man the deep-rooted depravity of his heart. "The heart," says Jeremiah, "is deceitful above all things and desperately wicked, who can know it." I think that what our blessed Lord said to the Jews of old, is applicable to every unconverted man under heaven—"But I know you that ye have not the love of God in you." Some of you may be more humane that others, more benevolent than other, more compassionate than other, as men, and as women, but one has as much of the love of God in him as others. "The carnal mind is enmity against God," against the being of God, against the government of God, against the gospel of God, against the purposes of God. The enmity of the human heart is unconquerable by any human agency whatever. It is mortal enmity, it strikes at the being of God, and, therefore, as President Edwards, of America, justly observes, "that when it found God in our nature, in our world, it put him to death on the accursed tree." Such, my brethren, is the enmity of the heart of man, such is its deep-rooted depravity, that in him there is no good thing. We can never speak too bad of what sin has done for us, and we can never speak too much, or too well, of what God has done for us, in the person of his Son, and in us, by the agency of his Holy Spirit.

Fourthly—The doctrine of human depravity may be proved from those passages which assert the universal necessity of redemption by Jesus Christ. "Thou shalt call his name Jesus," said the angel, "because he shall save his people from their sins," "In him we have redemption through his blood," says St. Paul, "even the forgiveness of sin according to the riches of his grace." Now, the work of redemption pre-supposes the sinful state of man, and implies a deliverance from that state and from the punishment to which man is exposed. Hence it is said of Christ, that he came into the world to save sinners, to seek and to save that which was lost, and that he died—the just for the unjust—that he might bring us to God. Now, if redemption by Christ is necessary, it is evident that man is a sinner; and, if man is a sinner, it is evident that man has a depraved nature. You cannot make anything else of it. Say what you like about man and about his excellencies, you must come to this conclusion, that he is a condemned and a depraved creature, or else he would not need redemption through the blood of our Lord Jesus Christ.

Fifthly,—The passages that assert the universal necessity of the new birth prove this very truth—"Except a man be born of water," said the Savior, "and of the Spirit, he cannot see the kingdom of God. Marvel not that I said unto you, ye must be born again." But if a man has some good in him, and if that good could be cherished, and be increased, and worked up so as to make men fit for heaven, what need of the new birth? what need of the Spirit of all grace to renew him in the spirit of his mind? Whenever, my brethren, you pray to God for the Spirit to change the human heart, whether you believe the doctrine or not, you imply it in your petition before the mercy-seat. They are represented by the sacred writers as having been called from darkness into light, as having an unction from the Holy One whereby they know all things, and those of them who have been called readily acknowledge that they were once foolish, once deceived and deceiving, once depraved—very depraved; and not only so, but the very best of Christians in the world confess with humility the depravity of their hearts, and I believe that the man who knows himself best is the man who is most ready to confess this and to humble himself before God—"Oh wretched man that I am, who shall deliver me from the body of this death?" And while Christians feel this, their language is, "Create within me a clean heart, oh God! and renew a right spirit within me; purge me with hysop and I shall be clean, wash me and I shall be whiter than snow." Apply the blood of sprinkling to my guilty conscience, and let the Spirit of all grace work in my polluted and depraved heart, and form me to the image of the Lord Jesus Christ, and meeten my immortal spirit for the inheritance of the saints in light, and of angels in glory. My dear friends, I need not say more. I should not think there is an individual here this afternoon who is not disposed to agree with me, when I say that man is fallen creature, is a depraved creature, is a condemned creature: he is under the curse of God's righteous law, and at the same time the subject of the reigning power of depravity, the subject of the effects of sin throughout his whole nature; and that, as a sinner, let it be recorded in high heaven there is no good in man's nature until God puts it there, and you will never be brought, by beloved hearers, into a right state of mind before God, until you are brought to feel that you have nothing, and that you must have all in the Lord Jesus Christ. "Oh! Israel, thou hast destroyed thyself!" But here are blessed tidings, "But in me is their help found." Does not this subject, my hearers, teach us, in the first place, the amazing long suffering of God towards our race. God might, as soon as man sinned, without the least imputation of injustice to his character, have cut him down, because the fall was the result of his criminal choice, and attended by the most aggravating circumstances; but God has borne with us, and is bearing still, which shows that he has no pleasure in the death of the sinner, but rather that he should turn from his ways and live. "Turn ye, turn ye, for why will ye die, oh! house of Israel?" And does not the subject teach us also the helplessness of man as a sinner? He is unable to atone for his sins or to renew his heart. Many attempts have been made to atone for human transgression, and to cleans and purify the human heart, but they have all failed, not one has succeeded. No sacrifice, short of an infinite one, could satisfy Divine justice and magnify the broken law. No power, short of the omnipotent energy of the Eternal Spirit, can renew the human heart. But, while man is a helpless creature he is not a hopeless creature. We do not say to him there is no hope.

Oh, no! I rejoice in that thought at this very moment. God has remembered us in our lowest state, he has laid help upon one that is mighty, one who, by his passive and active obedience, has magnified the law and made it honorable, satisfied the claims of Divine justice, so that God can be just, and the justifier of him that believeth in the Lord Jesus Christ; and while he made atonement for our transgressions, he has procured for us the Spirit of all grace to renew our nature, to transform us into the likeness of himself, and to prepare us in the use of means for the inheritance of the saints in light. Those of us who are made partakers of the Holy Ghost, and, I trust, most of us are—would to God that I could believe that we all are—let us pray for a larger measure of the Spirit, upon ourselves, individually, and upon the world around us. Surely, my hearers, my dear brother who has to occupy this platform, and who has to unfurl to you the banner of the cross, will need a large measure of the Holy Spirit. May He come upon his head, and upon his heart; and may he never ascend this platform but in His strength, and under His guidance, and in His light; may he never preach a sermon without its being blessed to the conversion of souls, and the building up of the Church; and may you, as a Christian Church, continue earnest in prayer for the Spirit to come, and it is the Spirit will reconcile us to each other, the Spirit will remove differences between Arminians and Calvinists, the Spirit will bring us to see, by-and-by, eye to eye, and this world will be filled with the glory of God. May the Lord command his blessing upon these remarks, for his name's sake. Amen.

The Meeting then adjourned till half-past six. After the friends had assembled—

The Rev. C. H. Spurgeon said,—I wish to make one or two observations before I introduce to you the speakers of this evening. Controversy is never a very happy element for the child of God: he would far rather be in communion than engaged in defense of the faith or in attack upon error. But the soldier of Christ knows no choice in his Master's commands. He may feel it to be better for him to lie upon the bed of rest than to stand covered with the sweat and dust of battle; but as a soldier he has learned to obey, and the rule of his obedience is not his personal comfort but his Lord's absolute command. The servant of God must endeavor to maintain all the truth which his Master has revealed to him, because, as a Christian soldier, this is part of his duty. But while he does so, he accords to others the liberty which he enjoys himself. In his own house of prayer he must and will maintain that which he believes to be true. He does not feel himself at all out of temper or angry when he hears that in other places there are some holding different views of what the truth is, who as honestly, and perhaps as forcibly, endeavor to maintain their views. To our own Master we stand or fall;

we have no absolute judge of right or wrong incarnate in the flesh on earth today. Nor is even the human judgment itself an infallible evidence of our being, for since the fall, no powers of mortals are free from imperfection. Our judgment is not necessarily a fully enlightened one, and we ourselves therefore let another man's judgment also be his guide unto God; but we must not forget that every man is responsible to the Most High for the use of that judgment, for the use of that mental power which God has given him, by which he is to weigh and balance the arguments of either side. I have found commonly that, with regard to the doctrine of grace which we preach, there are a great many objections raised. One of the simplest trades in the world is the raising of objections. You never need, if you wish to set up in that line of business, to look abroad for capital or resources; however poor and penniless a man may be, even in wits, he can easily manufacture difficulties. It is said "that a fool may raise objections which a thousand wise men could not answer." I would not hesitate to say that I could bring objections to your existence tonight, which you could not disprove. I could sophisticate and mystify until I brought out the conclusion that you were blind, and deaf, and dumb, and I am not sure that by any process of logic you would be able to prove that you were not so. It might be clear enough to you that you could both speak, and see, and hear. The only evidence, however, I suppose that you could give, would be by speaking, and seeing, and hearing, which might be conclusive enough; but if it were left to be a mere matter of word-fighting for schoolmen, I question whether the caviller might not cavil against you to the judgment-day in order to dispute you out of the evidence of your very senses. The raising of difficulties is the easiest trade in all the world, and, permit me to add, it is not one of the most honorable. The raising of objections has been espoused, you know, by that great and mighty master of falsehood in the olden times, and it has been carried on full often by those whose doubts about the truth sprung rather from their hearts than from their heads. Some difficulties, however, ought to be met, and let me now remove one or two of them. There are some who say, "Provided the doctrines of grace be true, what is the use of our preaching?" Of course I can hardly resist a smile while I put this splendid difficulty—it is so huge a one. If there are so many who are to be saved, then why preach? You cannot diminish, you cannot increase the number, why preach the Gospel? Now, I thought my friend Mr. Bloomfield anticipated this difficulty well enough. There must be a harvest,—why sow, why plow? Simply because the harvest is ordained in the use of the means. The reason why we preach at all is because God has ordained to save some. If he had not, we could not see the good of preaching at all. Why! we should come indeed on a fool's errand if we came here without the Master's orders at our back. His elect shall be saved—every one of them,—and if not by my instrumentality or that of any brother here present, if not by any instrumentality, then would God sooner call them by his Holy Spirit, without the voice of the minister, than that they should perish. But this is the very reason why we preach, because we wish to have the honor of being the means, in the hand of God, of calling these elect ones to himself. The certainty of the result quickens us in our work, and surely it would stay none but a fool in his labor. Because God ordains that his word shall not return unto him void, therefore, we preach that word, because, "as the rain cometh down and the snow from heaven, and returneth not thither, but watereth the earth and maketh it to bring forth and bud, even so doth the word of the Lord accomplish his purpose;" therefore, we would have our doctrine to drop as the rain and distil as the dew, and as the small rain upon the tender herb. But, there are some again who say, "To what purpose after all, is your inviting any to come, when the Spirit of God alone constrains them to come; and why, especially, preach to those whom believe to be so depraved that they cannot and will not come?" Ay, just so, this is a serious difficulty to everything except faith. Do you see Ezekiel yonder; he is about to preach a sermon. By his leave, we will stop him. "Ezekiel, where are you about to preach?" "I am about," saith he, "to preach to a strange congregation— dead, dry bones, lying in a mass in a valley." "But, Ezekiel, they have no power to live." "I know that," saith he. "To what purpose, then, is your preaching to them? If they have no power, and if the breath must come from the four winds, and they have no life in themselves, to what purpose do you preach?" "I am ordered to preach," saith he, "commanded;" and he does so. He prophesies, and afterward mounting to a yet higher stage of faith, he cries, "Come from the four winds, oh breath, and breathe upon these slain, that they may live." And the wind comes, and the effect of his ministry is seen in their life. So preach we to dead sinners; so pray we for the living Spirit. So, by faith, do we expect his Divine influence, and it comes,—cometh not from man, nor of man, nor by blood, nor by the will of the flesh, but from the sovereign will of God. But not withstanding it comes instrumentally through the faith of the preacher while he pleads with man, "as though God did beseech them by us, we pray them in Christ's stead to be reconciled to God." But if ten thousand other objections were raised, my simple reply would be just this, "We can raise more objections against your theory, than you can against ours." We do not believe that our scheme is free from difficulties; it were uncandid if we were to say so. But we believe that we have not the tithe of the difficulties to contend with that they have on the opposite side of the question. It is not hard to find in those texts which appear to be most against us, a key, by which they are to be harmonized; and we believe it to be utterly impossible, without wresting Scripture, to turn those texts which teach our doctrine, to teach any other thing whatsoever. They are plain, pointed, pertinent. If the Calvinistic scheme were the whole sum and substance of all truth, why then surely, if it held everything within some five or six doctrines, you might begin to think that man were God, and that God's theology were less than infinite in its sweep. What are we, that we should grasp the infinite? We shall never measure the marches of eternity. Who shall compass with a span the Eternal God, and who shall think out anew his infinite thoughts? We pretend not that Calvinism is a plumb-line to fathom the deeps; but we do say, that it is a ship which can sail safely over its surface, and that every wave shall speed it onwards towards its destined haven. To fathom and to comprehend is neither your business nor mine, but to learn, and then, having learned, to teach to others, is the business of each Christian man; and thus would be do, God being our helper. One friend kindly suggests a difficulty to me, which, having just spoken of, I shall sit down. That amazing difficulty has to do with the next speaker's topic, and, therefore, I touch it. It says in the Scriptures, that Paul would not have us destroy him with our meat for whom Christ died. Therefore, the inference is—only mark, we don to endorse the logic—the inference is, that you may destroy some with your meat for whom Christ died. That inference I utterly deny. But then, let me put it thus. Do you know, that a man may be guilty of a sin which he cannot commit. Does that startle you? Every man is guilty of putting God out of existence, if he says in his heart, "No God." But he cannot put God out of existence; and yet, the guilt is there, because he would if he could. There be some who crucify the Son of God afresh. They cannot,—he is in heaven, he is beyond their reach. And yet, because their deeds would do that, unless some power restrained, they are guilty of doing what they can never do, because the end and aim of their doings would be to destroy Christ, if he were here. Now, then, it is quite consistent with the doctrine that no man can destroy any for whom Christ died, still to insist upon it that a man may be guilty of the blood of souls. He may do that which, unless God prevented it,—and that is no credit to him,—unless God prevented it, would destroy souls for whom Jesus Christ died. But, again I say, I have not come here tonight to anticipate and to answer all objections; I have only done that, that some troubled conscience might find peace. This was not a meeting of discussion, but for the explaining of our views, and the teaching them simply to the people. I now shall call upon my beloved brother to take up the point of particular redemption.

2. ELECTION ("U" UNCONDITIONAL ELECTION)

(Delivered by Rev. John Bloomfield, of Meard's Court, SOHO)

My dear Christian friends, those who best know my cast of mind and ministry will readily believe me when I say I would rather have spoken on the majesty and mystery of the person of Christ, or I would rather have spoken on the perfection and intrinsic worth of the mediation of Christ, or on the great attraction of Christ as a gracious and omnipotent Savior, than on the subject that has been assigned to me. The subject that has been given me is that of the doctrine of eternal and personal election; I have to prove that the doctrine of election is a scriptural truth; and, at the commencement of my few remarks on this profound subject, allow me to say that I hold and firmly believe the Bible to be revelation from God, that the revelations of God's mind are essentially and infallibly true, that its ancient historical records are of the greatest value, that its prophecies are to be studied and to be venerated, that the doctrines of the Bible are in harmony with the majesty, wisdom, holiness and goodness of their Author. Now it should not be a point with us whether a doctrine is like or disliked, whether it is believed or disbelieved, but whether it is a doctrine according to godliness, whether it is the doctrine of the Word of God. Truth has never been popular in this world: Jesus Christ when on earth was by no means popular. Truth never will be popular in this world while men are influenced by sin, and enmity against God. Perhaps no doctrine has met with such bitter opposition as the doctrine on which I have to speak. It has been fearfully misunderstood for a want of prayerful and independent study of the Holy Scriptures, or perhaps from the miserable misrepresentations that have been given of it by some public men. It is a truth which has been bitterly opposed; we may oppose a doctrine which we cannot with all our puny efforts depose. We may dispute in our blindness and enmity a doctrine which we cannot refute. We believe firmly that the doctrine of election to salvation in Jesus Christ is a doctrine of the Scriptures. We believe in sovereign love, but not in sovereign hatred. We believe in salvation by the grace of God without works, but not in damnation without sin. We believe firmly in election to salvation by faith in the Lord Jesus Christ, but we discard from our creed the miserable, wretched doctrine of reprobation without sin. Is the doctrine of election a Scriptural doctrine? Can we prove it from the word of God? It is one thing to believe it to be a doctrine of Divine revelation, and it is another thing to have the sanctifying grace and power of it in our hearts. The election we read of in the Scriptures is inseparably connected with holiness, and we believe in no election to salvation without faith in the Lord Jesus Christ. He who has appointed salvation as an end has appointed the methods by which that end shall be accomplished. Perhaps no man possessed of his reasoning powers questions the truth that God has predestinated harvest as long as this world shall continue. But without sowing of seed, without the agricultural labor that is given to the land, we should have no harvest, because he who predestinated harvest predestinated the sowing of the seed as much. And God has appointed us not unto wrath, but to obtain salvation through Jesus Christ. I shall endeavor now to prove, from the quotation of a few Scriptures, that the doctrine of eternal and personal election is a Scriptural and Divine truth. Jesus Christ himself was said to be "chosen of God and precious." He is God's elect, for Jehovah himself says, "Behold my servant, mine elect in whom my soul delighteth." Angels that continue in their unfallen dignity and felicity are termed elect angels. Elect angels are employed as ministering spirits to those that shall be heirs of salvation. Elect angels will be employed in the gathering of God's elect into the heavenly world. The Jewish nation was a chosen nation, and as such they were privileged with the oracles of God, and stood as a representative people. They were chosen not because of their personal worth, they were chosen not because of their goodness, but they were chosen to be a separated people, a people that should be God's peculiar treasure, and should be holiness unto the Lord; of them it was said, "For thou art a holy people unto the Lord thy God—the Lord hath chosen thee to be a special people unto himself, above all people that are upon the face of the earth." Jesus Christ himself, in the 24th chapter of Matthew, speaks of certain days being shortened because of God's elect. The Psalmist craved to be remembered with the favor that God was pleased to bear towards his people, that he might see the good of his chosen. And Jesus Christ himself said to his disciples, "Ye have not chose me, but I have chosen you." And the Apostle Paul very often in his writings has brought out this great and profound doctrine. He says, "There is a remnant according to the election of grace." He speaks to the Ephesian Church, and says, "Ye are chosen in Christ before the foundation of the world that ye may be holy, and that ye may stand before God without blame in love." God hath in the exercise of his sovereignty chosen a people in Christ to salvation before time began—it was before the foundation of the world, here is its antiquity—it is in Christ according to the riches of God's grace, and it is to holiness and salvation. He, in his addresses to the Church at Thessalonica, said he could but thank God "that they were chosen to salvation through sanctification of the Spirit and the belief of the truth." Peter speaks of the people of God as a chosen generation and a royal priesthood. He wrote to the elect according to the foreknowledge of God the Father. More Scriptures might be given upon this subject, but I think they would be unnecessary. If we would only give our attention to the simple teachings of the Spirit of God by the prophets, by the Psalmist, by Christ, and by the Apostles, we could not have one moment's doubt as to the doctrine of Divine election being a Scriptural truth.

My second point is to show that God has chosen his people to the highest possible relation to himself, and to the enjoyment of the most precious blessings in Christ. All spiritual relations stand in Christ; all spiritual relations originated in God's grace; and all spiritual relations are standing manifestations of the sovereignty of God's favor and of the immutability of God's love. If we are the sons of God, what has constituted us the sons of God? We are sons of God by God's sovereign love; it is by an act of adoption, it is by an act of Jehovah's will, that we are constituted his sons and his daughters. Adoption is relation established to which we have no natural right; adoption is one thing, and the spirit of adoption is another. Now Christ is God's first-born, and all the family are chose in him; Christ is the glorious Head of the Church, and all the family of God are chosen members in him; Christ is the everlasting Priest of his Church, and he represents all the family, just as the Jewish priest represented by his breast-plate and in the fulfillment of his office the whole of the Jewish nation. All relation to God then stands in Christ, originated in the sovereignty of Jehovah's will, and is expressive of the infinite love of Jehovah's heart. We are chose to salvation—that is the end; the means by which that end is accomplished is by the "sanctification of the Spirit, and the belief of the truth." We are chose to usefulness; every Christian should seek to be useful; every Christian in his right mind is a witness for God; every Christian, as he is influenced by Christian principles, bears testimony to the dignity of the relation that God has established, and bears testimony to the holiness of the principles by which his heart is influenced; every Christian should be a living gospel, his life should bear testimony to the holiness of that Christianity that he studies and is influenced by. We are chosen to eternal life, but it is eternal life through Christ. Without faith there is no evidence of interest in Christ, without faith there is no enjoyment of salvation by Christ. Without faith, a man has no evidence of interest in the Lamb's Book of Life; but he who believes in Christ, however weak and trembling his faith has evidence in his own heart that his name is written in the Lamb's Book of Life; and his conduct corresponding with the holiness of the gospel, he carries in his life a witness to his interest in all the purposes of heaven, and in all the redemptive excellency of the Lord Jesus Christ. The great evidence of interest in election is holiness. A man to talk of believing in election, and going to heaven, because he is one of God's elect, and yet living in sin, and in enmity to God, this can never, never be. We are chosen unto salvation, it is said, "through sanctification of the Spirit and the belief of the truth;" and, without this sanctification of the Spirit and the belief of the truth, there is no holiness; and, "without holiness, no man can see the Lord." Without holiness, no man would be capable of serving God in heaven; without holiness, no man would be capable of beholding the glories of Jesus Christ there; without holiness, no man can serve God with power and success here; without holiness, no man can have fellowship with God, and so have fellowship with us, for truly our fellowship is with the Father and with his son Jesus Christ. It is only by practical life of consistency with faith in Christ Jesus, that we have evidence of our interest in election. We are chosen, not because we are holy, but that we might be holy; we are chosen, not because we are good, but that by the principles of the everlasting Gospel, we might become so; we are chosen, not because we are saved, but that we may be saved through faith in the Lord Jesus Christ. I hold, dear friends, that the great doctrine of election should be preached. It should be preached, because it is part of a grand system of truth. Truth is not one doctrine, but it is a grand system, and you cannot leave out one part without impairing its beauty, nor leave out one part of this system without weakening its strength. The beauty of truth lies in its perfection, and in that harmony of its connection; the strength of truth lies in the unity of its parts, and it is like gold dust—it is all precious. If Election be not a truth inspired by the Spirit of the living God—if it be not a truth proclaimed by the prophets that were inspired—if it be not a truth published by the Apostles—if it be not a truth found in the teachings of the word of God, let us never say one word about it; but if it was truth in the days of the Apostles, then it is no less a truth now. What the Apostles preached, I hold, we ought to preach in the spirit of love, in the spirit of faith, in the spirit of meekness, entirely depending on the power of the Holy Spirit to give us success in the conversion of immortal souls. One moment longer, and I have done. There is nothing in the doctrine of election that is discouraging to a penitent, seeking sinner. There is everything in the Gospel to welcome the returning prodigal to his Father's house; there is everything to meet the necessities of an awakened conscience; there is everything in the Gospel to satisfy the longing of a penitent soul. I know some may say, "I fear, Sir, I shall not be saved because I am not one of God's elect." Art thou a sinner? Art thou a penitent sinner? Art thou a seeking sinner? If thou art a seeking, penitent sinner, you cannot imagine how welcome you are to the provisions of infinite love. Every truth in the Gospel is open to you; every promise in the Gospel is open to you; every invitation in Scripture speaks to you. If thou art a sinner seeking mercy, let this cheer thy heart—that God delighteth in mercy. If thou art seeking salvation, Jesus is a willing and an able Savior, and he has said, "All that the Father giveth to me shall come to me, and him that cometh I will in no wise cast out." There is nothing, dear friends, in the doctrine of election as it stands in the Scriptures that should discourage any penitent in seeking after mercy through Jesus Christ. I know, in the miserable misrepresentation of this great and glorious truth, men might well be discouraged from seeking mercy through the Savior. But see it in its Scriptural connection; see it in the simplicity of it as it is put before us by the great Apostles; see it in the teachings of the Savior himself, and there is nothing in it but that which welcomes a penitent sinner. It is a great encouragement to a seeking soul. Does the farmer who sows his seed sow that seed with less or more encouragement because he knows that God has ordained that harvest shall be? He sows his seed with a heart brimfull with hope, because God has promised that a harvest shall be as long as the world continues. Only let the means be used according to the Holy Scriptures; only let the poor awakened, penitent sinner renounce everything but Christ and him crucified, mercy will roll into his troubled heart and fill his spirit with peace, and he shall come off more than conqueror, shouting, Victory through the blood of the Lamb—Victory, victory through Jesus Christ.

3. PARTICULAR REDEMPTION
("L" LIMITED ATONEMENT)

(Delivered by the Rev. J. A. Spurgeon, of Southampton)

I think it is well that the death of Christ and its consequent blessings should occupy one place in our discussion here tonight; for not only is it the central truth in the Calvinistic theory, but the death of Christ is the centre point of all history and of all time. The devout of all ages have stood and gazed with anxious glance into these deep mysteries, searching what, or what manner of things the Holy Spirit did by them testify and reveal; and we know that hereafter, in yon world of glory, the redeemed shall sing of these things forever, and shall find in the Redeemer and in his work, fresh matter for love and for praise as eternity shall roll on. We take our stand between the two, and I think the language of our hearts tonight is akin to all ages of the Church of Christ,—"God forbid that we should glory save in the cross of our Lord Jesus Christ."

Now the grand result of the death of our Lord—though not the only result—the grand result of that death, so far as man is concerned, is the redemption which it ultimately achieves; and, with regard to the extent of that redemption, we believe the Scriptures are plain and speak most clearly, when they tell of a final day of manifestation, when the redeemed from amongst men shall take their stand before the Redeemer, to sing of him who, as the good shepherd, hath laid down his life for his sheep, and has purchased unto himself a peculiar people—his body, the Church. Now, we believe that, in reaching that grand and final result there are many steps that must be taken, and we think that, from these preliminary steps, there are multitudes that gain rich handfuls of blessings who shall not however reap the full harvest of glory. We believe that the whole world is flooded with blessings, and that the stream rolls broad and clear from the hill-foot of Calvary, and laves the feet alike of the godly and of the ungodly, the thankful and the thankless. But from the riven side of Christ there comes forth one stream—the river of life, whose banks are trodden only by the feet of the multitude of believers, who wash and are clean, who drink and liver forevermore. We speak tonight of Christ's death in its various relations, so as to touch upon and include sundry things which cannot be properly classed under the title of particular redemption; but we feel we are driven to this course, so as to be able to do justice to ourselves and to our leading theme.

Now, we have three sets of truths before us, and these three sets of truths we must deal with. (1.) We have, first of all, a God holy and righteous, loving and gracious, a God who has been most grievously wronged and injured, and a God who must be honored alike by the giving him all the glory of which he has been robbed, and by the bearing of his just expression of holy indignation at the wrong that has been done unto him. We have a God jealous in the extreme, and yet, strange enough, declaring that he passes by iniquity and forgiveth transgression and sin. We have a God truthful, who has sworn "that the soul that sinneth it shall die," and who yet speaks to those souls, and says, "Turn ye, turn ye; for why will ye die." A God whom we know must be just, and must execute upon the ungodly that which they have justly merited, and who yet strangely says, "Come and let us plead together, and though your sins be as scarlet I will make them as wool, and though they be like crimson I will make them white as snow." That is one set of truths—strange, and apparently contradictory. Then we have another. (2.) We have a world lost, and yet swathed in an atmosphere of mercy. We have a world dark with the darkness of death, and yet everywhere we find it more or less under the influence of the beams of the Sun of Righteousness, which came a light unto darkness, that did not and could not comprehend it. And we have, moreover, a world rebellious, and serving another master than the right one, and yet nevertheless beneath the feet of him who has been made Head over all things for his body's sake, which is the Church. (3.) And then, once more, we have a Church peculiar in its unmerited privileges, chose from before all time to inherit the kingdom given to it before the world began—a kingdom that can never be trodden upon save by the spotless and the deathless; and yet the inheritors are by nature dead in trespasses and in sins—lost, ruined—without a God and without a hope in the world. How are all those strange and apparently contradictory things to be solved? One clue, we find, is in the cross of our Lord Jesus Christ. The work involves its ultimate end, which is redemption, and of that work we are about to speak here tonight.

We speak first of those blessings which come from the death of Christ, and are for all men; the whole world is under a mediatorial government, the whole spirit of which is a government of long-suffering, graciousness, tenderness, and mercy, such as could not have been exercised had Christ never died. A government there might have been, but it must be, we think, a government akin to that which is found in the place where those are found who make their bed in hell. We find, moreover, that the direct and indirect influences of the Cross of Christ have pervaded the whole world, and none can tell how full oft its gentle spirit has come like oil upon the troubled waters; or what man, with his wild passions, would have been without the ameliorating influence of the Cross. We possibly may be able to tell, when we look across the impassable gulf into a Gehenna beneath, and see sin unchecked working out its dire results; and, we believe that whatever comes short of that darkness, whose very light is darkness, is due to that light which radiates from the Cross of Christ, and whatever is short of hell streams from Calvary. And then, further still, we have a Bible, a revelation filled with the love and mercy of God to man—a Bible in which our Lord himself could show, beginning at Moses, and in all the prophets, that which did testify concerning himself; and, apart from Jesus Christ and his death, there could have been no such revelation of God's character unto the human race. A revelation there might have been, but it would have been a revelation of Sinai's horrors and terrors, without even the spark of hope which comes forth from that dispensation there set forth. There might have been a revelation, I say, but it would have been a revelation that would not have wound up as this does with a blessing. It would have ended like the Old Testament with a curse; it would have begun with the same. It would have been worse than Ezekiel's roll of woes which is filled all over with terrible lamentation, and with awful sorrow and woe. And again, there is a positive overture of mercy, a true and faithful declaration of good tidings unto every creature, and we do believe that it is our duty to preach the Gospel unto every creature; and the Gospel runs thus—"Believe on the Lord Jesus Christ and thou shalt be saved, for he who believeth and is baptized shall be saved." That overture we hold to be no mockery, but made in good faith; and that overture is not the overture of a shadow, but the presentation of solid, substantial blessings; and for the rejection of that, not God, but man is answerable, and for the rejection of that he will be lost. "For this the condemnation, that they have not believed on him whom God hath sent." And, then, lastly, we find that as the purchase of the death of Christ there is a Church, and that Church is sent forth into the world with orders to bless it and to do good unto all men. It is bidden to go forth as a light in the midst of darkness; it is bidden so to live as to be the salt of the whole earth. Now, we say that each one of these blessings is no small gift from God to man—no mean result of the death of our Master; and, combined, we think they would form a boon worthy of a God; and, as we put our hand upon it, we think we can give a full and true expression, and with an emphasis surpassed by none, to that glorious text—"God so loved the world that he gave his only begotten Son." And we think, upon our system, and upon ours alone, we can give full truthfulness and emphasis to the remainder—"That whosoever believeth in him shall have everlasting life." Now, upon redemption proper, the latter part of our theme, we will pass on to speak. And, first, what do we mean by redemption? Most certainly we do not mean the POSSIBILITY OF REDEMPTION, for we have learned to distinguish between the possibility of a thing and a thing itself. We feel this, that we do not preach and cannot preach, gathering our teaching from the Bible, a possibility of redemption. We proclaim a redemption. Nor do we mean by redemption a contingency of redemption, which, again, is contingent upon a third thing. We have learned to distinguish between a contingency and a certainty. We proclaim a certain redemption, and we speak of that which is not possible but positive, not contingent but certain. Neither do we mean by redemption such an outgrowth of the man's own power or goodness as shall enable him to burst his way through every bondage and to get forth free; such an elevation of human nature, whether by the education of others, or by his own works, as to enable him at last to stand free. If we meant that, we should use the word escape, but not the word redemption. And again, if we meant, as some, alas! have seemed to mean, God's foregoing his claim upon man; God's waiving man's liabilities, and God's giving up that which we believe, as a holy God, he cannot surrender; if we meant that, we should speak of emancipation—of pure pardon and forgiveness. But we do not. We mean redemption. And then, again, we do not mean by redemption the meeting of the debts, either in prospective or in the present. We do not mean that the man shall, either in the present or in the future, bear any part of the penalty; and, by some goodness, either in the present or foreseen, satisfy God's claim upon him. If we meant that, I think we should use altogether another word than the word redemption. What do we mean by redemption? We mean, by redemption, the work of one being which is done for another, but generally a helpless one, in order to give him a perfect freedom. And when we speak of redemption, mark you, we speak of a thing that is the result of that work. We distinguish between redemption and redemption work. What we mean, by redemption, is just this—the grand result and end of the work of our Lord Jesus Christ; and we could as well speak of redemption apart from the redeemed, as we could speak of life apart from a living creature. Life and living creatures are co-extensive, and so is redemption and the redeemed. If you take down any book that will give you an explanation of the word "redemption," I think you will find three things put therein. It is a ransom, a rescue, and a release. Now, I take the whole three words to be the fullness of the meaning of one word. It is such a ransom, and such a rescue, as result in a complete and full release. Whatever stops short of that thing, is, of course, not the thing itself; the thing itself that we mean, is the positively being redeemed and made free. Now, just by way of simplifying the subject, let me speak of the Redeemer, and of the redemption work, and of those who are redeemed.

First, the Redeemer, who is he? We believe him to be the Word that was with God, equal unto God, and was God,—who became flesh and dwelt among us. At the same time, the flesh did not become, in any sense, Deity, neither did the Deity, in any sense, become carnal. They formed another person, and that person the God-man, Jesus Christ, our Redeemer. Now, what is he? And here I just ask that question, in order to meet some objections, and, if I can, to put on one side two or three theories that seem to fight against ours. I hear a voice, saying, in reply to that question, what is he? Why, he is God's idea of humanity; he is God, who has taken up humanity from its fallen state, raised it up not only to the place where he first put it, but, beyond, even to the height to which he hoped it would ascend, or possibly something beyond it. And, now, from henceforth, such is the union betwixt common humanity, that the lost, in their degradation, have but to look to their common humanity exalted, realize their identity with it, and to feel themselves, by that deed, raised to the same standard, and redeemed, and free forevermore. To which, we reply, there is enough of truth in that lie to keep it alive, and that is all. We do believe that our Master did lay hold of humanity; we do believe that he has honored and dignified the human race, by taking that upon him, and by becoming flesh like unto ourselves. But we cannot see how that the gazing upon that can open blind eyes, unstop deaf ears, give live to the dead, and procure the discharge of our sins, any more than we can see how that the gazing upon an Olympic game would give to the physically lame, physical strength, or could give to those who were physically dead, life from their physical death.

And, again, I hear other voices replying to that question. They say, "he is the great example of self-denial, and of the submission of the human will to the Divine. And what redemption is, is this—that man now can look to that great display of selfdenial, can catch of its spirit, and can imitate it, and by that deed of subjection, making the will to succumb to the will of the Divine, they may, at least, emancipate themselves, and go forth free." To which we reply, once more, there is enough of truth in that just to cement the error together, and to give it a plausible appearance to the sons of men, but there is nothing more. It is true that our Savior was the Sent One of the Father. It is true, he came, saying, "Lo! I come to do thy will." He declares he was not doing his own will, but the will of him that sent him. And he winds up by saying, "Not my will, but thine be done." But, after all, we cannot, and dare not accept that submission of Christ's will to the Father, as being a satisfaction for sin; neither can we see, how, by the imitation of that, we can, in any sense, wipe away the sins of the past, or free ourselves from the penalty that is yet to come.

But now to answer for ourselves. What is our Lord Jesus Christ? And we say, that in life he is the great example and copy; in death, he is the substitute; and in both, the federal head—the elder brother and kinsman of his Church.

But now time warns me that I must pass on to the second thought—the work of redemption. First of all, we gaze at that part of the work which is Godward, and that we call atonement; and, when you ask me—What is the character of the atonement? I reply—It has a twofold nature, to correspond with the twofold character of sin. Sin is a transgression of the law, and a consequent insult to him who is the lawmaker. But it is something more than that: the power by which he has transgressed has been perverted; it was given to him to obey the law that he might glorify God. And to make, therefore, a satisfaction for sin, there must be a bringing to the law obedience; there must be the bearing of the sanction because of the disobedience; there must be the rendering to God the glory due to him; and there must be the bearing of his just displeasure and the expression of his holy wrath and indignation. That Christ has done: he came, and his whole life was obedience to the law, for he was obedient even unto death; and in that death he bore the sanction of the law—for he was made a curse, it being written, "Cursed is every one that hangeth on a tree." His whole life was spent to glorify God, and at its close he could say, "I have glorified thee, and I have finished the work which thou gavest me to do:" and his death was the bearing of the just displeasure of God towards the sinner, and in the agony of his heart he cried, "My God, my God, why hast thou forsaken me?" In these things we behold, therefore, the presentation of the obedience due, the giving to God the glory due, the bearing of God's displeasure, and the enduring of the curse of the law. And now the question would be put to me as to the value of atonement. We believe that its value depends not so much upon the Being appeased, nor upon the beings to be atoned for, as upon the Being who makes the atonement. The value of Christ's atonement is the value of himself. He gave himself for us. If he had stood as the surety for the whole world, he could not be more. He gave himself; what more could he bestow? The value of the atonement is the value of our Lord Jesus Christ. In his flesh he can take man's place, and by his Divinity he can give, and must give anyhow, an infinite value to the work that he, in mortal flesh, performs. For one soul, therefore, it must be infinite—for more or less it cannot be. Infinite it is, and infinite it must be, and we have no part or parcel with those who would say, that if Judas was to have been saved, Judas' amount of penalty would have had to have been paid, in addition to what has been borne and paid by Christ. He took the place, the room, and stead of the church, and then all that he was worth went in that church's place and stead. More he could not do, if he had taken the place of the whole world. But, you ask me, is there any limit to the atonement at all? I say I think there is; and the limit seems to be, not in the value, but in the purpose. The limit seems to be this theory—for whom did he die? in whose place and stead did he stand? If he stood in the place and stead of the whole world, then he made atonement for the sins of the whole world, and the whole world will be saved. If he stood in the place and stead of his Church, then he made atonement for his Church, and the whole Church will be saved. We believe that Christ took the place and stead of every believer, that the believer's sin was put on him, and thus the ex-sinner can go forth free. But I hear a voice saying, "I challenge substitution, and I object to that." So be it. I ask you, did Christ die for sin at all? It must be answered,—Yes. Then for whose sin did he die? If his own, then he suffered righteously. Did he die for the sins of the whole world? then justice cannot demand this again. Did he die for part of the sins of the whole world? then the rest of the sins will still condemn the world; then must have Christ died in vain. We believe that he took all the sins of some men. It was not a fictitious condemnation; it was not a fancy sin made for the occasion; it was a positive sin that had been committed by God's people, and is transferred from them to him who laid down his life for his sheep; loving us, and giving himself for and in the stead or in the place of his people.

But, then, we say this work of redemption comprised something more than thus paying down the ransom, and the bearing of the penalty. It is, moreover, a rescue; for sin has not only made men this to have insulted God and broken God's law, it has transferred them unto bondage under the allegiance of one—"the strong man armed." They must be freed from that. Christ came, has destroyed death, and through death him also who has the power of death, even the devil; making an open show of them upon his cross, ascending up on high a victor, leading captivity captive. And then, I think, there is yet something further. Sin has affected the man himself, made him to need in his own person a releasing from the dominion, power, and corruption of sin. This Christ has secured by his covenant with the Father. But that which I take to comprise effectual calling and final perseverance, I shall leave to my brethren who shall speak afterwards. And now as to the persons redeemed—who are they? The Church, we say, whether you look at the Church as elect from all eternity, or the Church believing in time, or the Church as glorified hereafter. We look at them all as one, and we say these are the redeemed, these are they for whom redemption has been procured. We cannot add to their number, we cannot diminish them; for we believe that those whom God foreknew, he did predestinate; that those whom he did predestinate, he also called: for whom he calls he justifies, for whom he justifies he also glorifies; the whole are one,—and for these redemption has been made.

Now, if I may be permitted the time, I will just touch upon one or two, objections, and then I will conclude. I hear some one saying, "But by that, sir, you surely must limit God's love." I reply, is God loving when he punishes any and doth not save all? Then is he loving also when he purposes to do that, for whatever justifies the deed justifies the purpose which gives the morality to the deed. And then I hear another objection—"How can you, sir, upon that theory, go to preach the Gospel unto every creature?" You have heard that answered—we have got the order; but, I reply yet further: I could not go and preach the Gospel upon any other theory, for I dare not go on that fool's errand of preaching a redemption that might not redeem, and declaring a salvation that might not save. I could not go and say to a man, "Believe on the Lord Jesus Christ and thou shalt be saved." And he would answer me, "Do you think you are going to heaven?" "Yes." "Why?" "Because Christ died for me." "But he died for us all, and my chances therefore are as good as yours." And he might reply to me after he had accepted my declaration, and after he had believed, and begun to rejoice, after all he might say, "Is there any real reason why I should rejoice, some for whom Christ died are in hell, and I may also go there. I cannot begin to rejoice in your news till I feel myself in glory. It is rather a faulty piece of good news, because it is nothing positive; it is a grand uncertainty you have proclaimed to me." Now, what we preach, is the Gospel to every creature, and that we take to be this—If you believe on the Lord Jesus Christ you shall be saved; if you do not, you will be lost, and lost forever. You are not redeemed—you are not saved,—there is not, in another word, salvation and redemption for those who are lost forever. But we add, "We are what we are by Divine grace; we have believed; if you believe on the Lord Jesus Christ you will be as we are—will be able to boast as we do, humbly in the Lord our God;" or in other words—If you believe, and are baptized, you will be saved; if you do not believe, you will be lost, and lost forever.

4. EFFECTUAL CALLING ("I" IRRESITABLE GRACE)
(Delivered by the Rev. James Smith of Cheltenham)

My Christian friends, our minds have been occupied today with some of the loftiest subjects that can engage the thoughts of man. Our attention has been directed to the infinitely wise and true God, and we have been endeavoring to conceive of him as the great, the infinite, the eternal; the great, the infinite, the eternal intellect, who, of himself, conceiveth the grandest schemes, and infallibly provides for their accomplishment, so that there can be no mistake, no failure. We know that every wise intellect forms its plan before it provides its mean, or attempts to carry out the idea conceived in the mind.

And the great doctrine of election, to which our attention was directed this afternoon, answers to the formation of the plan in the infinite mind of God. He foresaw, clearly, that the whole human race, represented by the first man, would fall into sin, and left to themselves, would certainly perish. To prevent a catastrophe so fearful, he determined in his infinite mind, to have a people for himself, a people that would comprise the vast majority of the fallen inhabitants of this world. They were all present before his mind; their names were registered in his book, which book was delivered into the hands of the Lamb, the Son of God, who accepted the book at the hands of his Father, and, as it were, signed it with his own name, so that it has been designated, "The Book of Life of the Lamb slain from the foundation of the world." And Jesus looked upon this act as the committing of the people to himself, on purpose that he might take the charge of them, on purpose that he might carry out the Father's will respecting them, and gain eternal laurels and honors to himself, by placing them in splendor, majesty, and glory before his Father's face forever. We therefore find him frequently when speaking with his Father, and referring to this act in the eternal counsels, saying, "Thine they were and thou gavest them me. Keep those whom thou hast given me by thine own name, that they may be one as we are." But election interferes not with man as standing in Adam, but with man as under sin the result of

Adam's fall. It ensured their restoration, but it did not interfere with their fall, and consequently the elect, with the rest, all fell in the first man. The entire mass of human nature became depraved, polluted, rotten to the heart's core; so depraved, so polluted, so rotten, that nothing could effect a change but the omnipotent energy of the omnipotent God. There is that in depravity in every form, that defies the touch of any one but the Infinite; that refuses to succumb to anything but to Omnipotence itself. The heart of man is foul as the heart of Satan; the nature of man is foul as the nature of Satan; and the sin of man is worse than the sin of Satan. Satan, the great archangel, that fell from heaven, did a tremendous deed when he set mind in opposition to Deity; but man set not merely mind, but matter with mind, in opposition to the eternal God. God could once look upon the world and say, "Though mind is in rebellion, matter is not in opposition;" but after the fall of man, mind and matter alike were corrupt, were depraved, were in opposition to the Eternal. Every man's heart steams with enmity against God; every man's spirit rises in rebellion against God; and, as you have heard tonight, the verdict of every man's conscience in its fallen state is, "No God, no God;" and if the Eternal could be voted out of existence by the suffrages of his fallen creatures, every hand would be up, every heart would give its verdict, and every voice would vote for the annihilation of the Most High. The will of man strong, the will of man stern, the will of man determined, and opposed to the will of God, will yield to nothing but that which is superior to itself; it laughs at authority, it turns with disgust from holiness, it refuses to listen to invitation, and, in this state, man—universal man, is found. In this state, man, the entire mass of man, with the exception of those who had been saved on credit, and had been changed by the sacred influences of the Spirit—in this state man was found when Christ came into our world. He came and, as ye have heard, assumed humanity, and united it with Deity. The two natures constituted the one person of the glorious Mediator; that glorious Mediator stood the representative of his people; that Mediator stood the Surety of his family; that Mediator stood the Substitute of the multitude of his fallen ones. That Mediator came to be the sacrifice to which sin was to be transferred, by which sin was to expiated and removed out of the way, that God's mercy might freely flow, and from the sinner's conscience, that he might have peace and joy.

But as the election of the Father did not interfere with the falling of man's nature, so the redemption of the Son did not change the nature that had fallen. It was therefore necessary, that as the Father sent the Son, the Son should send the Comforter; and as it required an infinite victim to atone for man's guilt, it required an infinite agent to change man's fallen nature. As to the Father, the atonement must be made as the moral governor, as the maintainer of the rights of the eternal throne; so from the Father, through the Son, must the Holy Spirit descend to renew, to transform, to remodel, to fit human nature to gaze upon the unveiled glories of Deity, and to render to God the homage due unto his name. And this just brings me to my point—EFFECTUAL CALLING. This implies, that there is a calling that may not be effectual. Yes, there is a call that extends to the whole human family. As it is written, "Unto you, O men, I call, and my voice is unto the sons of men." There is a call that refers to humanity as sinful, and to sinners as such, however fallen and depraved they may be. Repentance or a change of mind, repentance and remission of sins, are to be preached amongst all nations, and the disciples were to begin at Jerusalem; and, beginning at Jerusalem the slaughter-house of the Son of God, and the slaughter-house of the prophets, and of the saints,—beginning there, they said, "Repent and be converted, that your sins may be blotted out when the times of refreshing shall come from the presence of the Lord." But the people were like the deaf adder that stoppeth her ear, and refuseth to hear the voice of the charmer—charm he never so wisely. The Baptist had come and cried, "Repent," and sternly, and impressively he preached, but they paid little regard,—at least, little regard that tended to life. And the Son of God, with all that was soft, and winning, and captivating, came and preached; but they turned away, and he said, "To whom shall I like the men of this generation—they are like unto children sitting in the markets, and calling to their fellows—We have piped unto you, but ye have not danced, and we have mourned unto you, but ye have not lamented." Now, this call must be given, because God commands it; this call must be given, because God works by it. In giving the general, the universal call to all that hear the gospel, we obey the high mandate of the Eternal God; we do honor and homage to the authority of the Lord Jesus Christ, and we employ an instrument—a weapon, if you please—by which the Spirit of God operates upon the human mind; for the weapons of our warfare are not carnal, but are mighty through God, to the pulling down of strongholds, and the casting down of imaginations, and every high thing, and the bringing into subjection every thought to the obedience of Christ. The general call leads to the special, to the particular, or what we designate, the "effectual call." We speak to me as men, and we reason with them; we speak to sinners as sinners, and we expostulate with them; but while we reason, and while we expostulate, we have the promise of the presence of the Master—"I am with you;" we have the promised presence of the Eternal Paraclete, who was sent to empower, sent to accompany, and sent to work by the Lord's servants; and, while we speak and give the call as we are commanded and commissioned, the Holy Spirit works—the infinite power of the Eternal Spirit comes into contact,—direct, immediate contact, with the mind of man. There is a power that goes with the word—distinct from the word—when it is accompanied by the energy of the Eternal Spirit; and that power produces in the heart, life—a spiritual, a Divine, an immortal life—a life that man dead in sin had not; a life which a man once having loseth not, for it is eternal; a life that was given us in Christ before the world was; a life preserved for us by Christ all through the past ages that have rolled away; a life that is communicated from the loving heart of Him who is the great depository of grace, and conducted by the Holy Ghost into the heart that is called by grace. Has the Spirit accompanying the word produced life? From that life springs conviction: not the cold conviction awakened occasionally in the mind of man, by the reasoning of man, by reflecting upon his past misconduct, or by the flashing of the forked lightnings of the law; but a conviction that is produced by the Holy Spirit bringing the law into contact with the conscience—the Gospel into contact with the heart. In the sinner's conscience God erects a tribunal, in the sinner's conscience God sits as judge, and to the tribunal, before the just judge, man is summoned to appear; and in the heart, in the soul, in the nature of man, there is a miniature of the judgment that is to take place at the completion and winding up of the present dispensation. The man is arraigned as a sinner, the man is convicted as a culprit, the man is condemned as a criminal; he stands before God, and he has nothing to say; every excuse has withered like the leaves of autumn, every excuse is carried away like the chaff from the summer's threshing-floor, every rag that the man boasted of is torn from him, and he stands, a naked sinner, before a heart-searching God. The penetrating eye of the Omniscient darts into the innermost recesses of his soul, and the gentle fingers of the Spirit turns over one fold of the heart after the other; the process may be long, or the operation may be quick, but sooner or later the man is brought to this.—"In me, that is in my flesh, dwelleth no good thing." He had once started at the Scriptural representation of man's fallen and depraved nature; he had once wondered that from the lip of truth had proceeded the startling words, "From within, out of the heart, proceed murders, adulteries, blasphemies, false witnesses, and abominable idolatries." He never could have thought that evil so dreadful, he never could have thought that sins so fearful, he never could have thought that principles so diabolical, could have been found in a nature like his; but there they are, and he has nothing to object—but, under the power of the deep conviction that is produced, he is filled with terrible alarm. If he casts his eye back, there are the crimes of his life; if he casts his eye forward, there is the tremendous judgment; if he lifts up his eyes to Heaven, there is the pure and holy God that he has insulted; and if he turns his eyes within, all is dark and vain and wild. He is filled with alarm—alarm that perhaps keeps him awake by night, and haunts and harasses him by day, until he is prepared to do anything, prepared to go anywhere, if he may but escape the just judgment of his God. He is by this discipline prepared to submit to God's method of salvation; he is prepared to give up proposing conditions according to which he would be saved; he no longer goes about to work out a righteousness of his own, but he is ready to submit himself to the righteousness of God. Being, therefore, conscious of his criminality, burdened with his guilt, trembling at the prospect of his destiny, he falls prostrate before the high throne of the Eternal, smites upon his breast, and cries "God be merciful to me a sinner," as if no such a sinner had ever appealed to God's mercy, as if no such culprit had ever stood before God's throne; before God he says, "If there can be mercy in thy heart sufficient to reach a case so dismal and so desperate, God be merciful to me;" and after having pleaded with earnestness, after having supplicated with intense emotion, and after having, perhaps, become a little bold, he is startled at his own temerity, and receding, as it were, from the position that he had taken, he cries—

> "Depth of mercy, can there be
> Mercy in thy heart for me,
> O God of spotless purity?"

And, perhaps, like David, he groans in his heart, and mourns in his soul, until his bones wax old, through his roaring all the day long. But, no relief, no help is found, until, at length, he begins to make confession of his sin, and, as he confesses, the Spirit of God unveils and unfolds the gospel mystery, and, as in the days of the law, when the victim was brought to the Priest, and the man placed his hand upon its head, between its horns, and pressed with his might and confessed over it all his transgressions, all his iniquities, and all his sins, so the man lays his hand of faith upon the victim's head, and there confesses his sin. As he confesses, a change takes place in his feelings, the burden begins to disperse, a little bright light in the cloud attracts his attention, and, as he looks upward, he seems to catch the loving Father's eye, and feels an encouragement within him to approach unto God; and, as he approaches, still confessing, still pleading, still deploring, still resting his hand upon the victim's head, and trusting in the atonement you have heard of, and on that alone, he seems to hear strange music, delightful melody, and that music is the commencement of the sound of the trump of the Jubilee, when the oppressed one is to go free, and as he listens to the sound the chains drop from his hands, and the burden from his shoulders, the trouble is removed from his heart, and he lifts up his eyes, streaming perhaps with tears, to heaven, and says, "Oh Lord, I will praise thee, for though thou wast angry with me, thine anger is turned away, and thou comfortest me:" and looking around, on those about him, in the language of wonder, astonishment, and gratitude, he says, "Behold, behold a mystery, behold a miracle, behold one of the greatest wonders of the universe; behold, God is my salvation. I will trust, and not be afraid, for Jah Jehovah is my strength, and my song, he also is become my salvation." He has now peace flowing into his heart like a river, he has now a consciousness that God has accepted him in the beloved, and he now experimentally knows the truth, tastes the sweetness, and feels the power of the apostolic testimony, "Being justified by faith we have peace with God, through our Lord Jesus Christ; by whom also we have access into this grace, wherein we stand, and rejoice in hope of the glory of God." He has now experienced the effectual call. It has been a call from darkness into marvelous light, from bondage into glorious liberty; out of prison the man comes to reign; from the dunghill he is lifted up to sit among the princes, even among the princes of God's people. And, now, as I must conclude, just observe, the origin of this call is the free, the sovereign, the distinguishing grace of God. It originates, not in man's will, nor in man';s disposition, nor in man's station in society, but of His will, and of His will alone, who is the great sovereign ruler of the universe, is this change effected; of man it cannot be, for it includes a new creation; a resurrection; and the inhabitants of God. Generally speaking, the instrumentality by which God works is the gospel, but in every instance the agent that produces the change is the holy and eternal Spirit of God. He quickens the soul dead in trespasses and sins, he enlightens the understanding that was in the midnight darkness of nature, he disposes the will which before ran counter to the will of God; he teaches the understanding that was once averse to everything pure and holy, and then gently, and lovingly, and sweetly he leads the soul to the Cross to gaze upon the wondrous Sufferer, he then leads the soul to the Church to confess Christ and him crucified, and then leads it in the paths of righteousness for his own name's sake. The calling is high, for it is from the High and Holy One; it is heavenly, in contrast with the earthly calling of the descendants of Abraham of old; it is an evidence of distinguishing love; and thanks, eternal thanks to God, it is irreversible; for the gifts and the callings of God are without repentance. From death to life we pass; from darkness into light we come; out of bondage into liberty we spring; from sin to the knowledge and enjoyment of holiness we are introduced; then at last from earth to heaven. Into the grace of Christ we are called, and we stand in his favor. Into the fellowship of Christ we are called, and when Christ who is our life shall appear, we also shall appear with him in glory. The Father draws; the Spirit quickens; the Son receives; and when locked in the arms of the Son of God, our effectual calling is realized and enjoyed. Its author, is God; its subjects, are the elect; its nature, is holy; and its end, is glorious. Thus, you perceive, my friends, all originated in God's thought, which thought sprung into a perfect plan, to carry out which plan provision was made, and this plan will be perfectly carried out to the praise of the glory of his grace. Thus, whether you think of election, whether you think of redemption, or whether you think of effectual calling,

> *"Give all the glory to his holy name,*
> *For to him all the glory belongs;*
> *Be your's the high joy still to sound forth his praise*
> *And crown him in each of your songs."*

The Rev. C. H. Spurgeon—I think it was John Newton, who, speaking about good Calvinistic doctrine compared it to lumps of sugar; but he said, he did not so much give to his people the lumps of sugar, as diffuse the whole of it throughout his sermons; just as people do not eat sugar, but put it in their tea. Now, some of you have not yet grown patient enough to listen, I think, to a doctrine, however fully it may be brought out. Our people want anecdotes, illustrations, parables, and metaphors; even the best and sublimest things keep our minds on such a stretch when we listen to them, that there is good need that illustrations should yield us some relief. Today was set apart that these doctrines might be fully brought out; this has been done, and there remains but one, and that my friend Mr O'Neil is to take, namely the final perseverance of the saints. Before he speaks, just one or two words. Has it never struck you that the scheme of doctrine which is called Calvinistic has much to say concerning God? It commences and ends with the Divine One. The angel of that system stands like Uriel in the sun; it dwells with God; he begins, he carries on, he perfects; it is for his glory and for his honor. Father, Son, and Spirit co-working, the whole Gospel scheme is carried out. Perhaps there may be this defect in our theology; we may perhaps too much forget man. I think that is a very small fault, compared with the fault of the opposite system, which begins with man, and all but ends with him. Man is a creature; how ought God to deal with him? That is the question some theologians seem to answer. The way we put it is—God is the Creator, he has a right to do as he wills; he is Sovereign, there is no law above him, he has a right to make and to unmake, and when man hath sinned, he has a right to save or to destroy. If he can save, and yet not impair his justice, heaven shall ring with songs; if he destroy, and yet his goodness be not marred, then hell itself with its deep bass of misery, shall swell the mighty rollings of his glorious praise. We hold that God should be most prominent in all our teachings; and we hold this to be a gauge by which to test the soundness of ministers. If they exalt God and sink the sinner to the very dust, it is all well; but if they lower the prerogatives of Deity, if he be less sovereign, less just, or less loving than the Scripture reveals him to be, and if man be puffed up with that fond notion that he is anything better than an unclean thing, then such theology is utterly unsound. Salvation is of the Lord, and let the Lord alone be glorified.

5. THE FINAL PERSEVERANCE OF BELIEVERS IN CHRIST JESUS ("P" PERSEVERANCE OF THE SAINTS)

(Delivered by Rev. William O'Neill, New Broad Street Chapel, LONDON)

My dear Brethren and Friends,

Most unexpectedly did the kind invitation of my esteemed brother, Mr Spurgeon, come to me, to take part in the present service of this beautiful house. And after I had engaged to come I sincerely wished that I had not. I felt, however, that it would not be proper to retire from the engagement, but seek to meet in a becoming spirit, both towards God's truth and God's people. I will now try to do this. I utter here, of course, my own sentiments. As I am not responsible for anything that has been or may be said by another speaker, so I alone am responsible for what I shall say. But though I am not the delegate or representative of any church, denomination, or community, I doubt not that my declaration of faith on the matter at hand will be, in all substantial points, that of a very large number who love Jesus and are living in His service. That I desire to believe what the Bible teaches, and that I am sincere in my convictions, I know to be true: but that there are thousands of excellent Christians on the other side admits of no doubt, and should not be questioned by any one. Of their deep sincerity, love to God and his Gospel, zeal and devotedness in holy things, self-denying labors in the Divine service, and the cultivation and manifestation of Christian graces, I would and do speak with the most earnest approval. I give them as much credit for sincerity as I claim for myself; and I do this not as a favor, but as a piece of simple justice. Yet we differ—differ as to what the Sacred Oracles teach on the doctrine now before us; and it is competent and right for all men to examine, each one for himself, which of our opinions is that which is taught in the Bible, for certainly both are not taught there.

The question—Is it possible for sincere Christians, truly regenerated persons, to be finally separated from Jesus, to lose the favor of God their Father, and be eternally shut out from His smile and Home?—is one of no small moment. It involves issues of the most momentous nature, and cannot but be unspeakably interesting to every believer in Christ. We say, with unfaltering tongue, that of all the dead, every one who was ever renewed in heart is now in heaven; and that reconciliation with God on earth, through Christ Jesus, will, in every case, end in the everlasting salvation of the soul. Did God, then, tell us that all who are here now are His regenerated people, (would that they were!) we should believe that when the roll of the finally saved shall be called, every one of them would answer to that call by saying, "Here am I, Lord: Thy right arm, and the effectual operation of Thy Spirit and grace has done it all, and now I am to be forever happy, forever sinless, forever safe." It is hardly necessary to say, that we believe this view of the case to be in entire harmony with the teaching of God's Book. To the law and to the testimony, if we, or others, speak not on this and on all other matters according to that Word, it is because there is no light in us or in them. (Isaiah viii. 20.)

Having called public attention to this doctrine lately in a small book,* in which I have sought to obey the Master's command,—"Search the scriptures,"—I will now, with your kind permission, direct attention to a few portions of the Divine Word that, we believe, fully establish the doctrine of the saints' final preservation and perseverance. On each of those texts my words must be few, as the time allotted to me is short.

Hear then the Holy Spirit's teaching when speaking by the prophet Samuel:—"For the LORD will not forsake His people for His great name's sake; because it hath pleased the Lord to make you His people." (1 Sam. xii. 22) This, we think, is conclusive. What Christian does not know, and knowing, does not mourn over, the untrustworthiness of his own heart? And feeling fully assured that it is impossible for him to vanquish "the world, the flesh, and the devil," how welcome to his heart is the declaration, "The LORD will not forsake His people." No; He thought proper to renew their hearts, to quicken them into spiritual life, and He will mercifully continue to carry on His good work in their souls till it be perfected in glory. The reason why "He will not forsake His people" is stated here most explicitly; just as much so as is the declaration of His unchangeable love. It is not that they were less sinful by nature or practice than others; or because of any moral qualities that were found in them; but "because it pleased the Lord to make them His people." Hear another portion: God, speaking by his prophet Isaiah, says,—"Can a woman forget her sucking child, that she should not have compassion on the son of her womb? Yea, they may forget, yet will I not forget thee. Behold, I have graven thee upon the palms of My hands." (Isaiah xlix. 15, 16.) This we regard as a most interesting, as well as a most consolatory portion of Scripture. "Zion said, the LORD hath forsaken me, and my Lord hath forgotten me." This was not only an error in creed,—it was also a dishonorable estimate of the Divine character, and to it the Gracious One replies in these words:—"Can a woman forget her sucking child, that she should not have compassion on the son of her womb? Yea, they may forget, yet will not I forget thee." The affection of a right-minded mother for her tender and helpless offspring is one of the strongest that is experienced by human beings. But, though strong, very strong, it may, alas! give way. It is, at best, only a creature's love, and therefore changeable; while that love which is exercised by God towards His believing children is, like Himself, unchangeable. These words prove, and were designed to prove, most conclusively, that the love of the Divine Father towards His adopted sons and daughters is not a fluctuating or changing thing. What other, or what lower interpretation can we put upon the words, "YET WILL NOT I FORGET THEE?" And not forgetting them is, in this case, equivalent to His continuing to care for, to keep, and tenderly regard them.

Hear God again speaking by the same prophet:—"For a small moment have I forsaken thee; but with great mercies will I gather thee. In a little wrath I hid My face form thee for a moment; but with everlasting kindness will I have mercy on thee, saith the LORD thy Redeemer. For this is as the waters of Noah unto me: for as I have sworn that the waters of Noah should no more go over the earth; so have I sworn that I would not be wroth with thee, nor rebuke thee. For the mountains shall depart, and the hills be removed; but My kindness shall not depart from thee, neither shall the covenant of My peace be removed, saith the LORD that hath mercy on thee." These words deserve to hold a prominent place among those which God has spoken for the comfort and joy of His people. Their obvious design is—to sustain believers under the chastening hand of God, and to do this by considerations drawn from His own character, and not from anything in themselves. Vain, brethren, is it to trust, or put confidence in our own false hearts. They are weak as helpless infancy. To lean on them will only be evidence of our folly and of our sin. We are not to find consolation in our gifts, in our graces, in our labors, in our resolutions, or in our experience, nor by the grace of God will we do so. But when chastised by the everloving and good Father,—when smarting under his parental and deserved stripes,—we may feast our souls on His blessed words—words that fire those souls with confidence, hope, and love.—"In a little wrath I hid my face from thee for a moment; but with everlasting kindness will I have mercy upon thee. For the mountains shall depart, and the hills be removed; but My kindness shall not depart from thee, neither shall the covenant of my peace be removed, saith the LORD that hath mercy on thee." Such, brethren, are GOD'S utterances! These are the words of One who is unchangeable in affection; of One who says,—Oh! blessed be his adorable name for that saying,—"For I am the LORD, I change not; therefore ye sons of Jacob are not consumed." (Mal. iii. 6.)

I name another passage:—"For there shall arise," says Jesus, "false Christ's, and false prophets, and shall shew great signs and wonders; insomuch, that, if it were possible, they shall deceive the very elect." (Matt. xxiv. 24.) The plain and obvious meaning of this latter clause is, that it is not possible to deceive, or allure to their final ruin, the adopted sons and daughters of God, those whom He has chosen to be His. Nothing less, we believe, was intended by the Gracious Speaker, and we see not how any other meaning can be consistently given to the language which He here uses. The words, "If it were possible," only say, in another form, "It is not possible."

I now name such texts as connect faith, or believing in Christ, with salvation, of which the following are a few:—"God so loved the world, that He gave His only begotten Son, that whosoever believeth in Him should not perish, but have everlasting life." "Verily, verily, I say unto you, he that heareth My word, and believeth on Him that sent Me, hath everlasting life, and shall not come into condemnation, but is passed from death unto life." "And this is the will of Him that sent Me, that every one which seeth the Son, and believeth on Me hath everlasting life. I am the bread which came down from heaven: if any man eat of this bread he shall live forever." "The Gospel is the power of God unto salvation to every one that believeth." (John ii. 16, v. 24, vi. 47, 50, 51, 57; Rom. i. 16.) The plain teaching of these, and many similar passages, is, that every believer in Jesus hath everlasting life. They teach this or they teach nothing. Is this be not their meaning, what is? But, can that which is everlasting cease to be? Can it come to an end? No words can more plainly assert than these do, that whosoever believeth in Jesus SHALL NOT COME INTO CONDEMNATION; that all believers in him shall enjoy "everlasting life." We take these gracious assurances as proving, to the fullest extent, the doctrine for which we plead. If the belief of the Gospel be not followed, in every instance, by eternal blessedness, what did Paul mean when he said, "The Gospel is the power of God unto salvation to every one that believeth?" (Rom. i. 16.) If, at the last day, a single one be unsaved of those who had believed the Gospel, who had been united to Christ by faith in His name—the apostle's words must needs be falsified—his teaching is not true. This, at least, is our opinion. No amount of adverse criticism can set aside the evidence that such verses as these furnish in support of the blessed doctrine which we now defend.

Hear Christ again:—"My sheep," he says, "hear My voice, and I know them, and they follow Me: and I give unto them eternal life; and they shall never perish, neither shall any one pluck them out of My hand. My Father who gave them Me is greater than all; and no one is able to pluck them out of My Father's hand." We regard this entire passage as one of the most delightful and consoling in the Scriptures. It teaches most unequivocally,—in the plainest, strongest, and most conclusive terms,—that Christ's believing ones "SHALL NEVER PERISH;" that no enemy, human or hellish, shall be able to wrench them out of His or His Father's covenanted and secure grasp. Infinite power, no less than infinite love—both existing in their God and Savior—stand guarantee for their security! Neither men nor demons shall be able to defeat or overturn the purpose of Divine grace concerning them! Difficulties, many and sharp, may surround them; and temptations, fierce and fiery, may assault their souls; but Divine love, wisdom, grace, and power shall be ever on their side. Jesus, the "faithful and true witness," says, "THEY SHALL NEVER PERISH." Elsewhere He says, "Because I live, ye shall live also." (John xiv. 17) The spiritual life of believers is in HIS keeping, and He here declares that it is as secure as His own. If He dies, and continues not to be their "Advocate with the Father," (1 John ii. 1) their Intercessor "at the right hand of God," (Rom. viii. 34) then may they die also, but not otherwise. In perfect keeping with his Lord's words are those which Paul uses, when referring to the same subject. "For if," he says, "when we were enemies, we were reconciled to God by the death of His Son, much more, being reconciled, we shall be saved by His life." (Rom. v. 10) That is, we shall be preserved in that state of reconciliation by Christ's intercessory life at God's right hand in heaven. He, the God-man, lives there as Mediator, for them: He holds and exercises "all power in heaven and on earth" for the welfare and safety of His church. And they cannot die while He lives. The power that is to destroy the spiritual life of the weakest saint must first destroy the life of that saint's Head. "Their life," as the Holy Spirit by Paul elsewhere teaches, "is hid with Christ in God" (Col. iii. 3). Where, brethren, could it be safer, or as safe? In whose care or keeping could it be so secure? It is "hid with Christ in God." Not only so, but the Apostle goes on to say, "When Christ, who is our life, shall appear, then shall ye also appear with him IN GLORY." This, to say the least of it, is a glorious statement and declaration. Can language, we ask, go beyond that which is used in these texts to guarantee the eternal salvation of every believer in Jesus? The Head and members shall never be separated. They are bound up in an inseparable and an unchanging union.

Hear a Divine lesson given in another place:—"Moreover, whom He did predestinate, them He also called; and whom He called, them He also justified; and whom He justified, them He also glorified" (Rom. viii. 30).

When it is said, "Whom He did predestinate, them He also called," we must interpret the word "called" to mean very much more than invited; for the Apostle goes on to say, "Whom He called, them He also justified." We know that this is only true of those who believe in Jesus—who are effectually called or drawn, by the combined operations of the Word and Spirit of God, into the blessed fellowship and joys of the Gospel (1 Cor. i. 9). That those, and only those, who believe in Christ are justified, is the uniform lesson of the Divine Word (John iii. 16, 36; Acts xiii. 39, 40; Rom. i. 16, iii. 22, 28). Let it be noted that Paul affirms three things here. The first is—"Whom He did predestinate, them He also called." The second is—"Whom He called, them He also justified." And the third is—"Whom He justified, them He also glorified." What, then, does he mean by the expression "glorified?" Does he, or can he mean anything less than the enjoyment of everlasting life? We say, then, that were only a single individual out of the whole number of those who have been, or shall be "justified" by faith in Jesus, to come short of heaven, the declaration would not be true that "Whom He justified, them He also glorified."

Hear another Divine proclamation relative to the security of God's people:—"For I am persuaded that neither death, nor life, nor angels, nor principalities, nor powers, nor things to come, nor height, nor depth, nor any other creature, shall be able to separate us from the love of God which is in Christ Jesus our Lord" (Rom. viii. 38, 39). These, brethren, are notes of the most triumphant character, relative to the ultimate blessedness of believers in Jesus. The terms which are here used are such as leave no doubt as to what the Holy Spirit, speaking by Paul, meant to teach. We deliberately affirm that language has no power to assert the doctrine for which we contend more conclusively than is here done. Words have no meaning, nor are they of any use in communicating thought, if these words were not used by a man who believed as we do on the matter in hand. And we are entirely willing to believe or disbelieve with the Apostle Paul, neither more nor less.

I quote him again. Hear what he wrote to the Church at Philippi:—"Being confident of this very thing, that He who hath begun a good work in you will perform it until the day of Jesus Christ." I well remember how greatly this strengthened my own soul when, in the morning of my religious life, I was passing through much mental conflict. And are not these words well calculated to comfort the hearts of those who, through grace, have believed in the Savior? Is there any room for objecting criticism here, or is there any ambiguity in the language employed? No, there is none whatever: the Apostle was "confident of this very thing." What "very thing?" Why, that wherever the Divine Spirit had commenced this "good work" of grace in the soul, He would complete it. No other power could have begun it, and no other power is competent to carry it forward to completion. That He who commences that "good work" is able to finish it, no professing Christian will deny: that He will finish it, this verse most clearly teaches. The Apostle Paul was "confident of THIS VERY THING;" and so are we.

Let us give attention to other words of the same sacred penman. Addressing one of the primitive Churches, he says:—"We are bound to give thanks always to God for you, brethren beloved of the Lord, because God hath from the beginning chosen you to salvation, through sanctification of the Spirit and belief of the truth" (2 Thes. ii. 13). This is a most important portion of Scripture in relation to the question—What is the end of election? In what does it, or is it to terminate? What does it secure? Are its subjects merely chosen to enjoy the light of the gospel, the means of grace, and no more? Or, are they chosen to enjoy, in its full measure, everlasting life; the priceless favor and blissful fellowship of God here and forever? This question is definitely settled by the language of inspiration employed here. The Apostle declares that the choice is "to salvation;" or, in other words, which he also uses in this place, "to the obtaining of the glory of our Lord Jesus Christ." This means, of course, eternal life in heaven, as well as all that precedes and prepares for it on earth. But how can this be realized? How can it be said, they were "chosen to salvation," if they may all apostatize finally from Jesus, fall out of the Divine favor, and be forever numbered with the lost? The thing is, of course, impossible. If not saved,—fully and forever,—it would not be true to say they were chosen "to salvation."

I beg to name one passage more. Speaking of believers, a divinely inspired teacher says:—"Who are kept by the power of God through faith unto salvation" (1 Peter, i. 5). Here we are distinctly taught what the Divine Being is doing and will continue to do for His believing people. The Apostle asserts, that they are "kept by the power of God through faith unto salvation." If so, nothing is more certain than that they shall reach it, and enjoy it forever. Had Peter believed that it was possible for any number of them to become outcasts from God, and die in their sins, he would never have employed the language which is found here. The declaration that believers are "kept" or garrisoned in (for such is the meaning of the term here employed) "by the power of GOD through faith unto salvation," settles the point with us, and leaves us nothing more to desire in the shape of statement or promise. This is, indeed, a glorious declaration. Fellow pilgrims, let it fill you with the highest joy, as it gives you the fullest assurance that you are safe in the grasp and guardianship of Jehovah of hosts.

We hold and teach too, that the certain enjoyment of everlasting life is inseparably connected with continued faith in the Divine testimony concerning sin, Jesus, and His salvation. They shall be preserved in the exercise of faith in the Redeemer, until they shall enter upon the possession of the heavenly inheritance. This is clearly taught here, and nothing less.

I have now referred to a few out of the many portions of God's word which teach the doctrine for which we contend. God's people shall be preserved, and will persevere to the end, for they were given to Christ in the everlasting covenant, that covenant which is "ordered in all things and sure:" the stability of which is as safe as the oath, and promise, and power of God can make it (Psalm lxxxix. 30, 34; Heb. vi. 18, 19). They are "loved by Him with an everlasting love" (Jer. xxxi. 3); they are "chosen to salvation" (Eph. i. 4; 2 Thes. ii. 13); and God, their gracious and reconciled Father, "will rest in His love" (Zeph. iii. 17). Their safety, as believers in Jesus, is secured by the word and promise of the "God that cannot lie." He has said that He will never leave them nor forsake them (Heb. xiii. 2); that they shall never perish" (John x. 28); and that He will confirm them unto the end" (1 Cor. i. 8).

For this purpose the ever-availing intercession of Jesus is employed. He is at the right hand of God as their Brother, Representative, and Advocate. He prays for them that their faith fail not (Luke xxii. 32). They are, each and all, borne on His heart, and pleaded for in His gracious and ever-successful intercession. "Father," says he, "I will that they also, whom thou hast given Me, be with Me where I am, that they may behold My glory" (John xvii. 24). Oh, what priceless joy do these words afford to the believer's heart! No weapon that is formed against them shall prosper. Their Almighty King will vanquish all their spiritual foes. He will so aid them that they shall contend victoriously against "the world, the flesh, and the devil." They shall be more than conquerors through Him that loved them (Rom. viii. 37). They shall be the saved of His right arm, and the everlasting monuments and trophies of His grace, love, and power. They are "sealed with that Holy Spirit of promise which is the earnest of their inheritance, until the redemption of the purchased possession" (2 Cor. i. 21, 22; Eph. i. 13, 14). Having received the "earnest," the pledge which guarantees the fulfillment of their Heavenly Father's covenant to save them, they are perfectly and forever secure.

We build our faith in this doctrine on God's plain teaching. We extort no meaning from His word which cannot be found there by the simple and ordinary reader of it. We take its statements in their plain and grammatical sense, just as they would be interpreted by any unprejudiced expounder of language. We should be content to abide by the interpretation of them which would be given by any man, infidel or other, who felt no interest in our controversy, and who was entirely careless relative to our differences of opinion. One unequivocal passage teaching this doctrine would be, or should be sufficient to establish it, and to bring our opinions into harmony with Divine teaching; but we are not confined to one, or five, or ten; we have line upon line, promise upon promise, assurance upon assurance, and declaration upon declaration to this effect. So that we would fain ask,—If the doctrine be not taught in the portions of Scripture that I have named, what is taught in them? What is their import? What do they teach? Or, what language or terms would be thought sufficient to teach it? It is our firm conviction that no doctrine of religion is more clearly taught in the Bible than is this. It is expressed as plainly as words can possibly do it.

And are we, with these inspired declarations before us, to suppose it possible for wicked men or demons to say, when pointing to numbers of the lost,—"The Most High began to build up His kingdom in their souls, but He was not able to finish it! He quickened them into spiritual life,—renewed, pardoned, justified, and sanctified them; but now they are torn from His grasp, His enemies were able—contrary to the words of Jesus (1 John x. 21)—'to pluck them out of His hand,' and they have done it."

This would, indeed, make short work of many plain and positive declarations found in the Bible: it would prove, beyond doubt, that its promises, and assurances, and declarations are of very little value.

Let me, before I close, say—and say with the fullest emphasis possible—that we believe as firmly as any man living, as firmly as we believe any truth taught in the Bible, that "without holiness no man shall see the Lord" (Heb. xii. 14). We know no other evidence of being in Christ, or of being a Christian, than that which is furnished by a life and behavior becoming the Gospel. And though holiness is not the cause of God's first or continued love to His people, it is the effect and fruit of that love, and a main part of the salvation which is in Christ Jesus—that salvation to which they are chosen (Eph. i. 4); and he who is satisfying himself with the notion that he is safe for eternity, while he is living in any known sin, is turning the grace of our God into licentiousness, and is a deadly enemy of the Cross of Christ. The blessed doctrine which the Bible teaches, and in which we glory, is—the doctrine of the saints' final perseverance, and that doctrine was never designed to comfort any man who is not living a life of faith in the Son of God, intensely anxious to please God in all things, and to be the holy and happy subject of that mind which was in Jesus.

Very interesting, then, is the question, when asked in no wrong spirit—Are there few that be saved? If GOD does not hold up His people, if He does not keep them by His grace and power, they will be very few indeed—a child may count them, and, in fact, have none, not one, to count. But let no man charge our views with being "narrow," or "embracing only a few," or contemplating the eternal salvation of "a very limited number" of our race, for, according to the view which we hold and teach, they will be a numberless number. We believe, and our hearts swell with high and holy joy in believing, that every child of man who loved God,—every one of Adam's race who was renewed in heart,—all who were ever on the Lord's side,—will be found among the saved. Not one will be lost. Not one will be missed from the eternal banquet. Not one, will be outside the gates of the holy city. All, all shall be there, and there forever, and ever, and ever!

> *"The soul that on Jesus hath leaned for repose,*
> *He will not, He cannot, give up to His foes;*
> *That soul, though all hell should endeavor to shake,*
> *He'll never! no, never! no, never forsake!"*

ABOUT THE AUTHOR

Charles Haddon Spurgeon, often referred to as the "Prince of Preachers," was a prominent Baptist minister who left an indelible mark on Christian history. Born on June 19, 1834, in Kelvedon, Essex, England, Spurgeon's life was characterized by his powerful preaching, prolific writing, and unwavering commitment to the Christian faith.

Spurgeon's spiritual journey began early in life, influenced by his grandfather, who was a Congregationalist minister. However, it was on January 6, 1850, at the age of 15, that Spurgeon experienced a profound conversion to Christianity during a snowstorm that forced him to take shelter in a Primitive Methodist chapel.

At the remarkably young age of 19, Spurgeon was called to pastor the New Park Street Chapel in London. His powerful oratory and deep biblical knowledge quickly drew large crowds, necessitating a move to larger venues. Eventually, the Metropolitan Tabernacle was built to accommodate his growing congregation, seating 5,000 people with standing room for an additional 1,000.

Spurgeon's preaching style was characterized by its clarity, wit, and powerful application of biblical truths. He spoke extemporaneously, often preaching for 40 minutes to an hour without notes, yet his sermons were rich in content and practical application. His ability to connect with both the intellectual and the common person made his messages accessible to a wide audience.

Beyond the pulpit, Spurgeon was a prolific writer. He authored numerous books, including a seven-volume commentary on the Psalms titled "The Treasury of David." His sermons were transcribed and widely distributed, with his collected sermons filling 63 volumes, which stand as the largest set of books by a single author in Christian history.

Spurgeon's influence extended far beyond his local congregation. He founded the Pastor's College (now Spurgeon's College) to train ministers, established an orphanage, and was involved in numerous charitable works. His commitment to social causes was rooted in his deep faith and desire to see the practical outworking of Christian principles in society.

Theologically, Spurgeon was a committed Calvinist, adhering to the doctrines of grace. He vigorously defended these beliefs against what he perceived as the encroachment of liberal theology in the Baptist Union, leading to the "Downgrade Controversy" in the later years of his ministry.

Despite his many accomplishments, Spurgeon faced significant personal challenges. He struggled with depression and poor health throughout much of his adult life. These trials, however, seemed to deepen his faith and empathy, enriching his ministry and writings with a profound understanding of human suffering.

Spurgeon's influence continued to grow throughout his lifetime, and he became one of the most famous preachers in the English-speaking world. His sermons were translated into numerous languages, and he was invited to preach throughout Britain and beyond, though he rarely accepted invitations to leave London.

On January 31, 1892, at the age of 57, Charles Haddon Spurgeon passed away in Menton, France, where he had gone to recuperate from his ill health. His funeral in London was attended by tens of thousands, testament to the impact he had made during his lifetime.

Spurgeon's legacy continues to this day. His sermons and writings are still widely read and studied, and his emphasis on biblical preaching, evangelism, and social action continues to inspire Christians around the world. The Metropolitan Tabernacle still stands in London, and Spurgeon's College continues to train ministers and Christian workers.

Charles Haddon Spurgeon's life and ministry serve as a powerful reminder of the impact one person can have when fully dedicated to their faith and calling. His combination of powerful preaching, prolific writing, and practical Christianity continues to challenge and inspire believers more than a century after his death.

If you enjoyed
The Prince of Preachers
you'll love

In this volume, collected under one cover, are the very best gems of knowledge, wisdom and insight into Christ and the Christian life—culled for your convenience and blessing from the hundreds of literary works and transcribed sermons that Spurgeon produced.

ISBN: 978-1610100281

THE MISSION OF GREAT CHRISTIAN BOOKS

The ministry of Great Christian Books was established to glorify The Lord Jesus Christ and to be used by Him to expand and edify the kingdom of God while we occupy and anticipate Christ's glorious return. Great Christian Books will seek to accomplish this mission by publishing Gospel literature which is biblically faithful, relevant, and practically applicable to many of the serious spiritual needs of mankind upon the beginning of this new millennium. To do so we will always seek to boldly incorporate the truths of Scripture, especially those which were largely articulated as a body of theology during the Protestant Reformation of the sixteenth century and ensuing years. We gladly join our voice in the proclamations of— Scripture Alone, Faith Alone, Grace Alone, Christ Alone, and God's Glory Alone!

Our ministry seeks the blessing of our God as we seek His face to both confirm and support our labors for Him. Our prayers for this work can be summarized by two verses from the Book of Psalms:

"...let the beauty of the LORD our God be upon us, And establish the work of our hands for us; Yes, establish the work of our hands." —Psalm 90:17

"Not unto us, O LORD, not unto us, but to your name give glory."
—Psalm 115:1

Great Christian Books appreciates the financial support of anyone who shares our burden and vision for publishing literature which combines sound Bible doctrine and practical exhortation in an age when too few so-called "Christian" publications do the same. We thank you in advance for any assistance you can give us in our labors to fulfill this important mission. May God bless you.

Visit us for other

GREAT CHRISTIAN BOOKS

including additional titles

of inspiring Christian fiction.

www.greatchristianbooks.com

Join our email list and
receive free ebooks.

www.ingramcontent.com/pod-product-compliance
Lightning Source LLC
Chambersburg PA
CBHW060507090426
42735CB00011B/2141